D1566305

Missionaries of the State

Missionaries of the State

The Summer Institute of Linguistics,
State Formation, and Indigenous Mexico,
1935–1985

Todd Hartch

THE UNIVERSITY OF ALABAMA PRESS
Tuscaloosa

Typeface: New Baskerville

∞

The paper on which this book is printed meets the minimum requirements of
American National Standard for Information Sciences-Permanence of Paper for
Printed Library Materials, ANSI Z39.48-1984.

Library of Congress Cataloging-in-Publication Data

Hartch, Todd, 1967–
    Missionaries of the State : the Summer Institute of Linguistics, state formation,
and indigenous Mexico, 1935–1985 / Todd Hartch.
        p. cm.
    Includes bibliographical references and index.
    ISBN-13: 978-0-8173-1515-3 (cloth : alk. paper)
    ISBN-10: 0-8173-1515-2 (alk. paper)
    1. Summer Institute of Linguistics. 2. Missions—Mexico. 3. Christianity and
international affairs. I. Title.
    BV2370.S86H37 2006
    267′.130972—dc22

                                                              2005034154

Contents

Abbreviations Used in the Text

ACDLA   Anthropological Center for the Documentation of Latin America

CCI   Centro Coordinador Indigenista (Indigenous Coordinating Center)

CEAS   Colegio de Etnólogos y Antropólogos Sociales (College of Ethnologists and Social Anthropologists)

CNDE   Comité Nacional de Defensa Evangélica (National Evangelical Defense Committee)

DGAI   Direccion General de Asuntos Indígenas (Indigenous Affairs Section)

III   Instituto Indigenista Interamericano (Inter-American Indigenous Institute)

IMIL   Instituto Mexicano de Investigaciones Lingüísticas (Mexican Institute of Linguistic Research)

INAH   Instituto Nacional de Antropología e Historia (National Institute of Anthropology and History)

INI   Instituto Nacional Indigenista (National Indigenista Institute)

JAARS   Jungle Aviation and Radio Service

PRI   Partido Revolucionario Institucional (Institutional Revolutionary Party)

SEP   Secretaría de Educación Pública (Ministry of Public Education)

SIL   Summer Institute of Linguistics
WBT   Wycliffe Bible Translators
WCC   World Council of Churches

Introduction

North American adventurer Max Miller spent most of 1936 traveling through Mexico, searching for exotic sights and experiences. Near the end of his trip he heard tales about the "strange Hill People of Morelos" in southern Mexico, nomadic "tribes" who "had avoided the Conquest." Anxious for a glimpse of the "true primitive," Miller found a guide and interpreter and set out for what he had been told was the ancestral home of these Indians, the village of Tetelcingo.

After an arduous voyage through the mountains, Miller finally arrived in Tetelcingo. Far from being the first gringo in Tetelcingo, he had barely missed the departure of one "Thompson," an amateur linguist from the United States. This interloper not only had spoiled Miller's chance to be the first outsider in Tetelcingo but also had contributed to an irreversible process of acculturation in the village. The real problem was not that "Thompson" had taken advantage of anyone or done anything malicious. Miller found, in fact, that he was universally respected by the community. The issue for Miller was that even the positive actions that the linguist had taken, such as lobbying the Mexican state to donate a truck and producing a written version of the local indigenous language, set the stage for further changes in the town and thus for further loss of indigenous traditions. "The zest has been killed in me," he had to admit. Miller came to believe that wherever he went in rural Mexico he would find Americans and their damaging technological intrusions.[1]

In June 1979 more than eighty anthropologists and social scientists attending a conference at Mexico's National University would express a sentiment very similar to Miller's. They were upset that American linguists were to be found not only in Tetelcingo but also in dozens of remote hamlets all over Mexico. The omnipresent linguists were far worse than Miller had imagined, argued many at the conference. They were part of the Mexican government's "paternalistic and authoritarian" linguistic policy and were imposing the "dominant ideology" of the bourgeoisie onto indigenous communities.[2] Unlike Miller, however, these Mexican intellectuals were going to do something about the linguists. Due in large part to the angry protests of those in attendance at the conference, on September 21, 1979, the Mexican government severed its ties with the Summer Institute of Linguistics, the organization that "Thompson" had started in Tetelcingo and which had expanded throughout Mexico, Latin America, and the world.

"Thompson" was actually an American missionary named Cameron Townsend, who was learning what he called "Aztec" (a variant of Nahuatl) so that he could translate the New Testament into that language. In the years after he so disappointed Max Miller, Townsend had established a successful Bible translation operation that, surprisingly, worked closely with the Mexican state for over four decades. What began in the 1930s as a handful of American fundamentalists with big dreams became by the end of the twentieth century one of the world's largest mission organizations, the Wycliffe Bible Translators (WBT), and one of the world's largest scientific entities, the Summer Institute of Linguistics (SIL). By 2002 the SIL boasted over five thousand linguists working in more than fifty nations.[3]

This book will examine the history of the SIL in Mexico from its beginnings in 1933 until the growing crisis surrounding its activities in that nation led to the end of its official relationship with the Mexican government in 1979. From one perspective this book tells the familiar story of Americans using their power, wealth, and influence to dominate Mexico, leading eventually to resentment, disillusionment, and protest on the part of Mexicans. But this is not exactly the "same, old story." In this story, for instance, the Americans are not wealthy, powerful, or well connected. It is the Mexicans, or at least one group of Mexicans, who have the wealth, the power, and the connections. Finally, this is a story about Indians, Indians who confound our expectations by, often, rejecting these Americans and their new religion out of hand, and who confound our expectations still more by, occasionally, welcoming them and their new religion. In short, *Missionaries of the State* illustrates one of the more complex and surprising chapters in the long history of interactions between Mexicans and their neighbors to the north.

Far from God and Close to the United States

"Poor Mexico," dictator Porfirio Díaz is said to have lamented, "so far from God and so close to the United States." His words point to two reasons why the SIL's alliance with the Mexican state was so surprising: the religious conflict inside Mexico and Mexico's conflicted relationship with the United States. That the SIL established even a foothold in Mexico, much less a partnership with the Mexican state, was remarkable given the history of Mexico in the century before the SIL's arrival in 1931.

Because of the great power and influence of the Roman Catholic Church during the colonial era (1521–1821), Mexican liberals of the nineteenth century strove mightily to create a secular society in which the church's role would be severely circumscribed. By selling off church lands, abolishing the special legal privileges of priests and nuns, and establishing freedom of speech and education, liberals succeeded partially in limiting the church's role in public life. At the same time, they turned the church into an unflagging enemy of the Mexican state, resulting in an 1858–61 civil war between liberals and church-supported conservatives. After a costly victory, as the liberals began to rebuild the nation, they had to endure a second war. This time a French invasion forced liberal president Benito Juárez out of Mexico City and began the second civil war of the decade (1861–67). Conservatives and the Roman Catholic Church welcomed the French and eventually succeeded in luring an Austrian prince, Maximilian von Hapsburg, to the throne of the new Mexican "empire." Although Maximilian himself was not particularly conservative or Catholic, this second civil war resulted in a thorough loss of face for the church and its conservative allies. When the triumphant Juárez executed Maximilian in 1867, the message was clear—Maximilian and the Catholics and conservatives who had supported him were traitors.

Porfirio Díaz, the modernizing dictator who dominated Mexico during the period from 1876 to 1911, started out as a liberal hero but departed from liberalism in a number of ways, two of which figure in this discussion. First, he relaxed relations with the Roman Catholic Church, although he never allowed it anything like the power or influence it had enjoyed in the colonial era. Díaz saw conflict with the church as a distraction from the more important goals of political order and economic growth. Second, since he viewed foreign capital as an integral part of Mexico's modernization process, Díaz encouraged massive American and British investment in the mining, railroad, and oil sectors. Some Mexicans found this influx of foreign capital more troubling than Díaz's accommodations with the church, seeing domination of natural resources as an extension of the land grab of 1848, when the United States had forced Mexico to sell half of its territory after the U.S.-Mexican war of 1846–47. Particularly vexing were the many instances of American companies paying lower wages to Mexicans while Americans received higher wages for the same work.

In the years after Díaz the various contending factions in the Mexican Revolution (1910–20) showed a great deal of ideological variation, but there was a fair degree of agreement in the areas of church-state relations and U.S.-Mexican relations. First, as the new Constitution of 1917 firmly established, no church interference in public affairs would be tolerated. All church property would be transferred to the state; religious education would be prohibited; and priests and religious publications could no longer discuss politics or criticize the government. The revolutionary state would accomplish what the nineteenth-century liberals only dreamed of: a permanent weakening of the Roman Catholic Church. Catholic indignation burst forth in 1926, when some Catholics took up arms against the state in the bloody Cristero Rebellion. Although fighting ended in 1929, church-state relations remained quite tense through the early 1930s, with waves of anti-Catholic persecution and church resistance.

Second, the revolution—or, more precisely, the triumphant regime that emerged from the revolution—made clear its deeply nationalist credentials. Some U.S. investment would be tolerated, but foreigners would no longer be permitted to dominate any aspect of the nation. For instance, all subsurface mineral rights reverted to the nation—no longer would all of the nation's mineral wealth flow north—and only Mexicans had the right to own real estate. Similarly, no foreign priests or missionaries could operate in Mexico unless given special permission by the state. After a century of military, political, and economic humiliation at the hands of the foreigners and Mexican traitors, Mexico would at last be free and sovereign.

Thus, in 1933 Mexico had two distinctions that made it an unlikely candidate as the primary mission field of a new U.S. religious organization. Its revolutionary government had committed itself firmly to pushing its once-dominant religion out of the public square and into a thoroughly privatized, interior space. Of course, the regime's animus was reserved for the Roman Catholic Church, but all religious bodies were constitutionally restricted from owning land or playing any kind of public or political role. In fact, religious organizations of all kinds were constitutionally prohibited from having any kind of legal personality. Constitutionally and legally, they could not even exist. Revolutionary nationalism would replace Catholicism as the dominant ideology and would prevent the disastrous interventions and dominations of Mexico's past. Could any missionary organization operate in these conditions? The SIL showed that it was possible, but only through organizational contortions that no other missions were willing to copy and through an open and unreserved alliance with the Mexican state.

Fundamentalists Abroad

Before we get into what really is a Mexican story, we must digress to the United States to introduce the fundamentalist subculture from which the men and women of the SIL came. The meaning of the term *fundamentalism* has expanded in the past few decades, but this study will employ it as it was employed when it first became popular in the United States in the early 1920s to refer to "all sorts of American Protestants who were willing to wage ecclesiastical and theological war against modernism in theology and the cultural changes that modernists celebrated."[4] At the heart of this movement has always been a militant concern about the Bible. "They are fighting against modern interpretations of the Bible that they see as destroying most American denominations," writes George Marsden. "At the same time they are fighting to save American civilization, which they see as founded on the Bible."[5] Typical fundamentalist characteristics are "an intense focus on evangelism as the church's overwhelming priority, the need for a fresh infilling of the Holy Spirit after conversion in order to live a holy and effective Christian life, the imminent premillennial second coming of Christ, and the divine inspiration and absolute authority of the Bible."[6] Leading fundamentalist organizations would include the Moody Bible Institute in Chicago, Dallas Theological Seminary, and Charles Fuller's *Old Fashioned Revival Hour* radio program.

Some observers in 1925 assumed that the Scopes "monkey trial" in Dayton, Tennessee, signaled the last gasp of Christian fundamentalists. As early as 1931, H. Richard Niebuhr treated fundamentalism as if it had vanished from the face of North America by writing an article on the movement for the *Encyclopedia of the Social Sciences* that referred to it only in the past tense.[7] The reason why Niebuhr and others believed so strongly in the phenomenon's demise was that it had withdrawn from the view of much of mainstream American society during the second quarter of the twentieth century. During the twenty-five years after the Scopes trial, rather than dying a slow death, fundamentalism was going about the labor-intensive business of building its own churches, schools, magazines, colleges, seminaries, and missionary organizations. Since many major Protestant denominations had no place for them, fundamentalists created their own "parachurch" networks of institutions, including seminaries, Bible schools, radio stations, publishing houses, magazines, and retreat centers.

Contrary to the common stereotypes, fundamentalism was not confined to the South and the Midwest, nor was it composed predominantly of the disenfranchised rural poor. "Its origins and organizational centers were in the cities of the northeastern quadrant, from Chicago and St. Louis to Philadelphia and Boston," asserts Joel Carpenter. Although its adherents lived throughout the nation, in general it was composed of "Anglo-Americans and northern European immigrants of Protestant background." While fundamentalism seemed to appeal neither to the poorest sectors of the population nor to the wealthiest, it attracted the bulk of its support from the "upwardly aspiring and 'respectable' sector of the working class and . . . the lower middle class."[8]

Since fundamentalists had often fled or been expelled from mainstream Protestant denominations, they tended to cluster around Bible institutes, which became "denominational surrogates" providing "educational and other religious services, a support structure for fellowship and inspiration, and opportunities to participate in such 'Christian work' as evangelism and foreign missions."[9] Deprived of the many benefits that traditional Protestant denominations had once provided yet wary of committing themselves to a new denomination that might "go liberal," fundamentalists found in Bible institutes the kind of informal networks that allowed them to associate with like-minded Christians. Influential schools of this type, such as the Moody Bible Institute of Chicago, the Bible Institute of Los Angeles, and Columbia Bible College of South Carolina, trained generations of pastors and other leaders, including many future members of the SIL, and reached even more people through radio shows, magazines, and outreach programs.

"Because the missionary vocation was considered to demand the most radical self-denial and devotion to the evangelical cause," notes Carpenter, "volunteering for missionary service seemed a sure indication that one was a fully consecrated, Spirit-filled Christian."[10] Missionaries, therefore, were the fundamentalist first string, the movement's spiritual elite. For those who wanted to live a life of total commitment to Christ—and especially for women, who could not serve as pastors—there was no real alternative to foreign missions.

One of the great proofs of the vitality of fundamentalism from 1920 to 1950 is the life of Cameron Townsend. Born in 1896 into a struggling agricultural family that moved from town to town in rural southern California during his childhood, Townsend excelled in high school and went on to Occidental College in Los Angeles. To the dismay of his parents, who were hoping that he would become a Presbyterian minister, he dropped out after his junior year to become a Bible salesman and evangelist in Guatemala. From 1917 to 1932 Townsend traveled the roads and trails of rural Guatemala, selling Bibles, sharing the Gospel, and gaining a firsthand education in Latin American culture.

Unlike other evangelical missionaries working with him in the non-denominational fundamentalist Central American Mission, Townsend devoted much of his time to indigenous people and went so far as to translate the New Testament into Cakchiquel, a Mayan language. His attention to indigenous concerns, his willingness to socialize with Indians, and his insistence that Cakchiquels could run their own churches without missionary supervision led to tension with more traditionally minded missionaries, who believed that indigenous languages would soon die out and were therefore a waste of time. Eventually, Townsend's unconventional practices and visionary plans—he wanted, for instance, to use airplanes to reach remote villages—proved incompatible with the more conservative thrust of the other missionaries.[11]

Despite the tensions caused by Townsend's visionary and trailblazing style, the friends and acquaintances that Townsend made during his stint with the Central American Mission would stand him in good stead for the rest of his life. His marriage to a fellow missionary, Elvira Malmstrom, put him in direct contact with her home church, Harry Ironside's Moody Church of Chicago (affiliated with the Moody Bible Institute), perhaps the most influential fundamentalist empire in the United States. A developing friendship with the guest speaker at the Cakchiquel Bible Conference in January 1921, Leonard Livingston (L. L.) Legters, connected Townsend to the Pioneer Mission Agency, an organization dedicated to sending fundamentalist missionaries to new fields. When Lewis Sperry Chafer, the executive secretary of the Central American Mission, visited Guatemala in 1925, Townsend not only gave him a tour of rural Guatemala but also convinced the initially skeptical Chafer of the importance of translating the Bible into indigenous languages. When Chafer went on to found Dallas Theological Seminary, Townsend had a friend and ally at the head of what would become another of the most influential fundamentalist institutions.

Finally, Townsend befriended the Mexican educator and Protestant layman Moisés Sáenz when the two met in Panajachel, where Townsend ran a school for Cakchiquel children. Although Sáenz formerly had discounted the importance of indigenous languages, Townsend convinced him that the vernacular could play a meaningful role in the education of indigenous children. Because Sáenz was a Presbyterian he had no objections to the way in which Townsend combined evangelistic activities with education, and he invited his new friend to engage in the same kind of work in Mexico.

Thus, even though he experienced tension with other missionaries who did not believe in his innovative methods, by the age of thirty Townsend had developed strong relationships with some of the key personalities and institutions in North American fundamentalism—and with one of the few Protestants to have a significant role in Mexican education and indigenous affairs. Having resigned from the Central American Mission in 1933, Townsend turned his attentions to

Mexico, where, with the support of Legters, Ironside, Chafer, and other fundamentalist leaders, he swiftly built up his own hybrid missionary/scientific organization, known as the Summer Institute of Linguistics (and in the United States as the Wycliffe Bible Translators). In 1947, with the institute firmly established in Mexico, he shifted his attentions to Peru, where the SIL soon duplicated its Mexican success story. By the time Townsend died in 1982 at the age of eighty-six, the SIL's more than five thousand translators made it one of the largest missions agencies in the world.[12]

Making Sense of the SIL and Modern Mexico

Clearly, the SIL is a strange organization. As a U.S.-based fundamentalist missions organization that works closely with radical and nationalist foreign governments, starts no churches, and focuses on the arcane science of linguistics, it simply has no peers. It also has characteristics destined to perplex or offend almost everyone. For its fundamentalist constituency, linguistics is largely an unknown field of knowledge that few understand. The SIL's dealings with nationalist— often anti-American—governments alarms many, and its refusal to engage in normal missionary activity—preaching and starting new churches—concerns many others.[13] In the nations where it operates, the SIL provokes even more intense emotions. Nationalists oppose it as a representative of American imperialism. Secularists hate its religious mystification of fellow citizens. Those who advocate radical solutions to social problems see the SIL as diverting its converts from political action.

Despite multiple barriers to its success, the SIL managed to survive and thrive in Mexico and then in many other countries. The question, of course, is how it was able to do so. A closely related issue is what effect the organization had on Mexico and other host countries. The longevity of such a strange religious/scientific entity demands explanation and analysis. Not surprisingly, conservative Christians and secular observers have explained and evaluated the SIL's history in very different ways.

One of the most influential works about the SIL in recent years, especially among the organization's critics, has been Gerard Colby and Charlotte Dennett's biography of Nelson Rockefeller and Cameron Townsend, called *Thy Will Be Done: The Conquest of the Amazon: Nelson*

Rockefeller and Evangelism in the Age of Oil.[14] Years of research and a lively writing style make *Thy Will* an engrossing book to read, but the central implication of the work—that Rockefeller and Townsend were somehow working together to exploit the Amazon region—is never asserted, much less proved, making it strangely dissatisfying. Many readers, including supporters of the SIL, have jumped to the conclusion that Colby and Dennett have demonstrated some clear link between Rockefeller and Townsend, but it is obvious from the book that the two men never met.[15]

Others have found in *Thy Will* evidence of the SIL's complicity in international capital's willful destruction of indigenous societies.[16] Again, that is not exactly what *Thy Will* shows. It presents good evidence that the SIL was working in many of the same areas of the Amazon where Rockefeller was trying various schemes, but it presents no evidence that there was any conscious collusion between the SIL and Rockefeller enterprises. About the most that *Thy Will* can be said to prove is that in some cases prior exposure to the SIL might make some indigenous people more disposed to cooperate with capitalist forms of development. Colby and Dennett write too well to assert more than that. It is almost as if, having set out to tie Rockefeller and Townsend together, the authors found themselves in the awkward position of being unable to do so. Faced with a difficult choice between asserting more than their evidence actually supports or leaving the dots unconnected, they chose the latter, more honorable, course. In the end, though, we are left with biographies of two very different men with two very different projects who had little more in common than their interest in the Amazon.

An entirely different view emerges from the "hagiographies" written by friends of the SIL that tell the stories of latter-day Protestant "saints" in styles that evoke the New Testament book of Acts. They present the drama of missionaries trying to spread their message in hostile settings, the emotion of the first conversions, and the tragedy of violent opposition to the Gospel. They make no pretension to being academic histories and offer no more than fleeting glimpses of anything—such as politics or economics—that is not explicitly religious. As self-consciously devotional works these books are inherently limited in scope and perspective, and by themselves they will not satisfy anyone hungry for a scholarly analysis of the political and social impact of the SIL on indigenous communities. Nevertheless, because these works express a perspective from inside the SIL, they offer a wealth of information that is not otherwise available about how the SIL operates and what it values. Marianna Slocum's account of her work with the Tzeltals in *The Good Seed* and Hugh Steven's story of the early Chamulan Protestants in *They Dared to Be Different*, for example, are two extremely valuable (and underutilized) resources for the study of contemporary Chiapas.[17]

This book seeks to take a critical but not polemical, respectful but not hagiographical, approach to the SIL's history in one nation, Mexico. Like Colby and Dennett, I attempt to show connections between the SIL and major centers of power, but in this case the wielders of that power are Mexican political elites, not North American capitalists. I hope I have been more successful than they in presenting concrete evidence of those connections. Like the hagiographies, this book attempts to convey something of the drama and story of the SIL, but unlike them it also reserves the right to take up a range of political and social questions that do not always cast a positive light on the SIL. In short, rather than refuting all that has gone before, this study attempts to combine the best of the critical tradition—its questioning, investigative spirit—with the best of the celebratory tradition—its sense of the human drama that lies at the heart of the history of the SIL in Mexico.

The story told here is not exactly the "black legend" related by certain anthropologists; nor is it the kind of tale usually recounted in SIL publicity material. First, it attempts to cast new light on the presidency of Lázaro Cárdenas. Students of Mexican history may be hard-pressed to come up with a president less likely to open Mexico's doors to fundamentalist American missionaries. Students of American history might well list missionaries as the expatriates least likely to align themselves with radical, nationalist movements overseas. Both groups, then, have traditionally had difficulty making sense of the SIL's strange history. From the SIL's early days in the anticlerical Mexico of Calles and Cárdenas to its later institutionalized relationship with the Ministry of Education, its ties to the Mexican state have seemed strange, sinister, and suggestive of secret, backroom deals. Many wise observers have concluded that Townsend somehow tricked Cárdenas or that the U.S. State Department forced Townsend on Cárdenas or that the SIL was the tool of international capital. This book will argue against these interpretations and in favor of the simple but—to many—counterintuitive thesis that the relationship between the SIL and the Mexican state was a voluntary, generally sincere partnership in which each party understood and benefited from the identity and mission of the other.

A second point of emphasis will be the agency of indigenous people, that is, the idea that Indians of Mexico who interacted with the representatives of the SIL and the Mexican state in the period covered by this study (1935–85) responded to those outsiders rationally and according to what they viewed as their best interests. Some did their best to maintain the cultural boundaries of their communities, while others proved receptive to religious and cultural change. However they chose, indigenous Mexicans were not simply acted upon by the state and the SIL. Roads, public schools, and SIL linguists—often forerunners of outside influence—did not simply appear in indigenous communities because some government or missionary bureaucrat so ordered. Each of these inroads was the subject of conversation, negotiation, and sometimes resistance, both in indigenous communities and in urban centers of power. This is not to say that Mexican Indians had a great degree of power. They did not. But on many occasions they demonstrated enough power to keep the representatives of the SIL, at least, out of their villages.

Finally, the book seeks to illuminate a rather odd chapter in U.S.-Mexican relations, one in which middle- and working-class Americans —rather than economic or political elites—had the opportunity to interact directly with the Mexican state and Mexican citizens. One historian has argued recently that frequent difficulties in the relationship between the two countries were due largely to the fact that Mexico had to deal with American elites, who were not "representative of American diversity, especially in the development of democratic institutions and respect for Mexican sovereignty."[18] In the SIL's case, however, non-elite Americans provoked an angrier response than many industrialists and bankers ever did.

Chapter 1 looks at Cameron Townsend's early days in Mexico and his use of the concept of "dual identity" to differentiate the roles of the SIL and the WBT. In chapter 2 I seek to dispel the idea that Townsend somehow tricked Cárdenas into letting the SIL into Mexico. Internal and international political conditions in the mid-1930s were such that a North American evangelical scientific organization that worked with Indians had much to offer to the Cárdenas regime.

Chapter 3 emphasizes the ways in which Cameron and Elvira Townsend's support of Cárdenas's oil expropriation led to the development of the SIL's distinctive "submission theology." Chapter 4 examines the ways in which the SIL influenced Mexican indigenistas to identify linguistics as the solution to the "Indian problem." The SIL, of course, just happened to be the entity in Mexico best prepared to use linguistics in this way. In chapter 5 the religious conflicts that wracked Mexico in the 1940s are seen not to halt the rapid expansion of the SIL, due to its strong relationships with Mexican elites and its newfound linguistic legitimacy. Chapter 6 explains how the SIL managed to strengthen its position in Mexico during the 1950s, especially through a contract with the Ministry of Education. In chapters 7 and 8 we examine successful and unsuccessful SIL linguistics projects in different indigenous villages during the 1950s and 1960s. Changing emphases in anthropology in the 1960s and 1970s, especially the greater value being placed on the preservation of indigenous cultures, eventually doomed the SIL's official relationship with the Mexican government, as chapters 9 and 10 relate. The conclusion takes up some of the larger issues raised by the history of the SIL in Mexico.

Missionaries of the State

1

"All Things to All Men"

Adapting to Mexico

I have become all things to all men, that by all means I may save
some.
                    —1 Corinthians 9:19 (New American Standard Bible)

Cameron Townsend had an increasingly difficult time fitting into the
conservative, fundamentalist Central American Mission during his
later years in Guatemala, where he served from 1917 to 1932. The
problem was not that he was an ineffective missionary; in fact, he enjoyed a successful ministry and saw thousands convert as a direct result
of his work.[1] The difficulty lay in his convictions about the importance
of new tactics and strategies that seemed impractical to his colleagues.
For example, his desire to use airplanes to reach remote indigenous
villages seemed foolish and extravagant. Translating the Bible into
indigenous languages struck his colleagues as a poor allocation of resources, because each translation would take years to produce yet
would benefit only a small minority of Guatemala's population. Finally, his practice of giving Indian converts the opportunity to conduct their own affairs with limited missionary oversight ran afoul of
the Central American Mission's paternalistic policies.[2] Faced with the
mission's rejection of his new ideas, especially the translation of the
Bible into indigenous languages, Townsend returned to the United
States in 1932 and began discussing ways to implement his plans, perhaps in Mexico, with his friend and colleague L. L. Legters, the field
secretary of the Pioneer Mission Agency. Through a remarkable series
of events, Townsend managed not only to enter Mexico at a time when
the nation was barring new missionaries but also to secure the patronage of Mexico's president, Lázaro Cárdenas.

Guided to Mexico

During 1932 and early 1933, Townsend and his wife, Elvira, prayed
for guidance. They knew they wanted to translate the Bible for the

"wild tribes of Latin America," but they needed more specific direction. At the Victorious Life Conference on 10 August 1933 they received their answer. The leaders of the conference sensed that God wanted them to "set aside the schedule of meetings" and to devote the bulk of the day to prayer for Mexico. After L. L. Legters spoke of "the awful sin of American Christians in having neglected their next-door neighbor for so long," an "unusual burden of prayer" fell upon the audience. "Almost immediately," a participant at the conference later remembered, "the Lord revealed his will for Mr. Legters and Mr. W. C. Townsend of Guatemala to make a trip to Mexico City for the purpose of meeting with the government to get permission for sending men into the Indian tribes to learn the languages and to translate the Bible into those Indian tongues."[3]

This was easier said than done, for Mexico in the 1930s seemed inhospitable to religion. The nationalists who had prevailed in the revolution and written the Constitution of 1917 had viewed the Roman Catholic Church as one of their major rivals and Catholic religiosity as one of the major cultural barriers to their dream of a united, secular, modern nation. Persecution of the church and legal restrictions on a wide range of religious activities had commenced in earnest in the late 1920s, leading to the Cristero Rebellion, in which Catholics rose up against the Mexican state. Smaller rebellions continued in the early 1930s. Caught in the middle were Protestants, who, despite their general support of the regime, found their own properties nationalized and their own activities restricted.

Legters had recently returned from Yucatán and Veracruz and well knew that gaining such permission would prove almost impossible. With the tide of anti-religious activity at its high-water mark, there seemed little chance that he and Townsend would even be allowed to enter Mexico, much less receive permission to carry out their plans. Nevertheless, Legters believed that it was "perhaps the most important trip" of his life. "I think that all our future plans for Mexico will depend upon one thing—whether the authorities will give us permission to work among those tribes," he wrote Townsend. Even the Presbyterian Moisés Sáenz, who had met Townsend in Guatemala and invited him to duplicate his translation work in Mexico, believed that the anti-religious climate of 1933 would make it "very difficult" for a foreigner to get permission to work with the indigenous population. Still, Sáenz was not entirely dismissive. "Come to Mexico and see for yourself," he invited Townsend, "and I hope that after your visit we can find a way for you to stay."[4]

A New Identity

This "way to stay" was something Townsend and Legters began to think about as they planned their trip. The strategy they adopted responded to the Mexican situation in a surprising way: Townsend would renounce all his affiliations to missionary organizations so that he could say truthfully to Mexican officials that he was not a missionary. He therefore wrote a letter of resignation to the Central American Mission on 7 November 1933, explaining that he wanted to work with Indians outside Central America and that he wanted "to be able to work in Mexico," where he "would not be permitted to represent any religious organization."[5] Three days later he entered Mexico.

Because in later years critics decried similarly "flexible" approaches to identity as clearly intended to deceive, it is important to mention that at this time there was no Summer Institute of Linguistics. When Townsend resigned from the Central American Mission he was renouncing its financial support and its protection. It is also important to view his and Legters's decisions through the theological lens of American fundamentalism. In contrast to Roman Catholic priests, who view their priesthood as integral to their personal identity, Townsend and Legters felt free to divorce themselves from their "ecclesiastical" identities. Most likely they never even saw themselves as denying their missionary vocations. Any unease Townsend did express was related to the difficulties involved in the mechanics of constructing his new identity rather than guilt over its misrepresentation. "Having to be so careful makes me feel rather like a spy," he told some of his friends, "but I'd be even that in order to give the Message to those poor Indians."[6]

As devout fundamentalists, Townsend and Legters believed in the "priesthood of all believers," the idea that all Christian believers were called to evangelistic and ministerial activity. To them, any human identity beyond one's basic identity as a Christian believer was contingent and mutable, not intrinsic.[7] A position or title could be put on or taken off without enhancing or diminishing one's stature before God. In fact, it is probably fair to say that rather than the usual later dichotomies used to describe the SIL—science/religion, private/public, church/state—a more important distinction in the minds of both the SIL and their Mexican hosts was a theological one, the difference between clergy and laity. Mexico prohibited foreigners from being priests or ministers: Townsend and Legters's response was not to flout this command but to honor it. They would not preach or teach but would restrict themselves to the tasks that any layman could do. If this seems like the manipulation of a statutory loophole, it must be pointed out that this kind of individualistic, desacramentalized religion was exactly the kind envisioned by Mexico's Constitution of 1917 in its steep restrictions on clerical behavior. By prohibiting priests and ministers from voting, wearing clerical attire in public, or taking any kind of role in politics, the framers of the Constitution tried to push the clergy not only out of politics but outside public life altogether.

Using the letter from Sáenz, Townsend convinced skeptical border guards to let him into Mexico in the fall of 1933. At a dinner party in Mexico City, English anthropologist Bernard Bevans became intrigued with Townsend's project and offered to organize a luncheon at the Lady Baltimore Dining Room to introduce him to Frank Tannenbaum of Columbia University and other key American figures in Mexico. Demonstrating remarkable foresight, Townsend bought a copy of Tannenbaum's *Peace by Revolution* and asked Tannenbaum to sign it at the luncheon. Tannenbaum not only signed the book but also added some complimentary words about Townsend's work in Guatemala and gave him a letter of introduction to Rafael Ramírez, director of rural education for the Secretaría de Educación Pública (SEP; Ministry of Public Education). "It seems quite providential," he wrote to Elvira, "for it's the head of that department who is such a bitter enemy of evangelical work. I feel sure that God is going to use this contact to open the door for us."[8] Rather than wait for Ramírez to return to Mexico City, Townsend and Legters took a train to Monterrey, where Ramírez was scheduled to attend a meeting. Although impressed by Tannenbaum's recommendation and by their willingness to come all the way to Monterrey, Ramírez expressed disdain for the proposed program of Bible translation and asserted that the Bible had done enough damage to indigenous communities already. Townsend "was taken by surprise" that Ramírez already knew of his plans but replied that "the real trouble was that the priests had never given the Bible to the Indians." On hearing this, Ramírez's attitude "changed completely" and he promised to help "in every possible way."[9] When Townsend asked for permission "to study the rural school system and to write about it in the American press," Ramírez offered him a railroad pass to travel through central and southern Mexico.[10] It is hard to know what to make of this encounter and of Ramírez's generous offer, but the most logical explanation is that he admired Townsend's enthusiasm and saw him as a potential ally at a time when Mexico felt the need for good press in the United States.[11] Whatever his purpose, he knew of Townsend's religious objectives and had little sympathy with them, as is clear from a later meeting in which Ramírez "repeated that he wouldn't let the Indians have the Bible" and made Townsend promise "not to carry on any religious propaganda in the schools."[12]

Townsend's interactions with Ramírez reveal much about his pragmatic and personal approach to gaining access to Mexico. Townsend simply did not accept Ramírez's negative attitude toward Bible translation as a final answer.[13] Instead, he took Ramírez's openness to part of his project—helping indigenous people in a general sense—as the beginning of a relationship that would develop into something more to his liking. The restrictions on his religious activities and difficulties obtaining a visa were obstacles, but they could be surmounted. "Now it means that I must win the confidence of the officials fully before leaving Mexico," he told his wife, "and that our young men must be willing to come in merely to learn the languages and make personal contacts until such time as the officials have been won over to the wisdom of giving the poor Indians the Bible."[14]

After traveling five thousand miles through central and southern Mexico during the next seven weeks, Townsend returned to the United States and based himself in Sulphur Springs, Arkansas, where his brother Paul lived. There he began serious work on his two major problems. How would he obtain permission to translate the Bible in Mexico? With even Mexico's Protestants starting to despair about the anti-religious policies adopted by state and federal governments in 1934, there was little in the news to suggest that it was a good time to establish a religious mission in Mexico. But even if he obtained permission, who would perform the complex task of Bible translation into the many indigenous languages of Mexico? Learning an Indian language, creating a workable orthography, and then translating a multiauthored collection of gospels, epistles, and apocalyptic literature was hardly the kind of task that most Bible college graduates were prepared to undertake.

Townsend and Legters's answer to the second question took inspiration from the fundamentalist network of nondenominational schools, institutions, and training programs. In the new "Summer Training Camp for Pioneer Missionaries," in later years known as "Camp Wycliffe," fundamentalist youths would receive instruction in linguistics and practical missionary skills before entering their mission fields.[15] It was natural for Townsend and Legters not only to model their new institution after existing fundamentalist Bible schools and seminaries but also to see those institutions as potential allies in their project. Their translation camp was quite novel in its content and emphases, but once it gained the acceptance of evangelical leaders such as Lewis Sperry Chafer of Dallas Theological Seminary, Charles Fuller of the *Old-Fashioned Revival Hour,* and Harry Ironside of Moody Church, it received not only financial support but also a ready-made pool of potential missionaries.[16] Cameron and Elvira would start learning the language of "a new tribe" but would return to the United States every summer to direct the camp. "Spending eight or nine months of each year in Mexico and the summers here for the Camp work, I believe God will enable us to give the New Testament to another tribe in five years," he wrote from the second camp session.[17] While translating the Bible into one language, they also would be preparing translators for other languages.

As far as gaining permission to work in Mexico, Townsend's idea from the beginning seems to have been that individual Mexican officials were the key to entering the country. His unorthodox solution to the problem of winning their favor was to restyle himself as a valuable ally of the Mexican Revolution. This makeover would begin in the United States: he wrote favorable articles about Mexico to convince Mexican leaders of his sympathetic political attitudes and his usefulness as a representative of Mexican views in the United States. Townsend felt "lost trying to write secular articles," but he believed that, "having gained their gratitude through the articles," he could then "testify" to Mexican officials.[18] Thus, as soon as he got each of his three complimentary articles about Mexico published in the *Dallas News* and *School and Society,* he sent them to Ramírez and to Narciso Bassols, the Marxist head of the SEP. The articles painted a rosy picture of Mexico as a nation embarking on a "startling crusade" toward a "new world born of the revolution."[19]

Townsend did gain Ramírez's attention and appreciation through his writing.[20] More importantly, at the Seventh Inter-American Scientific Conference, in Mexico City in August 1935, Ramírez's thankfulness for Townsend's articles made possible some important contacts with other government officials. After the completion of the first training camp in Arkansas, Townsend had brought a group of students to Mexico to see the mission field for themselves. An American missionary told him that a major scientific conference, with a large section devoted to Indian affairs, was taking place at the Palace of Fine Arts. Townsend saw the conference as an opportunity to meet important officials and therefore attended with his group of "linguistic investigators." As he strolled around the conference, he told his colleague Ken Pike that he was experiencing "considerable tension" because he did not want to deceive Mexican officials about his intentions of translating the Bible. He wanted government support for his project but feared that most current government officials would dislike the religious side of his plans.[21]

When Pike asked how much they should divulge to other delegates, Townsend did not know what to say, but when he saw Ramírez at one of the sessions he was hoping to attend, he reacted boldly. "When I saw him I smiled and reached out my arms to give him an embrace," Townsend later remembered. "He got up and embraced me right there before those delegates."[22] Ramírez then introduced him to the delegates: "This is Townsend. He has come to translate the Bible."[23] At one stroke Ramírez had legitimized him and defused the tension that he had felt about revealing his religious plans. Townsend, Legters, Pike, and four others from their group were accepted as "foreign delegates" to the section of the conference devoted to indigenous affairs.[24] At the conference Townsend put his relationship with Ramírez on firmer ground and started a friendship with Mariano Silva y Aceves, the former rector of the National University and at that time director of the Instituto Mexicano de Investigaciones Lingüísticas (IMIL; Mexican Institute of Linguistic Research). He also became acquainted with Secretary of Labor Genaro Vásquez.

After the conference, Townsend managed to interest Vásquez, Silva y Aceves, and Celso Flores Zamora (the SEP's director of primary education) in a plan he had developed for the village of Tetelcingo, Morelos. "While working on the language we'll help the government in its welfare program for the Indians," Townsend strategized. "If we are able to satisfy the officials along this line it will be easy to get in ten fellows next summer for the same work."[25] He believed that if he could show good, practical results in Tetelcingo, his new friends in the government would allow him more freedom in the future. Apparently the officials liked what they heard, for Silva y Aceves's IMIL and Flores Zamora's section of the SEP agreed to publish a Nahuatl primer that Townsend had written and to distribute five thousand copies in Tetelcingo and other Nahuatl-speaking towns. Vásquez agreed to provide a used truck, funds for agricultural improvements, and a recommendation to the president that Mexico pay ten Americans to join Townsend in the work.[26]

Vásquez seems to have especially valued Townsend's efforts. When the latter wrote a booklet on literacy for him, Vásquez had the Ministry of Labor print ten thousand copies.[27] He also included Townsend, Pike, and Evelyn Griset (Townsend's niece) in a meeting he hosted to form the Sociedad de Amigos de Indios (Society of Friends of Indians), gave Townsend and Pike letters of introduction, and recommended Townsend to the SEP's division of indigenous affairs.[28] But his most helpful act was to pass on to President Cárdenas a copy of a report that Townsend had sent to U.S. ambassador Josephus Daniels.

Lázaro Cárdenas holds a special place in Mexican history, for he played a major role in restoring the legitimacy of the Mexican Revolution and the state that claimed to embody it. Whereas his predecessors had slowly moved away from the promises of the revolution, Cárdenas sided with the popular classes in three important areas. First, in agriculture he distributed more land to peasants than all of the previous presidents combined. Most of the millions of acres that Cárdenas distributed went to peasants in the form of *ejidos,* a kind of land tenure in which individual peasants received the right to farm a parcel of land but not the right to sell it, which protected them from the temptation to sell their land in hard times. Second, Cárdenas sided with labor unions in their confrontations with companies, thus improving wages and working conditions for many workers. Third, and perhaps most important, he took on oil companies from the United States and Great Britain and eventually nationalized the Mexican oil industry. He therefore serves as an icon of Mexican nationalism—a president who loved peasants and workers and who demonstrated beyond a shadow of a doubt that he would not bow to the United States or to exploitative capitalists.

Although the report that Daniels passed to Cárdenas ostensibly responded to Daniels's request for updates about Townsend's work, it seems to have been written as much for Mexican officials as for Daniels. It describes in detail the practical work Cameron and Elvira had done in Tetelcingo—planting gardens in the town plaza, growing vegetables, building a basketball court, giving sewing classes—but gives almost all the credit to various Mexican officials. For example, Javier Uranga, the spokesman for the Ministry of Labor, is described as "an unselfish and talented leader in revolutionary thought and action." All Townsend's contacts with "Mexican officialdom" inspired confidence. He concludes: "I doubt if there is a country in the world where more interest would be shown than this in helping a backward town."[29]

Cárdenas read the report and decided to check on this strangely pro-Mexican foreigner. He arrived in Tetelcingo on 21 January 1936, called Townsend by name, complimented his efforts at improving the town, and thanked him for his articles and his recent report. Since that report had started with Townsend's intention "to give the simple Bible to people with whom I came in contact" and "to see at least portions of this book of good will and brotherly love translated and published in all of the Indian languages," Cárdenas expressed no surprise when Townsend shared his religious plans with him.[30] Since 1936 was exactly the time when the president was easing the restrictions on the Roman Catholic Church, Townsend's clear articulation of his religious goal—the translation of the Bible but not the "propagation of sects"—actually may have worked in his favor. Here was a religious alternative to Catholicism that demonstrated real practical concern for rural Mexicans in a self-consciously pro-Mexican way. When Townsend asked if he could bring in more workers, Cárdenas's only concern was that they share Townsend's commitment to offering practical help for Indians. Assured that all Townsend's recruits would share this approach, Cárdenas encouraged Townsend to bring as many young people as he could.[31]

Legters thought it wise to have a "non-religious name" and suggested "American Linguistic Society." The shrewder Townsend put forward the less imposing "Summer Institute of Linguistics," which had the advantages of sounding unpretentious and avoiding reference to the group's nation of origin.[32] Eventually, the SIL family came to consist of three separate organizations: the Summer Institute of Linguistics (SIL), the Wycliffe Bible Translators (WBT), and the Jungle Aviation and Radio Service (JAARS). The SIL was the scientific organization that could contract its services to governments who might be hesitant to work with a manifestly religious organization; the WBT was the religious organization that openly solicited donations from churches and individuals for religious ends; and the JAARS was the technical support organization that was allowed to operate in some cases where the use of airplanes with overtly religious markings would have been frowned upon.

For simplicity's sake and because, in practical terms, the SIL, WBT, and JAARS functioned as one large organization, this study usually will refer to the SIL rather than to the other two entities. In a legal and theoretical sense the three organizations may be distinct, but they worked together so closely that there is no real way to tell where one started and the other began. While some critics cite the SIL/WBT dual identity (JAARS is usually left out of the picture) as evidence of the SIL's nefarious and subversive nature, this study will not focus on the issue, since it seems highly unlikely that any government official in Mexico was ever fooled into thinking that the SIL was a purely linguistic organization. Because the SIL never hid its desire to translate the New Testament into indigenous languages, and since Townsend could not stop himself from proselytizing whomever he met, it would have taken great faith in human nature and a fair degree of naïveté to suppose that the SIL translators were motivated to spend years of their lives in remote indigenous villages simply by the desire to advance linguistic science.

Dual identity functioned not as a subterfuge to slip Protestantism into Mexico but rather as a mutually acknowledged semantic concession to the political reality that no overtly religious organization could work hand in hand with the Mexican government. In 1979, when the SEP severed its agreement with the SIL, it did so not because some SEP official had suddenly discovered that the SIL was really a Protestant missionary organization but because the political cost of working with the SIL finally had become too high for the SEP to bear (see chapter 10 for more on this issue).

Serving the Revolution

The next major event in the growing alliance between the Mexican state and the incipient SIL was a banquet at Chapultepec Castle in Mexico City in early October 1936 in which the president offered almost unconditional support to the young linguists. But that banquet did not just happen. It was the culmination of the growing relationship between Townsend and Cárdenas that in turn resulted in large part from Townsend's unstinting efforts to cultivate that relationship. Starting with his first letter to the president—if he had loved the Mexican Revolution before meeting Cárdenas, now he felt "intimately identified with it and more resolved and committed to serve it"— and continuing throughout the following months, Townsend sent a steady stream of letters that emphasized themes of identification with Mexico and service to the revolution.[33] If these were words that few Americans, let alone American fundamentalists, would have uttered, that was just the point: Townsend was establishing himself as a "norteamericano raro," one who would put the interests of Mexico above those of his own nation.

Townsend made sure to assign two promising linguists, Max and Elizabeth Lathrop, to Cárdenas's home state of Michoacán and to ask the president's advice about which Tarascan community would be most suitable. In the spirit of French support for the American Revolution, he offered to organize a "brigade of university students" from Canada and the United States to serve in the "Mexican Social Revolution."[34] When Cárdenas responded favorably to his proposals, Townsend told the president that he was so "deeply inspired" that he had decided to travel through Texas, Alabama, Georgia, South Carolina, Tennessee, Kentucky, Missouri, and Arkansas to tell people about Cárdenas's "vast program" for the good of the masses.[35] Leaving Mexico would be like leaving home, so "glorious and idealistic" was the revolution's determination to bring justice to the indigenous population. It was "one of the greatest privileges" of Townsend's life to have served in the "redemption of an indigenous village." He was "an Indian at heart" and hoped to dedicate his life to "the race that has suffered so much and promises so much."[36]

Back in the United States, Townsend devoted himself to defending Mexico in the press and in conferences. He took pains to refute accusations that Cárdenas was a Communist, presenting him instead as a combination of the trust-busting Franklin Roosevelt and the slave-liberating Abraham Lincoln.[37] In fact, Townsend offered to write the biography of the man whom he believed would soon be known as the "Lincoln of Mexico," because "the sincere, unselfish and active friends of the poor are so scarce that one must introduce them to the world."[38]

Cárdenas responded favorably to Townsend's attentions. He found the idea of sending the Lathrops to the Tarascans "very satisfactory" and hoped "intensely" that Townsend could bring the brigade of students to Mexico. He promised that if they dedicated themselves to the same kind of practical work as Townsend had, his administration would take good care of them.[39] The president believed in Townsend's work enough to send 189 fruit trees, a ton of cement, two cows, and two pigs to Tetelcingo.[40] He noted and appreciated Townsend's defense of Mexico and himself in the press.[41] In sharp contrast to many other Americans in Mexico (the oil industry, e.g.), Townsend was making a concerted effort to praise Mexico, to obey its laws, and to work hand in hand with its authorities. In one letter to Cárdenas, for example, Townsend mentioned the help Tetelcingo had received from four different government agencies and six individual Mexicans.[42] It was no wonder that Cárdenas praised Townsend's "scientific and humanitarian" labors: it was almost as if Townsend was participating in a program designed by the Mexican state, rather than vice versa.[43] Cárdenas himself could hardly have designed a better "substitute" religion.

The dinner with the president in the fall of 1936 served to cement the budding relationship between Townsend and Cárdenas and to formalize the relationship between the Mexican state and the organization that was beginning to be known as the Summer Institute of Linguistics. On a symbolic level, the banquet at Chapultepec Castle for the Townsends and their ten young helpers, attended by the president and his wife, Amalia Solórzano, the governors of Quintana Roo and Michoacán, and the undersecretary of the Ministry of Foreign Affairs, indicated that Townsend and company had achieved official respectability. They were the friends and dinner guests of the president of Mexico. As Townsend and Cárdenas chatted, the president offered to pay rural teachers' salaries to any of the ten workers who needed financial support. When Townsend accepted on behalf of eight members of his group, a major milestone had been reached: the SIL literally was working for the Mexican state. A further formalization of relations occurred when Cárdenas acceded to Townsend's request that he be allowed to write a biography of the president: now the SIL was involved in public relations for the Mexican state.

Although this turn of events may have surprised some of the young linguists, it came as no surprise to Cameron Townsend. He had been working for just such a partnership between the SIL and the Mexican state for months, if not years. In fact, he had already asked the National University, the SEP, and the Ministry of Labor to sponsor or employ his workers.[44] Townsend had already written a number of favorable articles and had suggested the idea of a biography to the president's personal secretary in August 1936.[45] Far from being spur-of-the-moment decisions or sudden brainstorms, the teachers' salaries and the biography came as the result of a long period of courtship during which Townsend successfully demonstrated his organization's benefits to a long succession of Mexican officials.

It is important to note that Cárdenas was not blind to the SIL's religious purposes and that the SIL did not try to obscure its desire to translate the Bible. Townsend seems to have spent much of the evening telling the president about his religious beliefs and objectives. "We love the Bible; we believe the Bible; we try to model our lives according to the Bible; and we want to give the Bible to the tribes whose languages we study," he explained to the president. "Jesus Christ came not to be served but to serve and to give his life for others, and we wish to follow his example."[46] There is no record of how Cárdenas responded to these words of testimony, but we can surmise from his lifelong support of Townsend and the SIL that he found little in them that was objectionable. At the very least he saw this Bible-based religion as a superior alternative to Catholicism; it is even possible that he himself began to flirt with a privatized, Protestant-type faith.[47]

In fact, there was a surprising convergence between the beliefs of Cameron Townsend and those of Lázaro Cárdenas. When they looked at the indigenous people of Mexico, the American missionary and the Mexican president saw very similar problems. In his election campaign for the presidency in 1934, Cárdenas identified "language," "limited knowledge of agriculture," "the vice of alcoholism," and "fa-naticism" (a code word for Catholicism) as the most important barri-ers to the advancement of indigenous people.[48]

In his first Nahuatl primer, Townsend might have been paraphras-ing that same speech as he tells peasants to raise themselves from "ignorance, poverty and superstition." If they examine their customs, they will see that "drunkenness and fanaticism" are dragging them down but that government schools will guide them to a better life. "Learn to speak Spanish well," he encourages them, and "learn the laws of the nation."[49] Thus, although one was a conservative evangeli-cal from the United States and the other was the leading revolutionary nationalist in Mexico, the two men supported education, especially the learning of Spanish, and opposed drunkenness and "fanaticism." Both men similarly believed that the application of modern science to indigenous Mexico had the potential to solve formerly intractable problems. Both men also were impatient with the esoteric intellectu-alism and political posturing that had not led to real action on behalf of the Indians.

Townsend's desire to convert indigenous people to evangelical Christianity by means of linguistics and vernacular literacy was also not so different from Cárdenas's desire to wean them from Catholi-cism by means of state-sponsored education, which he believed was the "key to solve their problems." If the two men differed over exactly what kind of education would be best for indigenous people, they could identify a common enemy in "fanaticism." Consequently, Town-send offered Cárdenas two important weapons in the fight to improve the lot of the indigenous campesino: first, his theory about the impor-tance of the use of the vernacular promised to provide quicker and better education in the growing network of rural schools, leading eventually to the growth of Spanish and thus the unification of the nation; and second, the presence of his Protestant linguists in isolated indigenous communities would tend to impede the influence of those "enemies of the Revolution," Catholic priests.[50]

The services that Townsend and the SIL provided for Tetelcingo with the help of the SEP, the Ministry of Labor, and the IMIL might not have been exactly what residents wanted, but they definitely ap-pealed to the modernizing, nationalizing notions of Mexican elites like Cárdenas. The sheer quantity of projects that Townsend began in his first year in the town was notable. His schemes included installing an irrigated garden in the central plaza, beginning a literacy campaign that taught fifteen people to read, and planting 189 fruit trees. On other occasions he managed to find different agencies and individuals who would provide needed equipment and facilities for the town, such as books and utensils for the local school, instruments for a barbershop, and eight hundred tiles for the roof of a kindergarten. The broad appeal of charitable acts like these made possible some more controversial activities, such as the distribution of partisan political literature and "a moderate and discreet campaign against fanaticism."[51]

President Cárdenas liked what he saw in Tetelcingo so much that he authorized a generous grant to the town in 1937 that included 15,000 pesos for an irrigation project, 2,941 pesos for a pool, 19,139 pesos for the construction of the "Institute of Community Directors," and 2,614 pesos for the construction of a telephone line from Cuautla to Tetelcingo. He ordered that ejidal land be given and distributed to the members of the community and authorized the Forestry Department to donate ten thousand orange and lime trees "for planting on the lands of the ejido, for the good of the Community."[52] Cárdenas saw the work in Tetelcingo as so important that he sent the secretaries of agriculture and education to meet there with delegations from local communities.[53]

Cárdenas also paid the salaries of seven members of the Inter-American Service Brigade from 1939 to 1941. Like the Townsends, the members of the brigade devoted themselves to multiple programs in Tetelcingo: personal lessons in agricultural techniques, classes in horticulture, special consultations on fruit growing and animal husbandry, a campaign against pests, sale of milk at cost, raising of hogs and poultry, a cooperative for the making and packing of peanut butter and of tomatoes, a sewing class, a hygiene campaign, a cooking class, Saturday-afternoon games (before which all participants would sing the national anthem), a cooperative store selling items from Mexico City at cost, and the introduction of chemical fertilizers for local fields.[54]

Failure and Success in Tetelcingo

Yet all this effort by the SIL and different ministries of the Mexican government did not accomplish as much as Townsend or Cárdenas had hoped. Because of local resistance, neither the evangelistic plans of the SIL nor the modernizing schemes of Mexican elites bore great fruit. Part of the problem was that the municipio of Cuautla, where Tetelcingo was located, experienced much unrest during the 1930s as rival towns fought for the land of Hacienda Calderón, which each hoped to add to its own ejido.[55] This was one of many rural regions in Mexico where the post-revolutionary era was one of conflict as different social groups used various means, ranging from dialogue to violence, to gain access to land. In the official story of the revolution the ejidos solved the nation's agrarian problem, but in many rural communities the creation of an ejido led to new conflicts and divisions, and often to new caciques (political bosses).[56] Giving land to Tetelcingo's peasants would mean denying it to other communities. At the same time, Tetelcingo's cacique and ejidal commissioner, Francisco Carrillo, opposed Townsend's plans for the town "on religious grounds" and because the direct links to government agencies that Townsend was offering threatened his power base and his control of the community's best irrigated land.[57] Carrillo's band of "mestizos allied together to defend their political interests" threatened Townsend by firing shots over his house, and they intimidated Javier Uranga, Cárdenas's designated supervisor of the projects in Tetelcingo. Even with "many soldiers at his home and also in town," Uranga feared for his life, according to one observer. Uranga himself noted that "the politicians frequently obstruct the work of the Government with their tendency to trample social needs for their political interests." That Carrillo and his allies were not particularly astute or hardboiled antagonists—his henchman Geraldo had been on his way to kill Townsend's main local ally, Martín Méndez, when he accidentally shot himself in the hand and foot and proceeded to beg Méndez to come and help him—makes their ability to alarm a heavily guarded representative of the federal government that much more remarkable, and indicative of the relative weakness of the federal government.[58]

Because he controlled the positions of ejidal commissioner, president of the agricultural credit society, and judge, Carrillo steered almost all of the previously irrigated land in the new ejido to himself and his cronies. He also managed to divert most of the water from the newly constructed irrigation system so that his fifty-four hectares of "magnificent" rice fields contrasted sharply with the "almost completely devastated" rice fields of the village's other one hundred families. The ejidatarios lived in fear of losing their parcels of land; many families, in fact, had no land at all and had to work as peons for Carrillo, who exploited them more cruelly than the hacendado of the old Hacienda Calderón had. When an official of the Bank of Ejidal Credit arranged for three tractors to be used for the planting of sugarcane, Carrillo expressed his displeasure and the three tractors simply sat in the fields, with locals and federal employees alike afraid to oppose his wishes.[59] Finally, in 1940 Uranga boasted that he had managed to distribute ejidal lands more fairly and that he would be seeking employment elsewhere. He left the impression that things were still not altogether equitable, though, when he mentioned that his replacement might want to engage in "a complete reorganization of all the ejidos" and would require "full authorization" to carry out such an endeavor.[60]

Ultimately it was not so much the resistance of Carrillo's armed band that hindered the plans of the government and the SIL for Tetelcingo. For one thing, as Townsend expanded his vision to reach all the indigenous groups in Mexico and then oversaw the SIL's expansion into Peru, Tetelcingo received less and less of his attention. Although the Townsends and their colleagues did enough obviously religious work to attract the attention of the Roman Catholic Church, which "sent three priests and a bishop to conduct a special mission" against the Protestant interlopers, they never saw mass conversions or great interest in the religious side of their work.[61] While most SIL linguists found that duties beyond Bible translation distracted greatly from their primary task, Townsend always had a full agenda of other commitments. As the SIL's growth increased his responsibilities, he wanted to set an example by continuing his fieldwork in Tetelcingo, but he simply could not give the town the kind of day-to-day attention that Bible translation or effective evangelism demanded.

When Cameron and his second wife, Elaine (Elvira died in 1944), moved from Mexico to Peru in 1946, they left behind an uncompleted translation and effectively ended Tetelcingo's bonanza of government attention. Without Cameron's motivating and engaging personality, there was simply little reason for government officials to lavish the town with projects. At the same time, members of the community do not seem to have been particularly eager to apply what the Townsends and the Inter-American Service Brigade had taught them or to maintain the various "improvements" they had received. By Townsend's own admission, the park in the town plaza that had so impressed Cárdenas on his first visit "only lasted a year and a half."[62] After the multiple projects of 1936, Townsend had to confess to Cárdenas that "in large part your efforts to help this pueblo and those of the Department of Labor and of myself have failed."[63]

Although Townsend might have regretted that more had not been accomplished in Tetelcingo, he definitely rejoiced in the expanding influence of the SIL. The park, for example, was not a total failure. "As soon as we had gone away the cattle came and destroyed most of it," he later admitted, "but it was beautiful while it lasted and it had its effect."[64] The most important "effect" was that many officials who did not share Townsend's religious convictions nevertheless endorsed (quietly) his evangelistic aspirations because of what they had seen in Tetelcingo. For example, Carlos Basauri of the SEP had confided to him that he wanted to see "evangelical pastors among all the Indian congregations because . . . the human heart demands religion, and Indians should have a more decent religion than the one they have." Cárdenas liked what he saw so much that he suggested that evangelicals extend their work to the Indians of South America too. "Many of the officials consider us missionaries," Townsend reported. "This does not seem to affect their friendship towards us in the least."[65] Thus, although Tetelcingo did not succeed greatly as a missionary enterprise, it did have lasting benefits for the SIL. For Basauri, Secretary of Labor Vásquez, and other officials, it would serve as a shining example of enlightened missionary activity. For Townsend and company, Cárdenas's friendship alone was worth all the effort that had been put into the town.

Mexican officials' positive response to Tetelcingo also convinced Townsend that practical service was absolutely essential to the SIL's ministry. This was not always a popular policy, for the SIL linguists already struggled with the requirement that they avoid traditional evangelistic activities. In the United States, liberal Protestants had moved away from the evangelism that fundamentalists believed was an essential part of the Christian life and had replaced it with the "social gospel" of service to the poor. Consequently, adding activities that smacked of the "social gospel" to their responsibilities was almost too much for these good fundamentalists to bear. In the face of widespread complaints and, even worse, neglect of practical service, Elvira mailed all the translators copies of the report that Cameron had sent to Ambassador Daniels and Secretary Vásquez in 1935. "We are sending you each a copy of the report that you may know more correctly the basis on which we have been given such a hearty welcome to Mexico," she wrote, "and that we may all continue to work as SER-VANTS for Jesus' sake along the same principles as outlined in the report."[66] When linguists objected that "little projects" took time away from translation work, Cameron replied that he would listen to almost any advice about how to care for a horse, "but when you say to cut off one of its legs, how can I listen? If you take away from the SIL the policy of service, how could I possibly follow your advice?"[67] Even when it seemed to fail from the standpoint of evangelism, Tetelcingo-style practical service was the kind of activity that Mexican elites responded to, and it therefore needed to be part of the SIL's repertoire.

Cárdenas Had His Reasons

*Why a Nationalist President Embraced
American Fundamentalists*

The SIL's many early successes may make sense to readers disposed
to see the providential nature of the SIL's beginnings, but to those
familiar with the labyrinthine nature of Mexican politics, the seemingly miraculous ability of the almost penniless Cameron Townsend
to gain the favor of one Mexican official after another may seem suspect. How could one rather poor American get so close to Mexico's
most influential leaders? Why would notoriously anti-religious officials
such as Rafael Ramírez have anything to do with an American missionary, much less sponsor his activities? What could have motivated
Lázaro Cárdenas, one of Mexico's most nationalistic presidents, to
welcome and support an American missionary enterprise in the indigenous heart of Mexico? Since the SIL account sounds contrived
and simplistic, observers have concluded either that Townsend somehow tricked numerous Mexican officials or that he had the support
of powerful U.S. sectors that forced Mexican officials to bend to their
desires.[1] One Mexican writer, for instance, suggests that the SIL's entrance into Mexico may have been arranged by the Bucareli Street
agreements of 1923, in which Mexico made a number of concessions
to U.S. interests in return for recognition from the Coolidge administration.[2]

The context of 1930s national and international politics makes
such speculations unnecessary. This chapter will demonstrate that
Mexican officials such as Ramírez, Vásquez, and Cárdenas had good
political reasons for their decisions to open doors to Townsend. The
Mexican regime's openness to the SIL sprang from the specific political and social circumstances between 1931 and 1938: the Mexican
state's ongoing conflict with the Roman Catholic Church and Mexico's
great economic and political dependence on the United States. This
chapter also introduces the political and religious landscape of Mexico
in the 1930s, a landscape that had a profound effect on the evolution
of the SIL's relationship with the Mexican state.

The Ongoing Conflict

One of the major reasons why Cárdenas and others welcomed the SIL was the religious conflict that raged throughout the country from 1931 to 1936. Often the religious issues of the mid-1930s have fallen under the shadow of the Cristero Rebellion, agrarian reform, socialist education, and oil expropriation, as if religious issues had been laid to rest with the agreements of 1929 that ended the Cristero Rebellion. The fact is, though, that conflict between the state and the Roman Catholic Church dominated the Mexican scene for much of the decade. In fact, it seems difficult to make much sense of Cardenista policies, including openness to working with Townsend and the SIL, without taking account of the religious politics that were so important to the period.

The basic elements of the conflict between church and state were, on the one hand, the government's restrictions on the number of priests allowed to officiate, its taking of church property, and its educational reforms, and, on the other hand, the Roman Catholic Church's responses to these programs. Each side leveled strong allegations against the other: the church claimed that the Mexican government was systematically persecuting priests and nuns, going so far as rape and murder; the government accused the Catholic hierarchy of fomenting an armed rebellion. Both sides' claims seem to have been at least partly true.[3]

These tensions were nothing new, since various colonial and national governments had battled the church for centuries. The 1920s, however, had brought a new intensity on the government's part. Whereas the liberals of the nineteenth century had sought to wrest supremacy from the church, the post-revolutionary regimes went so far as to seek the elimination of the church. Plutarco Elías Calles, as president (1924–28) and then as the nation's so-called *jefe máximo* (1928–34), made the war against the church one of the government's top two or three priorities. He so hated the Roman Catholic Church, perhaps because of feelings of shame and anger related to his own illegitimate birth, that the mere mention of religious topics would provoke him to violent action.[4] At the same time, the war against the church proved less costly than the implementation of the social programs (especially agrarian reform) promised by the revolution. Warring with the church became a way to preserve a radical reputation without the expense of substantive reform. Thus, strong hatred of the church and the desire to deflect attention from the dying revolution led Calles to an intentional provocation of the church in his 1926 Ley Calles, which nationalized church property, expelled foreign priests, and closed Catholic schools. When Catholic bishops responded by suspending church services throughout the nation, Calles almost encouraged the church to take more extreme measures. Thousands (eventually more than fifty thousand) of Catholic partisans took up arms in 1927. Because the Mexican state proved unable to defeat the Cristero rebels, in 1929 it had to accede to a peace settlement brokered by U.S. ambassador Dwight Morrow in which religious restrictions would stay on the books but would not be enforced.

In 1931, after two years of relative calm in relations between church and state, President Pascual Ortiz Rubio opened the year with the bluntly provocative decision to hand over Corpus Christi Church in Mexico City to the schismatic Iglesia Católica Apóstolica Mexicana. Then the state of Veracruz not only restricted the number of priests allowed to officiate to one for every one hundred thousand residents but also fired all of its Catholic schoolteachers. Yucatán and Chiapas followed suit with similarly restrictive laws, including Yucatán's prohibition of children under thirteen from churches, only to be surpassed by Tabasco's ban on all priests within its borders.[5] Other states followed suit, so that by early 1932 legislatures in every state but one had instituted new restrictions on the number of priests.[6]

Undeterred by these restrictive measures, the Mexican hierarchy took a number of bold, perhaps foolhardy, steps to preserve its power and influence. Archbishop Leopoldo Ruiz y Flores refused to name the eleven priests that would be permitted under the new Veracruz law and told priests not to leave their parishes until forced out.[7] Pope Pius XI's encyclical *Acerbi Animi* of 30 September 1932 counseled Catholic peacefulness but threw more fuel on the fire by claiming that the state had neglected to honor the agreements of 1929, fortifying Catholics in their indignation and convincing anticlericals that he was calling for another Cristiada.[8] The church fought back in the courts, then decided to celebrate the four-hundredth anniversary of the appearance of the Virgin of Guadalupe, Mexico's patron saint, with a series of massive public festivals. The combination of the regime's obsessive hatred of the church, on the one hand, and the hierarchy's recklessness, on the other hand, ignited the conflict once again. While José Vasconcelos's challenge in the presidential elections of 1929 had forced Calles to accept a negotiated peace to the Cristero Rebellion (to prevent Vasconcelos from joining forces with the Cristeros), by 1931 Calles and the more anticlerical state governors felt free to devote their energies once more to defeating the church.[9]

To Calles and his allies, the Guadalupan celebrations seemed like a direct violation of the agreements negotiated in 1929 and thus a perfect excuse to violate the accords themselves. Wanting to send a clear message, the government responded swiftly: in late December 1931, less than two weeks after the end of the celebrations, the Mexican congress passed a law limiting the number of priests in the Federal District and in all territories administered by the federal government to one for every fifty thousand people. At a time when there were over one million inhabitants and more than four hundred churches in the city, the legislature had effectively lowered the number of legally officiating priests in Mexico City to twenty-four.

To make matters worse, these restrictions were coupled with the continued confiscation of church properties, most of which became schools or government administrative offices. As if to make clear that confiscation was a matter not merely of using resources efficiently but of punishing enemies and rewarding allies, in 1933 Mexico City's Santa Catalina de Sena Church was given to the Presbyterians and made into a Protestant church. Then, in 1934, the regime's support of the schismatic Iglesia Católica Apóstolica Mexicana continued with the gift to that body of a chapel in the Colonia Obrera neighborhood of Mexico City.[10]

In Catholic eyes, these attempts to weaken the church by antagonizing its personnel and giving its property to its religious rivals were disagreeable enough, but they paled in comparison to new government education policies, which went beyond the public realm into the sacred domain of the family. First, a 1932 law stripped private schools of any kind of religious content, depriving Catholic parents of the ability to educate their children as they saw fit. Then, in 1933, Secretary of Education Narciso Bassols called for the implementation of a sexual education program, and the ruling Partido Nacional Revolucionario proposed to liberate children from "religious dogmatism" by making all public education "socialistic." If this was not enough to confirm Catholic fears that the field of education would become the next battlefield in the contest between church and state, Calles soon issued his famous "Grito de Guadalajara." In that impassioned speech of 1934 he went beyond the usual revolutionary rhetoric about the importance of the public education to assert that Mexico's children actually *belonged* to the revolution. He condemned as selfish and reactionary any idea that children belonged to the home or to the family, for only the revolution could "form the new national soul."[11]

In 1932 and then again between 1934 and 1936, Cristero rebels took up arms in Veracruz, Querétaro, and Jalisco. In Mexico City, Catholic parents removed their children from public schools and began a protest that led to Bassols's resignation in May 1934.[12] In late 1934 only fifteen of the twenty-eight Mexican states permitted religious services. Of those fifteen, at the permissive end of the scale, San Luis Potosí permitted seventy priests to officiate and Jalisco allowed fifty. At the other end of the spectrum, Querétaro, with two priests, and Nayarit, with five, conceded no more than a token presence to the church. Furthermore, in some of those fifteen states few or no churches remained open.[13]

Restrictions on the church, Catholic defiance, government reprisals: this was the political and social reality of Mexico from 1931 to 1936. The limits placed on priests and the closure of churches meant that in an overwhelmingly Catholic nation most people were being forbidden to practice the central rituals of their faith. To have even one state where no religious services were being held would be remarkable, but to have thirteen marks what must surely be one of the boldest steps in social engineering ever taken in Mexico. This situation of profound religious tension did not seem especially auspicious for the establishment of a new religious enterprise in Mexico, but both Cameron Townsend and Lázaro Cárdenas proved adept at adapting fundamentalism to the context of revolutionary Mexico. Cárdenas wanted to reduce the level of confrontation with the Roman Catholic Church while still chipping away at its power and influence. He saw in Townsend someone who had the potential to help him in this more understated version of the Mexican state's continuing attack on Catholic power and influence.

Obedient Protestants

Cárdenas also had good reason to believe that converts to Protestantism would be good political allies of his regime. Starting in the 1820s with the first real Protestant missionary to Mexico, James Thompson of the British and Foreign Bible Society, Protestantism in Mexico had always had a liberal, anticlerical flavor. Because of the long association of Roman Catholicism with conservatism, monarchy, and the status quo, conversion to Protestantism was not simply a religious act but a political one as well. Serious Protestant evangelism from the north began in the 1860s when Baptist missionaries began working in northern Mexico. They were followed in the 1870s by Methodists and Presbyterians, and by 1890 there were at least fifty thousand Protestants worshipping in about 470 congregations. By 1913 only five Mexican states lacked a Protestant missionary station, and there more than six hundred Protestant schools. These Protestants were not numerically powerful, but their networks of schools and churches produced thousands of liberal thinkers (it was virtually impossible for a Mexican Protestant to be politically conservative) who were quite ready to join the revolution when it came and to support the revolutionary regime afterward.[14] As the foremost historian of Mexican Protestantism has concluded, Protestantism often led to "active political participation in opposition [to Porfirio Díaz] that was particularly meaningful when one took account of the extreme minority status of the movement."[15]

Although Catholics liked to portray Mexican Protestants as stooges of North American imperialism, most Protestants were fiercely nationalistic.[16] During the revolution most missionaries left Mexico, so these already-nationalistic Protestants gained a further sense of independence as they ran their churches for years without missionary control. When those missionaries met in Ohio to formulate the Cincinnati Plan, in which denominations received exclusive rights to certain geographical regions, Mexican Protestants felt left out of an extremely important and far-reaching decision. Their bitterness about the Cincinnati Plan in large part scuttled the plan's effectiveness and marked another step in many Mexican Protestants' gradual separation from missionary influence. Most Mexican Protestants believed that they should control their churches and that good relations with the Mexican state were more important than pleasing their missionary patrons.[17]

"They never lead or promote mobs; they never attack the Government officials; they never issue subversive and flaming manifestoes. . . . Protestants understand the meaning of the law and quietly obey it." This statement from a 1926 booklet by Methodist writer Gonzalo

Báez-Camargo expressed the Mexican Protestant understanding of post-revolutionary religious conflict: it was all the Catholics' fault. Báez-Camargo contended that there was no religious persecution in Mexico, that the government was doing a wonderful job of modernizing the country, and that Catholic truculence and avarice were the only barriers to democracy and prosperity. In contrast to Catholic rebelliousness, he offered Protestant submissiveness. Even though they were experiencing major losses of their own property and severe restrictions on their religious mission because of the Catholics' sins, Protestants would continue to support the revolutionary government that they admired and respected.[18] Protestants continued to present this rhetoric of Catholic rebelliousness and Protestant submissiveness in public and private, in Mexico and the United States, throughout the 1920s and 1930s. Especially during the Cristero Rebellion and the troubles of the mid-1930s, this rhetoric contrasted sharply with official Catholic pronouncements rejecting the Mexican Constitution.

Protestant support of the Mexican regime was not based on unqualified agreement with the regime's policies. In fact, Mexican Protestantism was severely damaged by the restrictions on religion, which were not confined to Catholicism. The U.S. consul in Guaymas, Sonora, for instance, reported in 1934 that "every single church," including Protestant churches, in Sonora had been closed and that the churches in the state of Sinaloa were expected to be closed soon. He related the case of a Baptist missionary whose church in Empalme, Sonora, had been confiscated by the government to be used as a home for the federal school inspector and as a meeting place for labor organizations. This missionary "was very pessimistic about the situation in general, stating emphatically that the so-called Socialist teachings in the schools and the frequent meetings of laborers which are being held for the ostensible purpose of advancing socialist ideas are really nothing more than an attack on the churches."[19]

Although most Mexican Protestants and American Protestant missionaries had welcomed the revolution and had endorsed the measures taken to limit the power of the Roman Catholic Church, they had expected their support to garner them more favorable treatment from the state. Instead, they now found their work restricted, their 250 schools closed, their twelve hospitals incorporated into the state system, and some of their property taken away. They ultimately chose to tolerate these losses not because they deemed them just but because they believed that these laws might hobble their Catholic rivals.[20] Protestants responded to these reversals with a rhetoric of submission that was somewhat at odds with the spirit of the revolution and somewhat at odds, even, with the boldness with which Protestants themselves had taken up arms. Still, it was a shrewd appeal to a government that needed allies in both Mexico and the United States.

Mexican officials welcomed Protestant support, especially when it influenced American public opinion. Their real worry was that Catholics would persuade Protestants that the "religious issue" was more than a parochial Catholic concern, that it touched on profound matters of rights and human dignity. Ambassador to the United States Francisco Castillo Nájera was thus disturbed that Catholic priests and bishops were trying to build bridges to American Protestants. He need not have worried, for American Protestant leaders, especially those with missionary experience in Latin America, seemed quite willing to support the Mexican regime. Samuel Guy Inman, a Protestant missionary spokesman and distinguished scholar, worked tirelessly during much of the 1930s to counteract "propaganda against Mexico," going so far as to organize the Mexican-American Cultural Relations Association specifically for this purpose. When socialist education began to generate negative publicity in 1934, Inman worked behind the scenes to restrain a number of organizations from adopting resolutions that might have cast Mexico in an unfavorable light. He stressed to these bodies that the situation in Mexico was "very different" from that in the United States and that the same standards could not be applied to both countries.[21] Consequently, the Mexican embassy welcomed a meeting with officers and pastors of the World Baptist Alliance in 1935, even though it recently had refused to meet with the secretary of the National Catholic Welfare Conference.[22] Protestants, in short, were proven allies of the Mexican regime. Cárdenas and other Mexican leaders knew of and valued Protestant support and were thus predisposed to take Cameron Townsend seriously as a potential ally.

Uncomfortable but Necessary

The other dynamic that Townsend and Cárdenas had to take account of was the relationship between the United States and Mexico. Mexico was quite aware, as Ambassador Castillo Nájera pointed out to the

Academy of World Economics in 1936—that Mexico was only the United States' seventh-largest trading partner but that of all Mexican exports, 52 percent went to the United States. Mexico was also vulnerable on the other end, since 61 percent of its imports came from the United States.[23] Any significant drop in American purchases or sales could bring the fragile post-revolutionary economy to its knees. At the same time, as a cash-poor nation that wanted both to develop social programs and build a strong industrial base, Mexico still coveted U.S. investment. "Do not let social reforms frighten you," advised Castillo Nájera. "Without them the transformation of Latin America—I should rather say, of my country—is impossible." He then quoted President Cárdenas to make clear that this was an official policy: "Foreign capital will be welcome, provided it recognizes the economic rights of the workers and does not seek special privileges, such as are not accorded Mexican capital. . . . Nothing is more useful than capital which is willing to share in our own destinies."[24] As much as Mexican officials may have hated to admit it, the relationship with the United States had to be kept on good terms or all of Mexico would suffer the economic consequences.

Many former combatants in the revolution had hoped to achieve some measure of independence from the United States and from American capital, but even the most nationalistic among them recognized the serious nature of the situation. A significant drop in U.S.-Mexican trade would put the hopes and dreams of the revolutionary regime in jeopardy. Mexico might have felt free to act independently if other Latin American nations had stood with it, but only the liberal government of Colombia showed anything approaching sympathy for Mexico's revolutionary project. The oligarchs and dictators of the other Latin American nations remained uncomfortable with Roosevelt's New Deal liberalism, never mind Mexico's more radical designs.[25]

This need for strong relations with Washington thus serves as the backdrop to all that follows. Mexican leaders might have wanted to plot their own political course and ignore their neighbor to the north, but they knew they needed to maintain at least a civil relationship in order to keep American markets open. Similarly, if they were going to ally themselves with another nation in the Americas, the United States under Franklin Delano Roosevelt seemed a far better choice than South American dictatorships. The point is not that Mexico had to follow every wish and whim of Washington—Cárdenas's 1938 oil expropriation surely puts that idea to rest—but rather that Mexican leaders always had to take serious account of Washington's views.

And what did the United States want from Mexico in the era of the New Deal and the Good Neighbor Policy? The Roosevelt administration's fundamental policies toward Mexico in the 1930s involved three main objectives: first, to maintain a fairly cordial relationship that did not hinder the economic ties between the two countries; second, to implement the Good Neighbor Policy, in which the United States would treat Latin American nations as friends and allies rather than as American fiefdoms; and third, surprisingly enough, to work quietly for religious freedom in Mexico. If the first two objectives had somewhat higher priority for Roosevelt and Secretary of State Cordell Hull, the "church situation" held special interest for Ambassador to Mexico Josephus Daniels, who in 1936 remarked to Undersecretary of State Sumner Welles: "Of the various problems we have before us, there is nothing I follow more closely."[26] Mindful of Mexico's resentfulness of foreign interference in its internal affairs, Daniels always insisted that he "never injected into official dealings American requests for action as to church matters." This was a bit disingenuous, for he stated in his next breath that he took every occasion to express his conviction that "democracy, freedom of religion, and public education" were necessary to the health of any country. Daniels had many "heart-to-heart talks" with Cárdenas in which he expressed the hope that Mexico would soon allow true religious liberty.[27] Supporting Townsend's evangelistic linguistic project thus allowed Cárdenas to demonstrate his support of religious freedom, his openness to the United States, and his willingness to take seriously the concerns of the Roosevelt administration at the same time that he was advancing his own subtle attack on Catholicism.

It is no wonder that the revolutionary state looked with favor on Protestantism. In the United States, Protestants were the key to counteracting Catholic propaganda; in Mexico, Protestantism might well be a good substitute for Catholicism. Cárdenas and other key officials could not help but notice that Protestants from Mexico and the United States took great pains to assert their religion's compatibility and kinship with revolutionary nationalism at a time when the Catholic hierarchy embodied incompatibility and opposition.

Consequently, despite the religious conflicts and often generally anti-religious atmosphere of Mexico in the 1930s, a number of factors made it an auspicious time for the establishment of an organization such as the Summer Institute of Linguistics. Alerted by Catholic talk of widespread religious persecution, American politicians were charging the Mexican regime with across-the-board attacks on religious people of all creeds. Mexican officials, as we have seen, still harbored grave suspicions about the Catholic hierarchy, but they received a fair measure of support and sympathy from Protestants in both the United States and Mexico. In this situation, allowing Townsend and the SIL into Mexico had a number of advantages for the regime: in one move it could show the United States its tolerance for religion, gain the sympathy of Protestants, and strike a further blow at the Roman Catholic Church by introducing Protestantism into the traditionally conservative countryside.

Cameron Townsend proved particularly well suited to working in Cárdenas's Mexico. Unlike other American Protestants who wanted to work there, he was willing to give up a great deal of traditional Protestant missionary practice and a great deal of his identity as an American in order to gain official Mexican sanction for his project. This kind of pragmatism made Townsend and company welcome in Mexico when other would-be missionaries were being turned away. In an era when the Mexican state needed American allies and still hoped to weaken the power of the Roman Catholic Church, an American Protestant of any stripe was a helpful ally, but a Protestant who identified as easily with the hopes and dreams of the revolution as Townsend did had particular value to the regime.

An Indirect Approach to the Religious Issue

When Cárdenas became president in December 1934, he chose to rely on education and other strategies of replacement or substitution in the revolutionary state's ongoing battle with the church rather than on the more direct approaches (closing churches and limiting priests) that Calles and his allies had favored. Socialist education served as the most obvious official alternative to Catholicism, but the regime was ready to aid many different non-Catholic faiths and ideologies. A few of these efforts include the following: in May 1936, the Mexican government welcomed Greek Orthodox Christian leader Atenágoras, to the capital with a "squad of special police" and provided him with the use of a Catholic church for his "pontifical" mass; during his presidency, Cárdenas tried to foment a new kind of Mexican Freemasonry for workers and peasants, although without great success; in addition to the already-mentioned gift of a Catholic church in Mexico City, the state gave the National Presbyterian Church two Catholic churches in Yucatán.[28]

The large indigenous population posed perhaps the greatest barrier to the regime's plans to "defanaticize" its people. Often living in communities that lacked not only schools but also any significant contact with proper "scientific" ideology, these unfortunates were, many officials believed, particularly susceptible to the dangers of superstition and priestly domination. One of Mexico's leading educators, Moisés Sáenz, who earlier had met Townsend in Guatemala and invited him to Mexico, believed that the state should promote music, dance, drama, and other cultural practices as replacements for indigenous Catholicism. The religious problem would be addressed by the "positive means of substitution" instead of by the old means of "suppression and persecution."[29] Sáenz saw no possibility of eliminating religion; to him, even attempting such a course would have been misguided, unwise, and probably futile. Instead, he proposed the secular infiltration of indigenous religion and the capture of indigenous customs for the state. It is no surprise, then, that Sáenz expressed great interest in Townsend's religious and educational work with the Cakchiquels of Guatemala. His invitation to come to Mexico was thus not merely a courtesy to a fellow Protestant but also an expression of a general Cardenista policy of religious replacement. As we shall see, Townsend's willingness to tailor his organization's activities to the state's liking made his project particularly appealing.

Unlike Calles, the new president did not see religion as the major issue facing the nation. Although no friend of "fanaticism," Cárdenas chose to emphasize public education rather than direct confrontation in his attempts to limit the power of the church. Catholicism was for him a superstition that would pass when Mexicans were properly educated rather than the specter that haunted Calles's every waking moment. If he had had his way when he succeeded to the presidency in December 1934, he probably would have ended the most blatant forms of persecution. Cárdenas could not immediately institute his own policies when he took office, however. He needed time to consolidate his power and to wrest power from Calles before he could replace state governors and make other drastic changes. Since state governors had the authority to enforce key aspects of the Constitution's restrictions on religion, the differences between Cárdenas's more subdued approach to anticlericalism and Calles's obsessive style were not readily apparent until the spring of 1936.

In February 1936, Cárdenas's new approach became evident as the government loosened its restrictions and opened a number of churches.[30] In early March, Cárdenas made a decisive break with the policies of his predecessors in an address to teachers in Guadalajara. The religious issue would no longer dominate the revolutionary agenda: "It is not the job of the Government to undertake anti-religious campaigns that accomplish nothing but waste the effort of public servants, cause resistance, and postpone indefinitely the achievement of the economic and social goals necessary for the well-being of the people."[31] The state of Campeche followed the president's lead by opening a number of churches.[32] On 30 March 1936, Cárdenas's secretary of the interior, Silvano Barba González, announced that, since all religious buildings belonged to the federal government and since the federal government had never ordered their closure, all those churches that had not been retired from religious service (converted into schools, offices, etc.) could now be reopened. The federal government had not *commanded* the reopening of the churches, but it had given a strong signal to state governments that such was its desire. This new official policy produced "a considerable lessening of tension" throughout the country as churches began reopening in state after state and "Catholics observed Easter with complete liberty, in the capital, at least."[33] It is important to recognize that this "lessening of tension" by no means indicated an elimination of conflict between church and state. Cárdenas would continue the state's long conflict with the church, but with more stealth and much more success than his predecessors by using surrogates like the SIL.

Was Cárdenas fooled? Was allowing a fundamentalist missionary from the United States to work with the Mexican government a grave mistake? Did this icon of revolutionary nationalism fail to grasp who Townsend really was? We can answer in the negative to all three questions. Cárdenas knew what he was doing. He knew who Townsend was; he knew about Townsend's religious agenda; and he knew that supporting Townsend's work would bring Protestantism into indigenous communities all over Mexico. In the 1930s Cárdenas and other Mexican elites had very strong reasons to be welcoming to American Protestants. They had even more reason to welcome Townsend and the organization that would become the SIL, for Townsend was eager to adapt himself and his organization to the needs and desires of the Mexican regime.

3

Identifying with Mexico

> Let every soul be subject unto the higher powers. For there is
> no power but of God: the powers that be are ordained by God.
> Whosoever therefore resisteth the power, resisteth the ordinance
> of God.
>
> —Romans 1:1–3 (King James Version)

When President Lázaro Cárdenas nationalized the Mexican oil industry on 18 March 1938, he was taking a calculated risk. His justifica-
tion for his decree, which transferred the land, oil, and equipment
of seventeen U.S. and British companies to the Mexican state, was
reasonable—the foreign companies, after all, had refused openly to
comply with a decision of the Mexican Supreme Court—but the companies exercised tremendous influence in their home countries. It was
not impossible that the oil companies could convince their respective
governments to intervene economically, politically, or even militarily.
In fact, Theodore Roosevelt's Corollary to the Monroe Doctrine had
asserted the United States' right to act as a police power in the Western Hemisphere to preserve "order," and the United States had not
been remiss in applying the corollary in the Caribbean and Central
America in the decades since it was issued in 1904. Dozens of times
in the three decades prior to 1933 the United States had intervened
militarily in nations such as Nicaragua, Haiti, and Mexico itself. In
1914, for instance, President Woodrow Wilson had ordered the invasion of Mexico's main port of Veracruz in response to a trivial incident involving the arrest (and quick release) of American sailors. Two
years later Wilson had sent six thousand soldiers under Gen. John J.
Pershing into northern Mexico to capture and punish Pancho Villa
after the revolutionary's infamous raid on Columbus, New Mexico.

Cárdenas was gambling that in 1938, with the depression still
plaguing the U.S. economy and with conflict looming in Europe and
already raging in Asia, President Franklin Roosevelt would be very
hesitant to use military force. The unsuccessful Pershing expedition

twenty years earlier had run through $130 million in less than a year, and the retaking of the Mexican oil fields would be a much larger operation. At the same time, Cárdenas was gambling that most Mexicans would support his action, that Mexican nationalism would surge in this confrontation with greedy foreign capital. The cost of misjudging the American reaction to oil expropriation would have been extreme for Cárdenas and for Mexico. If Roosevelt had sent in the Marines, the Mexican military would have had a very low probability of prevailing. What the Mexican president needed in this situation was as much support inside the United States as possible.

If Cárdenas ever wondered whether he had made a wise decision in allowing Townsend and the SIL into the interior of Mexico, the oil expropriation crisis confirmed to him that he had. In the spring of 1938, all other concerns within the bilateral relationship faded for the diplomats and officials of the two countries. Religious persecution was already in abeyance by then, but it might as well have dropped off the map. Ambassador Josephus Daniels, Ambassador Francisco Castillo Nájera, and their staffs seem to have devoted almost all their attention to negotiating some kind of an oil settlement. Cárdenas and Roosevelt wrote worried letters to their negotiators while the oil companies shifted their publicity campaigns into high gear. Mexican officials began to feel more and more alone. When it came to choosing between U.S. companies and the Mexican government, it seemed to the Mexicans that even the most liberal New Dealers moved instinctively to close ranks around the American capitalists.

President Cárdenas found the U.S. response to the expropriation and other financial matters extremely disappointing. "The continual intervention of the American Ambassador in Mexico or of the Department of State in each one of the conflicts that involves North American citizens who have business here seems excessive to us," he complained. "All it takes is for one company to have a conflict with its workers and we start receiving protests from the American government, even before our competent authorities know what is going on."[1] Similarly, Castillo Nájera believed that one of Mexico's only friends in Washington was President Roosevelt, who had a sincere desire "to avoid disastrous consequences in the relationship between Mexico and the United States."[2] On the other hand, after talking to those politicians whom he previously had considered friends of Mexico, the ambassador decided that none of them was ready to take any concrete action on Mexico's behalf. "The only one," he admitted, "who shows decided good will in our favor is President Roosevelt, and, in a less committed fashion, Undersecretary Welles."[3] Thus, both Castillo Nájera and Cárdenas had lost faith in almost every U.S. official and former ally except for Franklin Roosevelt. In a time of crisis and decision it appeared that old friends had deserted them and chosen to back North American capital over the Mexican worker.

A conspicuous exception to this wholesale desertion was Cameron Townsend. Unlike most Americans, and especially unlike most conservative Protestants, Townsend came out squarely for the expropriation. He not only made his views public in Mexico but also toured the United States trying to drum up support for the Mexican government. At a time when "friendly" politicians seemed unwilling to lift a finger to help Mexico, Townsend went out of his way to provide support.[4]

Defending Mexico

During the summer and fall of 1937, Townsend had demonstrated continued allegiance to President Cárdenas and to Mexico. He had given the biography of Cárdenas such a high priority that he handed over most of the teaching responsibility at "Camp Wycliffe" to Ken Pike and Eugene Nida, the emerging linguistic "stars" of the SIL. By the end of the summer he had mailed seven chapters to Cárdenas's close friend Ramón Beteta, undersecretary of the Ministry of Foreign Affairs, and received word that he was "proceeding with the proper spirit and style."[5] When he returned to Mexico he tried to organize some other Protestant missionaries there to devote themselves to "service of a social and regenerating nature among the masses, setting aside to a greater degree ecclesiastical matters and adhering more closely to the spiritual and material needs of the peasants and the proletariat."[6] So appreciative of these efforts was the president that he sent the Townsends twenty-five hundred pesos to build a better house in Tetelcingo and gave Cameron the pen he had used to sign most of the agrarian reform legislation.[7]

On 31 March 1938 the president breakfasted with Townsend at Los Pinos (the Mexican presidential residence) and asked him for a favor: he wanted Cameron and Elvira to return to the United States to publicize Mexico's side of the oil conflict. If evangelical missionaries were not exactly the kind of powerful figures that Cárdenas might have chosen to influence public opinion in the United States, the president and his advisers Ramón Beteta and Secretary of Communications Francisco Múgica believed that they needed all the help they could get.[8] The Townsends had proved themselves extremely loyal to Mexico. On the specific issue of the oil industry, Cameron had congratulated Cárdenas twice for his "patriotic and valiant" defense of Mexican sovereignty and already had offered to help in any way he could.[9] They also had a proven track record in doing public relations work for Mexico. During the summer of 1937, for example, while Cameron was writing his biography of Cárdenas, Elvira had "traveled extensively and given many lectures before many important groups" to counteract negative propaganda against Mexico.[10]

Cárdenas was so eager to put the Townsends to work in 1938 that he gave them a thousand dollars to buy a new car for their travels.[11] "We now feel that he is counting on us for help," Elvira wrote to friends. Although she and Cameron felt that they had little to offer the president, she continued, "We should do the thing he feels would be of great help to him and his country, that of our going up to the States and making known the facts as they are, to our friends."[12] Elvira discerned God's voice in Cárdenas's request: "The President is making the trip possible, so in spite of the fact that personally I would prefer staying in the village with our Indians, the indications seem clear and of the Lord for us to leave here in the middle of next week."[13] After getting a note of introduction to President Roosevelt from Ambassador Daniels, the Townsends left immediately for the United States, bought a new Chevrolet, and started their campaign. Elvira would use the car to travel through the southern and central regions of the country; Cameron would focus on the East Coast and on writing.[14]

During the next six months, from April to October 1938, the Townsends went beyond even the president's expectations in their efforts to defend Mexico. In the first month Cameron traveled from Mexico City to Dallas to Philadelphia, gave more than twenty lectures, explained Mexico's point of view to the editors of six different publications, revised the biography of Cárdenas, met with the treasurer of Gulf Oil, and recruited an Inter-American Service Brigade of youths who would serve Mexico in practical ways.[15] He gave a luncheon presentation on "Mexico, her Indian problem and her President" to "forty leaders" at the Empire State Building in New York City and "of course" mentioned the oil issue.[16] By the end of July the two Townsends had traveled more than fifteen thousand miles on their publicity tour.

Cameron's approach to publicity was simple, direct, and, at times, naive. He saw Roosevelt's Good Neighbor Policy as a serious proposal to rework hemispheric relations on a more equitable basis, and he believed that Mexico would be happy to join with the United States to confront the growing international problems of the late 1930s. "All that Mexico asks in return for her friendship is a due respect for her sovereignty," he stressed. He therefore expressed dismay at the oil companies' disrespectful attitudes toward Mexico and was shocked that the State Department could side with the obvious villains in a unequivocal contest of right and wrong. The violator of the administration's clearly articulated Good Neighbor Policy was American capital, not the Mexican government. American investors had profited greatly from Mexico's natural resources "without paying living wages to their peons," he argued.[17]

The Townsends had much to be proud of by the time they returned to Mexico in October 1938. They had given ninety lectures and had had countless personal conversations in defense of Mexico and the oil expropriation. They had recruited seven young Americans to serve Mexico in the Inter-American Service Brigade. They had received word from Cárdenas himself that their efforts were "very important" and that they had done as much as they possibly could have done for the cause of understanding between the two nations.[18] Nevertheless, in many ways their trip had failed—and that failure set the course for the future trajectory of the SIL.

After having consorted with the uppermost echelon of Mexican politicians—the president, cabinet members, and the highest-ranking government officials—Townsend was shut out of similar circles in the United States. Notwithstanding his letter of introduction from Ambassador Daniels, Roosevelt would not see him, nor would Secretary of State Cordell Hull. Business leaders generally avoided him. When he scheduled a meeting at the Oilman's Club in Dallas, he was told at the last minute that it had been canceled because he was going to present Mexico's side of the conflict. Newspapers and magazines would not accept his writing. "As regards my articles," he explained, "some have been published but most of them have been rejected due to the fact that the editors feel that I simply cannot be right in view of the tremendous amount of literature they read from other sources which tells another story."[19]

Denied both the public square and the corridors of power, Townsend had expended much effort and energy and accomplished little more than a growing personal sense of outrage.[20] Before leaving Arkansas to return to Mexico, he wrote Secretary Hull a caustic letter in which he asked why the United States was pressing its poor neighbor for a debt when European nations owing far more were being treated with kid gloves. He cautioned the secretary that the American people would not tolerate a government that sucked the lifeblood from malnourished Mexicans. Then, after returning to Mexico, mindful of his own experiences with the American press, he applauded the Mexican government's decision to expel the *New York Times*'s Frank Kluckhorn and warned the paper that it needed to dispense with its "highly biased picture of Mexico." As he asked President Cárdenas, how would the American people ever learn the truth, "when the press is capitalist and twists the facts?"[21]

Townsend's less-than-triumphant return to his "adopted land," as he now called Mexico, in 1938 marks the beginning of a new era for the SIL. It was not so much a turning point as a time when a number of important ideas in Townsend's understanding of his mission seem to have come together in more solid form. What had been hinted at and implied in his thinking now became explicit. A long stream of events and experiences from his different lives in Guatemala, Mexico, and the United States rearranged themselves in his mind. Jolted by the indifference or hostility that his defense of Cardenismo had produced in the United States, Townsend consciously began to identify himself with Mexico. This mental and emotional recentering had implications not only for Townsend as an individual but for the SIL as an organization. Most importantly, as far as the ministry of the SIL was concerned, what had been provisional tactics now became established principles.

The principles that Townsend now perceived looked something like this: the SIL's mission was to translate the Bible, not to plant churches or start denominations; the SIL would accomplish this task by openly (not surreptitiously) seeking the help and approval of the Mexican government; and it would go out of its way to identify culturally and politically with Mexico, not with the United States. To a large extent, Townsend had been engaging in these practices all along, but his difficult experiences in the United States in 1938 had "Mexicanized" him. They had convinced him that the American alliance between government and industry was wrong, that the Mexican state was right, and that the future of his organization lay in identifying with Mexico. These practices *were* his mission; they were what he was supposed to be doing. They were not just a ploy to bide time until he could undertake "real" missionary work. The SIL's charge in 1938, just as it had been in 1935, and just as it would be years in the future, was to translate, to seek the Mexican states' help and approval, and to identify with Mexico. The tasks of traditional missionaries—preaching, teaching, administering churches, building denominational bodies—were not a far-off goal that the SIL was heading toward. They were something the SIL simply would avoid altogether.

Needless to say, Townsend's emerging conception of his and the SIL's mission had little in common with traditional American fundamentalism. The many ways in which his understanding of the SIL's calling confronted differing expectations and frustrating opposition help to explain why, starting in the fall of 1938 and continuing into 1940 or 1941, an angry tone—the tone of an enlightened teacher trying and failing to hide his frustration with the willfully ignorant—slipped into much of Townsend's correspondence. It crept into his letter to Secretary Hull and popped up intermittently for a few years as he struggled to reconcile the clarity of his own vision with the blindness of those around him.

Townsend, for instance, expressed real anger when Rafael Ramírez, the architect of Mexico's rural education system, suggested "in front of various people" that his linguists were not university-trained. Twelve of them were university graduates, Townsend explained, and Ken Pike was about to get his doctorate. As to the suggestion that he himself was not a *universitario,* this was "very contrary to the truth," as Ramírez could have discovered if he had "written to OCCIDENTAL COLLEGE, LOS ANGELES, CALIF, E.U." He hoped that his explanation had made clear the "great injustice" that Ramírez had done him. Since a number of the SILers were not in fact university graduates, since few of them had majored in linguistics, and since Townsend himself had not graduated from Occidental, his anger makes the most sense as a response not to injustice but to fear. Specifically, Townsend feared that his plans, which depended on cooperation between the SIL and the government on the basis of the former's linguistic expertise, could be undone by Ramírez's attitude.[22]

As the fledgling SIL attempted to formalize its policies, Townsend expressed frustration that other Americans kept trying to run the organization like a normal evangelical mission. He could not understand, for instance, why the group's executive committee had proposed "to take the risk involved in including Bible and Seminary credentials as standards in the articles of organization of a linguistic society."[23] He could not understand why L. L. Legters had made the "mistake" of raising money to publish the New Testaments that the SIL was in the process of translating, since publishing was not the SIL's job at all.[24] The fact was that to American evangelicals, the course that he was proposing was not self-evident. Using linguistics, practical help, and personal relationships to enter Mexico was one thing, but devoting an organization to those tasks even after it had entered the country was quite another. The problem was twofold: first, to most evangelicals from north of the border, the government of Mexico seemed too radical; second, practical help (agricultural, educational, etc.) and government relations were simply not part of their conception of missions. Even Bible translation was not the goal of most evangelical missionaries: it was a means to the more important end of evangelism. To focus on translation seemed to make a peripheral task central. Working closely with a government perceived as atheistic and socialistic was simply too much for many of the young fundamentalists. Already one couple, John and Isabel Twentyman, "after much prayer and meditation," had come to the conclusion that they could not "work with the schools under the present arrangements."[25] Another member, Richmond McKinney, continued to raise objections about the direction the organization was taking, especially its work for an "unbelieving" government.[26]

When one of the members of the Inter-American Service Brigade spent a sleepless night over legislation pending in the Mexican congress that would have prohibited religious schools, Townsend did what he probably should have done earlier: he wrote a letter to the SIL membership explaining "our policy of cooperating with governments and scientific organizations." To start with, worries about socialist education were ridiculous. "Why should we be alarmed over a law which *may* be passed which will prohibit religious schools?" he asked. They were in Mexico "to serve and not to dictate policies to the government." It was Mexico's own affair if it wanted to teach its children "to share with one another as sincere socialists should." The SIL had a simple job—to give "the Word of God" to the people—and should not let itself be distracted from that task. "After all," he asked, "who called us to pass judgment upon rulers? Are we not commanded to obey and pray for them? Let us be consistent. If anyone feels obliged to hold himself aloof from the Government as regards cooperation, let him also hold himself aloof as regards criticism." In fact, even the passage of a more radical law would not have changed his attitude of cooperation, because he had come to Mexico "not to oppose socialism, but to give the Word to people who have never received it."[27]

Townsend went even further a few days later. First he defended the proposed educational law as a reasonable response to Catholic pressures. Then he turned the tables on his critics. The real problem was their failure to identify properly with Mexico: "You have more contact with the American colony, which is generally very alarmist in its views, than you do with the Mexican element that is responsible for the laws." His opponents gave too much heed to critical views of the government: "Many of you read *Excélsior,* and that is like trying to get a fair view of Martin Luther from reading histories compiled by the Jesuit fathers." Townsend found it "absolutely necessary" to point out that it was "very unbecoming" for people who had received so many courtesies from the government of Mexico to take such a critical attitude. He concluded: "Will you not respond to this in the right spirit, recognize your mistake and look up with a new faith and trust in the One who is going to visit Mexico with a great spiritual awakening if we but continue faithful."[28]

The membership must have been a bit taken aback by the vehemence of Townsend's letters. Unlike the American intellectuals and leftists who admired Mexico specifically because of its progressive politics, these "middle Americans" could not help but find Cardenista policies threatening.[29] How, for instance, would they have known that they were supposed to spend their time with Mexican lawmakers and to avoid fellow Americans? How were they supposed to have known that even certain *Mexican* newspapers were off limits? More to the point, it is hardly surprising that fundamentalist missionaries would take a while to comprehend the limited and yet innovative nature of their mission in Mexico. If it had ever been in doubt, now it was clear:

the Summer Institute of Linguistics was not just another evangelical mission.

Dual Identity

The tension within the SIL itself over its identity and the proper tasks of its members makes this a good spot to examine the dual identity of the SIL and Wycliffe Bible Translators. As is evident in the preceding section, Townsend's vision was difficult to understand even for those who had committed themselves to his project in Mexico. The concept of dual identity—that is, of being part of two overlapping but different entities, one religious, one secular—was easy enough to grasp; much more difficult for both insiders and outsiders was the fact that Townsend was serious about the restrictions that the SIL would impose on its personnel. Some early members apparently saw these restrictions as mere subterfuges that could be abandoned once the SIL had entered Mexico, but Townsend had no such intention. To him, the trick was not that the SIL would turn into a more traditional missionary organization after it had secured its position in Mexico, but rather that through translating the Bible into indigenous languages and personal influence the SIL could accomplish the goals of fundamentalist evangelization.

It was as if both Townsend and his critics within the SIL were saying that the SIL should enter Mexico with one hand tied behind its back. For the critics, this was just a ruse. They had planned to starting using that hand again as soon as possible. Townsend viewed the hand tied behind the back as a permanent sacrifice, but he also believed that the SIL could accomplish its objectives without use of that hand. The problem was not that Townsend and his critics disagreed about the goal; the problem was that he and his critics disagreed about minimum missionary activity necessary to achieve that goal. For Townsend, translating the Bible was an acceptable minimum; for his critics, more activity—preaching, public proclamation, church planting—was necessary.

Consequently, throughout this history I will treat the SIL as an organization whose goals were primarily spiritual, as implied in this book's title, *and* as an organization that operated more or less in accord with its own restrictions on traditional missionary activity. The only reason why fundamentalist young people were willing to join the organization and to spend decades of their lives in remote locations, and the only reason why churches across the United States were willing to support these individuals financially, was that they all believed that they were participating in the "Great Commission," Christ's parting charge to spread the Gospel around the world. It is in this sense that SIL linguists were missionaries, and I occasionally will refer to them as such, but by calling them missionaries I do not mean to imply that they functioned as traditional missionaries. SIL linguists did not go from town to town "preaching the Gospel"; they did not serve as pastors or preach in town squares; they did not plant churches or start Christian schools. They learned indigenous languages, translated the Bible, and had personal relationships. The restrictions that SIL linguists had to tolerate were accepted as trade-offs for greater access to restricted areas of the world. SIL linguists thus sacrificed much of traditional missionary activity (and even the ability to refer to themselves as missionaries) because they believed that such sacrifices would ultimately aid the larger task of world evangelization. "To the Mexican government, it does not matter whether we are missionaries, but we must be linguists," argued the SIL's Richard Pittman. "Many of our friends at home do not care whether we are linguists, so long as we are missionaries."[30]

It is important to recognize both sides of this equation. SIL linguists really did give up many traditional missionary activities (many critics of the SIL have failed to see this), *and* the only reason for the existence of the SIL was to fulfill the missionary goals of conservative Protestant Christianity. Despite being distinguished by its innovative approach and, eventually, worldwide presence, the SIL was in one essential way entirely representative of the North American fundamentalism from which it arose. Its reduction of the missionary enterprise to the translation of the Bible is a profound expression of the central place of the Bible in American fundamentalism. For missionaries, to assume that the translation of the Bible is worth decades (often entire adulthoods) of labor is to assume not only the centrality of that text in their faith but also its power to accomplish evangelization. It is not surprising, therefore, that Roman Catholic and liberal Protestant missionary organizations have rarely devoted the time and effort that the SIL did to translating the Bible.

A recruiting letter from SIL executive director Ken Pike in 1956 exemplified dual identity perfectly. "The urgency of the missionary task is greater than ever," wrote Pike on SIL letterhead. "Forces of darkness have crowded back messengers of the gospel to narrower confines." What must missionaries do to prepare for difficult situations that awaited them? According to Pike, many of them would need "instruction in modern linguistic techniques" and would benefit from the SIL's summer courses at the University of Oklahoma and the University of North Dakota even if they ended up serving with missions other than the SIL.[31] The letter is utterly inexplicable without the basic understanding that Pike and the SIL viewed the "missionary task" as their priority. At the same time, the letter makes clear that the SIL was like no other missionary organization. In the world of evangelical Christians, nobody else had the expertise in linguistics and translation that the SIL did, and nobody else saw the translation of the Bible into vernacular languages as the primary means to the goal of evangelization.

Perhaps, then, it would make more sense to refer mainly to the Wycliffe Bible Translators, with the Summer Institute of Linguistics as the junior partner. This is how David Stoll chose to treat the organizations in his book *Fishers of Men or Builders of Empire? The Wycliffe Translators in Latin America.* I have chosen not to do so because this is a book about Mexico, and in Mexico the organization represented itself primarily as the SIL and was known to others primarily as the SIL. If I had written a book focused on the United States, I would have used the Wycliffe terminology. The use of the name "Summer Institute of Linguistics" is not meant to deny the missionary aims of the organization; the term *missionary* is not meant to imply that the SIL functioned like other missions or that its members were hypocrites.

Submission Theology

A key element of Cameron and Elvira Townsend's ongoing "Mexicanization" and of their developing understanding of the SIL's role in Mexico can be traced directly to their relationship with President Cárdenas. The great importance of this one relationship to the success of their work in Mexico seems to have given them a personalistic understanding of power that shaped the SIL's philosophy of "government relations." So crucial had Cárdenas been to the SIL's initial and ongoing successes, and so involved had the Townsends become in Cárdenas's life, both through their friendship and through writing his biography, that they began to view him as a sort of divinely ordained figure. From this conception of Cárdenas's providential role in Mexican history and in the expansion of the Gospel, Cameron and Elvira developed a more general philosophy of how the SIL should relate to those who held positions of power.

At first the Townsends simply admired Cárdenas's personality. After touring Morelos with the president in 1937, Cameron told friends, "It was a great privilege to see the man work. I don't know whether he is a Christian or not but I do wish that my life were as Christlike as his was all day under tremendous strain and pressure."[32] Soon Townsend came to believe that Cárdenas was becoming "sympathetic" to his "spiritual objectives."[33] Then, admiration and appreciation turned into a conception of Cárdenas as a divine agent. "We believe," Cameron told his father in 1938, "that General Cárdenas is called of God to become a mighty instrument in his hands."[34] As noted previously, when Cárdenas asked the Townsends to do public relations work for him, Elvira responded to his request as if God himself were speaking.[35]

Struck by Cárdenas's "Christlike" behavior, and meditating about the link between presidential power and Christian commitment, Townsend soon came to believe that his friend had converted to Protestantism. Despite Cárdenas's failure to declare such a conversion, Townsend interpreted his actions at a picnic for U.S. supporters of the SIL and Mexican government officials in 1939 in Tijuana as evidence enough. "The way that the President shook Mr. Nyman's hand and thanked him for his personal testimony about the way that God had changed his heart of stone into one of flesh," he reported to a Mexican friend, "convinced Mr. Nyman (who has a long history of personal evangelistic work) that the President is a saved man now, if not before. After the President's words to me, he removed all doubt from my mind."[36]

Townsend's theology of submission helps to explain his occasionally overly subservient attitude toward Cárdenas. For instance, when Cárdenas started to use the informal "tu" when addressing him, Townsend explained that he was honored but would continue to address Cárdenas with the more formal "usted." Being addressed as "tu" made Townsend feel favored with Cárdenas's special "protection and affection," while calling Cárdenas "usted" linked him to the former president's "care and friendship" in an appropriately "polite and cordial manner."[37]

Growing convictions about God's plans for Cárdenas and Mexico led Townsend to formulate what might be called a "theology of submission" that emphasized submission to rulers as God's agents. In 1938 Townsend had already come to a new understanding of his mission that emphasized policies of working with the state, Bible translation, and practical service. The theology of submission provided a philosophical rationale for those policies. If government officials really were God's agents, then submissive policies toward the state were not only expedient but morally required. Although this theology had grown out of Townsend's interaction with Cárdenas in response to the specific circumstances of Mexico in the 1930s, he soon began to assert its universal validity. "If you and I lived in Russia," he told the members of the SIL in 1939, "we would find that the life of God in our hearts would be ample preparation for living under that regime and it would be less exacting than the Sermon on the Mount." Although most American fundamentalists believed that resistance to the communistic, atheistic Soviet state was a moral obligation, Townsend pointed them to the Bible, which, he believed, called for submission to all governments, including the most despotic ones. In fact, Townsend could envision himself living peacefully in the Soviet Union: "If they let me teach the Bible in Russia, I would gladly abstain from censorship of their policies that I did not like. After all, who called us to pass judgment upon rulers? Are we not commanded to obey and pray for them?"[38]

As Townsend made clear in a letter to Brainerd Legters in 1940, the scriptural basis for his theology of submission was chapter 13 of Paul's letter to the Romans. Legters had threatened to disregard the Mexican government's policy of using a phonetic orthography developed by Morris Swadesh (an American linguist working for the Mexican government) for vernacular alphabets because he and the rest of the SIL were trying to use alphabets as similar as possible to Spanish, to facilitate the learning of Spanish for those who were literate in vernacular languages. Instead of resisting Swadesh's proposals, Townsend counseled Legters to "mark time until the end of the year," when he believed that a new government would put Swadesh out of power. To oppose Swadesh before then, though, would be a violation of Romans 13:1, which says, "Let every soul be subject unto the higher powers." He did not want Legters to end up like another SIL linguist, Richmond McKinney, whose resistance to government plans for the Otomi alphabet had incurred "cordial dislike" among Mexican officials.[39] The fact that McKinney ended up in jail for "propagating religion rather than doing linguistic research" only served to convince Townsend of the wisdom of his policy of submission.[40]

Soon Townsend came to the point where he was able to treat the requests of government officials as requests from God himself. When Mexican officials asked that linguists be sent to the Lacandones and Seris, two Indian groups with extremely small populations, Townsend heard God speaking to him about "giving the Word to all the tribes of Mexico." God's challenge seemed to be, "Call upon Me and I will answer thee and thrust forth workers for every unreached tribe in Mexico, small or large."[41]

Rather than formulating a plan based on rational, doctrinal, theological, or biblical criteria and then submitting it for government approval, as other missionary organizations might do, the SIL was now letting the Mexican state set its missionary agenda. If the state suggested a certain course, Townsend, at least, was prepared to hear the voice of God. Such an approach to mission goes beyond what would seem to be required by Romans 13, but it is not necessarily antithetical to it.[42]

The SIL's interpretation of Romans 13 obeyed the command to submit as a matter of course but added its own wrinkle to verse seven, which says, "Render therefore to all their dues: tribute to whom tribute is due; custom to whom custom; fear to whom fear; honour to whom honour." Under Townsend's guidance, the organization came to see this verse as a command not merely to treat government officials with respect but as a charge to cultivate relationships with specific officials whom God had brought across their paths. In his early years in Mexico (c. 1940), Dick Pittman, for instance, suggested once that it might be wise to meet a certain influential Mexican figure. Townsend replied in the negative, but he did not dismiss the importance of such contacts. "We do not 'try' to meet influential people," he responded. "But when God brings them our way and/or gives providential encounters with them, we try to be faithful friends." Pittman would later cite the Townsends' long relationship with the Cárdenas family as a good example of living out Romans 13:7 and as a model for would-be Bible translators.[43]

Part of this philosophy was that translators must go through the proper channels. "There are many Christians who would like to do Bible translation in countries which are not their own without rendering to the government authorities of those countries the recognition which is their due," Pittman warned. Translators in foreign countries might be tempted to "circumvent established protocol" by dealing only with friendly Protestant officials, but to do so would be a serious mistake. "Not only the 'powers that be' but also their ranks in their hierarchy are ordained by God," Pittman continued, "and part of what God has ordained in our day is that, in relations with expatriates, at least, the State is over the Church."[44] Unlike most other missionary organizations, the SIL would therefore put most of its efforts (other than its primary efforts in the field of translation) toward the political elites they encountered in their work. "We feel called to witness to the upper classes because God has opened the door to them through our going to the Indians," said Pittman. "We invite them to our homes. We have probably two or three people of that type to one visiting missionary from some other organization."[45] Townsend, a teetotaler who had supported the Prohibition Party as a youth, was so intent on befriending important Mexicans that he was willing not only to enter a saloon with a "prominent official" but also to pay for the man's drink.[46]

Throughout his life Townsend tried to follow this model—and to teach his colleagues to do the same. At every level of government, he believed, the SIL was "commanded" by Romans 13 to "pay respect" to the local authority figure, whether mayor, or chief, or governor. He realized that a local chief could be "untaught, ignorant, maybe a killer," but his experience was that such a man "appreciates deference so much that he will not try to use his authority over you. If you recognize the authority, he will not use it." To illustrate his point, Townsend gave the example of a short stopover he had on an airplane flight in the 1940s in Tuxtla Gutiérrez, Chiapas. Although he had a limited amount of time, he decided to visit the governor of Chiapas to inform him about the SIL's new training camp in Yaxoquintelá. "I felt it was only right—a bunch of foreigners out on their frontier with Guatemala—a rather delicate frontier," he explained. "They could wonder what we were doing—especially if we were using radio." This visit sharply distinguished the SIL from missionary organizations that never contacted Mexican officials. "As a consequence," Townsend concluded, "they give us red carpet treatment."[47]

Mexico in the 1930s offered some significant barriers to would-be fundamentalist missionaries. Neither its predominantly Roman Catholic population nor its nationalist anti-Catholic political leadership seemed likely advocates for a wave of evangelism from the north. At a time when many U.S.-owned mines, railroads, and ranches had been seized by the Mexican state, it was not clear that it was a propitious moment for any sort of American endeavor in Mexico.[48] There were, however, a few glimmers of possibility. American Catholics, their allies in Congress, and Ambassador Daniels were lobbying hard for the generic concept of "religious freedom." Cárdenas and other high officials needed to keep relations with the United States on a firm footing but were convinced that another Catholic revolt was still a real threat. Their solution to this problem—easing religious restrictions while simultaneously trying to use socialist education and other religious and ideological substitutes to continue the attack on Catholicism—made them receptive to Mexican and American Protestants, both of whom had a strong record of supporting the Mexican state.

Cameron Townsend and the incipient Summer Institute of Linguistics adapted shrewdly to these conditions. If Protestants in general seemed to offer a good alternative to Catholicism, the SIL offered an even more appealing option. Because Townsend and company renounced traditional missionary activities (especially any kind of denominational ambitions), performed nontraditional activities (agricultural, educational, and linguistic work) in harmony with the revolutionary ethic, and adopted a posture of cooperation toward the Mexican state, they far surpassed other Protestant groups in their attractiveness to revolutionary elites. Townsend's willingness to befriend, praise, and cooperate with Mexican officials sharply distinguished him from other Americans and from other missionaries. In his support of Mexico in the months following the oil expropriation, Townsend made it clear that he was willing to put Mexico's interests above those of his native land and that he would do so publicly. Few, if any, other missionaries would go so far.

Townsend's responses to a specific, highly contingent situation created the SIL's strange "submission theology." A context of religious unrest and international tension might seem unlikely to provide generalizable principles for a missionary organization. In fact, the truly extreme conditions under which the SIL was founded provided it with experiential and philosophical resources that allowed it to survive and eventually to thrive in a variety of apparently unpromising environments in Mexico and beyond. As will be seen in the next chapter, its ability to embrace—and more importantly, to be embraced by—the important philosophical/political project known as *indigenismo* sprang directly from its unorthodox approach to Christian mission. Even as the Roman Catholic Church struck out at Protestantism and attempted its own rapprochement with the state in the 1940s, the SIL's principles of cooperation and identification made it remarkably resistant to attack. The SIL prospered because it was adopted into the "Revolutionary family," a clan that protected its own and which would safeguard the SIL from even the most determined attacks for decades to come. Only when the regime suffered an irreversible blow to its own legitimacy (when it murdered hundreds of student protesters at Tlatelolco in 1968) did the SIL's revolutionary pedigree begin to show signs of wearing thin. Even then, a new generation of enemies underestimated the degree to which the interests of the state and the SIL had become intertwined.

4

How Linguistics Became the Solution to Mexico's "Indian Problem"

"The Indian problem is our preeminent problem," contended Mexican intellectual Pablo González Casanova in 1935.[1] A year later, President Cárdenas stated that "the principal obligations" of his government were to indigenous people more than to any other group.[2] González Casanova, Cárdenas, and other leading public figures in Mexico during the 1930s could not agree on the solution to Mexico's "Indian problem," but they did agree that *something* needed to be done. The Mexican educators, politicians, scientists, and intellectuals who pondered the fate of their country's indigenous populations and formulated any number of plans to incorporate, integrate, and assimilate them into their nation's larger mestizo populations stood at the vanguard of an intellectual and political movement known as *indigenismo* that spread through many of the nations of Latin America.

The partisans of this movement, known as *indigenistas,* approached the issue from a primarily nationalistic perspective. Their rhetoric of uplift and improvement was not necessarily cynical or manipulative, but at heart they were interested in indigenous people as a means to the further end of national unity. Basically, the existence of large groups of people who did not share in the national language or culture seemed to impede the attainment of true nationhood, which was considered to depend upon uniformity of language and culture. It is in relation to hopes and dreams about the nation that Mexico should become that Indians assumed such importance in the minds of non-Indians.

It is not clear whether Cameron Townsend even knew what indigenismo was when he arrived in Mexico in 1933. It was certainly not a central concern of the evangelical youths who chose to work with the SIL. But Townsend quickly learned to identify himself and his organization with indigenismo. His ability to do so successfully is demonstrated by his organization's long history of cooperation with Mexico's major indigenista organizations. Despite the SIL's commitment to Bible translation and the Mexican government's constitutional commitment to strict separation of church and state, agencies such as the Instituto Nacional Indigenista (INI; National Indigenista Institute), the Instituto Indigenista Interamericano (III; Inter-American Indigenista Institute), and the SEP worked with the SIL for decades.

Clearly, these were odd partnerships. Mexican nationalists veered dangerously close to self-contradiction in their use of foreign missionaries in so sensitive a project. Conversely, Christian missionaries risked the loss of their distinctive religious commitments to the totalizing project of the state.[3] These obvious risks for both sides raised doubts and objections, but they were largely overcome (until 1979) because the SIL's greatest strength, linguistics, lay in an area that many indigenistas believed held the answers to Mexico's "Indian problem." Since linguistics was still a new and developing field in the 1930s and since there were very few academically trained Mexican linguists until the 1960s, the SIL's offer to perform linguistic work in exchange for access to indigenous communities seemed too good to refuse. Mexican indigenista agencies never had large budgets in relation to the mammoth tasks they faced, so for many years the SIL's willingness to supply linguistic information, to produce grammars and primers, and to teach some classes on linguistics meant that indigenistas could devote their scarce resources to other areas.

As indigenistas saw it, the central problem facing Mexico's Indians was a linguistic one. There might be other factors separating Indians from the rest of the nation, but none seemed so obvious or overwhelming as Indians' inability to speak Spanish.[4] An editorialist in 1936, for example, was shocked by Mexico's "lack of linguistic unity, by the variety of indigenous dialects, a living museum of languages, and by the extremely high number of Indians that live at the margin of the life of the nation because they do not know Spanish. . . . They do not know our history, our ideals, or our economic, scientific and artistic achievements," he continued, "and they make up foreign populations within the body of Mexicans."[5] Thus, nationalist dreams confronted the harsh reality of Mexico's indigenous populations.

Starting in the late nineteenth century and continuing well into the twentieth, indigenous languages seemed like the great gulf Mexico had to cross to become a modern nation.[6] The teaching of Spanish in public schools was widely perceived as the bridge across that chasm: schools would civilize, nationalize, and modernize mestizos and Indians alike, primarily by teaching Spanish.[7] Despite these desires, by the

1930s public education had reached only a miniscule percentage of Mexico's indigenous communities.

Linguistics in Revolutionary Mexico

One of the first attempts to rectify the problem came from the National University in Mexico City, which established the Mexican Institute of Linguistic Research in 1933.[8] Mariano Silva y Aceves, the institute's founder and director, believed that linguistics was the key to the incorporation of the Indian, a vision that would mesh well with the talents and dreams of the small group of Americans known as the Summer Institute of Linguistics. "Our goal is that vernacular languages be known, be preserved and be used as tools for education and progress," he stated in 1937. The goal was to use an indigenous person's own language "as a means of gaining his confidence." Then, argued Silva y Aceves, "we can communicate to him what we want him to learn."[9] The most interesting part of Silva y Aceves's approach was his call for the conservation of indigenous languages and for their active use in Indian education. Although this idea was not itself new—Roman Catholic missionaries had used indigenous languages for education as early as the sixteenth century—it was a departure for the twentieth-century Mexican educational establishment and a timely opening for the like-minded linguists of the SIL. It was also an idea that the SIL had long been encouraging Mexican linguists to adopt.

Silva y Aceves had met Townsend in 1935 at the indigenismo section of the Seventh Inter-American Scientific Conference and had asked him to work with his institute. Silva y Aceves also introduced Townsend to another indigenista interested in the use of vernacular languages, Celso Flores Zamora, head of primary education for the SEP. Together, Silva y Aceves's institute and Flores Zamora's section of the SEP published a Nahuatl primer written by Townsend. In 1936, at Townsend's urging, Silva y Aceves recommended to the rector of the National University that he make SIL linguists official researchers of the university. Townsend also suggested that the SIL co-sponsor a "linguistics week" with the institute and with the SEP, both to publicize Silva y Aceves's linguistic efforts and to demonstrate that the SIL was a legitimate scientific entity.[10]

Because very few linguists were actually working on indigenous languages in Mexico, members of the SIL formed the majority of the featured participants in the celebration of Linguistics Week. Papers read by participants such as the SIL's Gene Nida, L. G. Christiansen, Walter Miller, Max Lathrop, and Cameron Townsend on their work among various Indian groups convinced *El Nacional*'s reporter that the application of linguistics to indigenous languages would lead to the "incorporation of various millions of inhabitants of the Mexican nation."[11] For Townsend, the week was "quite a success" because it accomplished two major objectives. "We intend to make every effort to make the work of our entire group thoroughly scientific and the linguistic conference was a big help in that direction as well as putting us in better than ever with the authorities," he wrote soon afterward.[12] Silva y Aceves had been lobbying the university for a graduate program in linguistics, and the publicity surrounding Linguistics Week helped him demonstrate the importance of his discipline. "He became so grateful," Townsend reported, "that he persuaded the University to hold a banquet in honor of the different linguists who had taken part, our group being in predominance." The program also "further fomented" relations with the director of the SEP's Indigenous Education section, Carlos Basauri, by similarly giving him positive publicity.[13]

Silva y Aceves was quick to seize upon Townsend's experiences in Guatemala as a concrete example of the efficacy of vernacular literacy as a bridge to Spanish.[14] Townsend himself emphasized that vernacular literacy, far from hurting efforts at teaching Spanish, actually made learning Spanish much easier. "A person who can read one language will easily learn to read another," he argued. "Once he has learned to read his own language the resulting confidence and ambition will keep him in school until he learns the national language."[15]

This idea of vernacular literacy as a bridge to Spanish proved compelling to many indigenistas. Between 1933 and 1937 this belief in the power and importance of vernacular literacy promoted by Silva y Aceves and Townsend helped launch the creation of organizations devoted to the study of the major vernacular languages, including La Academia de Nahuatl in Mexico City, La Academia de Otomí in Ixmiquilpan, Hidalgo, and La Academia de Maya in Mérida, as well as a new concentration in aboriginal languages at the National University. At the same time, Silva y Aceves's linguistics institute published Nahuatl and Otomi dictionaries and started a linguistics journal.[16] Unfortunately for Mexican linguistics, however, the linguists and amateur enthusiasts attracted to the science tended to cluster in the "classical" languages such as Nahuatl, Otomi, and Maya. Most had little interest in the dozens of less-known and less-common languages that most needed linguistic work. Despite this imbalance, Townsend's and Silva y Aceves's ideas did have great impact in the theoretical realm. Their advocacy in the 1930s paved the way for the widespread acceptance in later decades of the idea that vernacular literacy was the key to teaching and learning Spanish.

Until approximately 1930, most indigenistas had believed that the best way to achieve a universal language for Mexico was to teach Spanish by means of the "direct method," in which teachers with no knowledge of indigenous languages used only Spanish in the classroom. The advantage of this approach was its simplicity: it required only that teachers know Spanish. Its disadvantage lay in the hardships it imposed on monolingual indigenous children, who often found their submersion in Spanish frustrating and unconducive to learning. Bilingual education had the obvious disadvantage of requiring not only bilingual teachers but also bilingual educational materials. It thus represented a stupendous investment in teacher training and the preparation of indigenous language materials in what were then thought to be Mexico's forty indigenous languages.[17] Bilingual education did have the compelling advantage of offering young students the comforts of gradualism, however. After beginning their studies in their own language, they could make a slow transition to Spanish.

The proponents of the use of the vernacular comprised a greatly varied group. At one extreme were those who viewed the vernacular as of absolutely no worth except as a means to learning Spanish. They followed in the tradition of Porfirian education minister Justo Sierra, who actually spoke of teachers learning indigenous languages with "no other object than to destroy them, to teach everyone the Spanish language and to surmount this formidable barrier to the unification of the Mexican people."[18] This kind of "bilingualism" conceded the necessity of some use of the vernacular but saw it as having no intrinsic worth. At the other end of the spectrum were Marxists such as Vicente Lombardo Toledano, who, taking a cue from Stalin's "little nationalities" policy, believed that vernacular literacy was an end in itself. In his mind, "the promotion of vernacular languages" and the creation of alphabets for the languages that did not have them should rank right beside "absolute political autonomy" and "the end of private property" as priorities for the state in its policies toward the Indians.[19] Between these extremes there were a number of more moderate voices. As we have seen, Undersecretary of Education Moisés Sáenz came to support bilingual education for practical reasons. He had witnessed Cameron Townsend's successes in Guatemala and believed that the same results could be attained in Mexico. Other educators, without necessarily wanting to use indigenous languages in education, were coming to the conclusion that the vernacular was valuable in itself. For instance, Josefina Ramos, one of the speakers at a conference for kindergarten teachers in 1934, "argued for the necessity of linguistic unification, but without destroying or forgetting Indian languages, because only by preserving his language would the Indian be able to express his feelings and needs and way of thinking."[20] Propitiously for the SIL, and in large part through Townsend's efforts, bilingual education became a live issue in the 1930s. By the end of the decade the belief in vernacular literacy as the gateway to learning Spanish had solidified into an article of faith for many indigenistas.

Two professional conferences helped cement the gains made by the proponents of vernacular education. The Third Inter-American Education Conference, in Mexico City in 1937, featured a spirited confrontation between Carlos Besauri's espousal of education in the indigenous languages and Rafael Ramírez's defense of the direct method. But the real turning point for vernacular education occurred in 1939, when the Assembly of Philologists and Linguist rejected the direct method as a cruel vestige of the policy of incorporation and endorsed its replacement with instruction in the vernacular.[21] Although this was theoretically a conference for Mexican linguists, President Cárdenas had made it clear that he wanted all the members of the SIL to attend. They participated actively, siding with the majority on the role of the vernacular but butting heads with another American, Morris Swadesh. Significantly, the controversy raged not over the issue of the use of the vernacular, which by now was accepted by the majority of delegates, but over alphabets. Swadesh wanted to employ a phonetically accurate but extremely complicated alphabet for all indigenous languages, whereas the SILers argued for the importance of keeping the orthography as close as possible to Spanish.[22]

Whatever their reasons, by the late 1930s many indigenistas had come to similar conclusions about the importance of indigenous languages, although some of their colleagues remained unconvinced.

Even though the conflict between the direct method and the bilingual approach would continue well into the 1960s, by the late 1930s Townsend and Silva y Aceves had won over a large number of indigenistas and educators. The widespread adoption of the principle of vernacular education would put the SIL into a prominent position in indigenista circles because it was the only organization in Mexico, including the state itself, that possessed any real experience of teaching vernacular literacy.

The International Dimension

Nationalism, of course, is not merely a matter of internal goals and programs. It has its competitive aspect, the desire to gain prominence or dominance in the larger community of nations. Not surprisingly, Mexican indigenismo, as a true child of Mexican nationalism, manifested an international dimension. In the 1930s Mexico's revolutionary legacy sharply distinguished the state from other Latin American nations still in the hands of dictators. The social ideals of the revolution convinced many Mexicans that they had an important role to play as examples to their less enlightened neighbors to the south. One of the most important Mexican political figures to seize on indigenismo as a means to assert his country's leadership in Latin America was Townsend's friend and fellow Protestant Moisés Sáenz. In 1936, Sáenz described an upcoming Congress of Americanists in Mexico City as a "magnificent opportunity for suggestion and propaganda" for Mexico. He hoped to use the conference as a showcase that would demonstrate to all of Latin America "what Mexico is, what it wants to be and *what one day will be Indo-America under the spiritual direction of Mexico.*"[23]

In Sáenz's thinking, indigenismo thus served not only as a policy designed to unify Mexico but also as a means to assert Mexico's leadership in the international sphere. Sáenz believed that Mexico could blaze the trail for the rest of Latin America: "By elaborating a Mexican culture that is loyal to its native roots and enriched with white affluence, we can achieve the miracle of producing in our land a pattern of Indo-Latin civilization that can serve as a model for mestizo America."[24] Although his premature death in 1941 meant that many of his dreams were never fulfilled, Sáenz did live to see the Inter-

American Indigenista Congress of 1940, at which Mexico hosted indigenistas from North, Central, and South America.

The congress honored Mexico in many ways, but it also put the nation under pressure. The honor came in the form of both word and deed: the newly created Inter-American Indigenista Institute would be based in Mexico and would be headed by a Mexican, Sáenz himself.[25] The pressure arose from having to live up to the expectations raised by the conference, especially in the area of vernacular education. One of the major developments at the congress was the endorsement of vernacular languages for indigenous education. As anthropologist Gonzalo Aguirre Beltrán notes, this was a coup for Cameron Townsend and a demonstration of the influence he had exercised in the indigenista community: "William C. Townsend was not a delegate, but his influence was present in the resolutions on the use of vernacular languages."[26] The importance of the vernacular in indigenous education was now accepted by many, but Townsend's experience in Guatemala was probably the only concrete evidence that conference delegates could point to as an example of successful vernacular indigenous education.

The endorsement of vernacular languages for indigenous education by the Inter-American Indigenista Congress may have been a victory for the proponents of the vernacular, but it was in many ways an unrealistic goal even for Mexico, the acknowledged leader of the indigenista nations. Even though the Mexican delegates supported the idea of vernacular education, the government afterward found the policy difficult to implement because it lacked linguists willing and able to do the necessary kind of descriptive linguistics. It had been easy to endorse bilingual education. It sounded logical and had the support of the most progressive indigenista thinkers. Much harder was the actual practice of bilingual education.

While the direct method could make use of one set of textbooks to educate the whole nation and could use teachers from the cities to educate children anywhere in the nation, bilingual education required not only teachers who spoke indigenous languages but also written materials in those languages. Before such education could take place, written languages needed to be created where none existed, textbooks needed to be written, and bilingual teachers needed to be trained to read the vernacular themselves and then in methods of spreading literacy to others. Still, the resolutions of 1940 were not unimportant: they made the huge psychological admission that indigenous languages were legitimate languages of instruction, an important step in Mexico's journey to self-understanding and a milestone in its attempts to bring equitable treatment to its indigenous populations. As a practical matter, however, the nation's economic situation meant that it could do little more than adopt "vernacular education" as a slogan.

Even if Mexico had had the money to fund vernacular literacy programs, another barrier to such plans arose from the lack of trained Mexican linguists. Since few Mexicans were qualified, much less willing, to embark on the necessary linguistic prerequisites to vernacular education, most indigenous languages lacked the attentions of linguists willing to do the time-consuming work of learning the language, creating an alphabet, and producing written material. Silva y Aceves had hoped to train such linguists and send them out to the far corners of the nation. The sad fact, however, was that before his death in 1940 he had trained only a handful of people. Mexican linguistics was still in its infancy and simply could not supply the hundreds of trained specialists who were not just an integral part but a necessary prerequisite for a widespread program of bilingual education for the country's indigenous peoples. Even those linguists who had been trained did not necessarily want to spend years of their lives in indigenous villages, learning languages. Unlike some other types of linguistics, the descriptive linguistics required to create alphabets in preliterate languages could only be practiced in the field. If the languages were to be learned well enough to produce primers and textbooks, two- or three-week visits would not suffice, but linguists willing to spend years of their lives in indigenous villages were rare creatures indeed.

When one considers both Mexico's commitment to bilingual education and its inability to support this program, another reason for the nation's willingness to work with the SIL falls into place. Mexico, after all, had essentially staked its leadership of indigenismo on its ability to implement bilingual education. If the ideological commonalities that the SIL and indigenismo shared made cooperation possible, the linguistic problem, once it was recognized as the prerequisite to indigenous education, made cooperation almost a necessity. Who else could do the job? Even more importantly, who else would do the job for free? The irony was that the SIL in no small part had created this fait accompli for Mexico by advocating bilingual education at a time when there was no reasonable way for the state to implement such a policy. No one but the SIL had any feasible way of overcoming the linguistic obstacle to Mexico's nationalist dreams and international commitments.

5
Expansion in a Time of Conflict

On 10 July 1944 the Mexico City newspaper *El Universal* printed an article entitled "Independent Republics within Our Republic." Mexican "explorers," it said, had recently discovered the presence of foreign missionaries in the most isolated areas of the nation, including a group that had been "studying the indigenous languages for some years" and was "already editing Bibles in some of these languages." Although the work of these missionaries was praiseworthy in many ways, they did not understand Mexico or Mexican customs and were introducing "other customs, other habits and other cultures." "The danger," concluded the article, "is that, despite the enormous populations that exist within the territory of the nation, Mexico does not have one citizen among them who knows even superficially what our land is in terms of territory or institutions and therefore they are learning what these missionaries teach them."[1]

The next day, Cameron Townsend wrote to José Pavia Crespo, a government official who had been cited in the article, to refute the charges. The linguists of the SIL, he explained, "identify themselves with their adopted land in all its aspirations, and help the Indians whose language we study to be better citizens of Mexico." They followed rules established by various government agencies and had been complimented on their performances by those agencies. "Other institutions have expressed themselves in equal manner, to the extent that we now feel that we are Mexicans."[2]

Historians of Mexico generally present the 1940s and 1950s as decades of peace when the revolutionary state consolidated its power and control. One aspect of the relative peace that characterized this era was the regime's modus vivendi with the Roman Catholic Church. Whereas the Callista and Cardenista governments had tried to destroy or supplant the church, their successors chose a policy of accommodation. For the vast majority of Mexicans this détente paid great dividends by eliminating much of the friction and open conflict that had characterized relations between church and state during the 1920s and 1930s, but for Protestants it was a disaster. The general social stability achieved by the Mexican regime between 1940 and 1952 resulted to a certain extent from the sacrifice of loyal Protestant allies. The regime's decision to pursue better relations with the Roman Catholic Church (symbolized best by Manuel Ávila Camacho's statement that he was "a believer") opened the door for a widespread pattern of anti-Protestant violence and intimidation. Reluctant to risk its growing relationship with the Catholic Church and hesitant to antagonize the vast majority of Mexicans to protect the rights of a small minority, the Ávila Camacho and Alemán administrations denied Protestant requests to open churches and generally failed to protect Protestants when they were attacked and intimidated. Historian Enrique Krauze acknowledges that during the presidency of Miguel Alemán (1946–52) "there were incidents—usually at the instigation of a village priest—where Protestants were attacked and beaten and their homes burned," as happened in Tlacochahuaya, Nuevo León, in 1949 and in San Pedro Ixtlahuaca in 1950. "But," he goes on to say, "despite such moments, the country in general enjoyed a climate of religious tolerance." While Krauze deserves credit for pointing out the existence of "incidents" between Protestants and Catholics, like other scholars he underestimates the extent of religious conflict and its importance as a test of state power.[3]

The 1940s were a dangerous decade for Mexican Protestants, yet they were also an era of rapid expansion for the SIL and other Protestant groups. Persecution and government indifference did not seem to hinder the double-digit annual growth of many Protestant denominations, especially Pentecostal ones.[4] Even as a revitalized Catholic Church stepped up an ideological attack on Protestantism that emphasized themes of betrayal and imperialism, the SIL managed to continue the work it had started in the 1930s and began dozens of new translation projects in indigenous villages throughout the nation. Ironically, the SIL's rapid expansion and the conflicts between Catholics and Protestants that wracked the nation were two sides of the same coin: a rather weak federal government was trying to consolidate its power, on the one hand by coming to terms with the Catholic Church, on the other hand by attempting to make its varied indigenous groups into a more homogeneous, Mexican population.

Thus, religious factors profoundly influenced the process by which the state gradually extended its reach into new segments of Mexican society during the 1940s and 1950s. Improved relations with the

Catholic Church greatly eased the state's position in relation to popular culture, for the ruling party no longer rejected the traditional religiosity of the Mexican people. Détente with the church was a religious kind of state formation in which popular culture had wrung a concession from the state. In a sense, popular religiosity had deflected and redirected the anti-Catholic trajectory of the post-revolutionary state.[5] The state's alliance with the SIL was another religious kind of state formation, one in which the state took a more active role by using Protestant missionaries to expand into indigenous communities. In the Otomi community of San Antonio el Grande (examined in chapter 8), for instance, SIL linguists not only translated the New Testament but also served as liaisons between the village and various government agencies.

Although the SIL found itself caught in the cross fire of increasingly unfettered Catholic opposition to Protestantism, it managed to survive by sticking closely to its protectors within the Mexican state. While most Protestants had to defend themselves with appeals to abstract constitutional principles, the SIL could call on specific branches of the federal government, as Townsend did in the letter to Pavia Crespo. Although the educational and indigenista agencies with which the SIL had allied itself often lacked the clout to enforce their will in a given indigenous community, they usually had enough power to get SIL linguists into *some* indigenous community and to make them uninviting targets for the violence that was often meted out to less-well-connected Protestants. The SIL's connections to the state were buttressed and maintained by its personnel's tireless efforts to befriend Mexican officials, its institution-wide emphasis on "Latin American courtesy," and its increasingly successful attempts to present itself as a legitimate, scientifically rigorous linguistics institute.

The Catholic Offensive

The Catholic hierarchy had long opposed the advance of Protestantism, seeing in it not only a religious rival but a danger to national unity. The archbishop of Mexico City, Pascual Díaz, for example, called in 1930 for all Mexicans to cooperate so that the "divisive propaganda of Protestantism" would be "totally rejected."[6] In 1931 the archbishop of Oaxaca suggested that Protestantism threatened to damage Catholicism and to destroy the national character of Mexico.[7]

However, as government-sponsored persecution broke out against the Roman Catholic Church itself at this time, the ideological contest with Protestantism receded in importance for a number of years. Only with the end of open persecution during the last Cárdenas years and with the ever-growing tolerance for church activities during Ávila Camacho's presidency did the Catholic Church rebound. "Against the letter of the Constitution, Roman Catholic Schools began to flourish openly," noted one Protestant writer. "Great religious festivals began to take place once more with big public demonstrations."[8]

Part of the revival of Catholicism was a new offensive against Protestantism, which found its most organized expression in the lay Catholic movement known as the Unión Nacional Sinarquista (1937–48). The Sinarquistas grouped Protestantism with communism, Judaism, revolution, and North American imperialism as foreign impositions that should be opposed by patriotic Mexicans.[9] Although most of the Catholic hierarchy distanced itself from the fascist leanings of the Sinarquistas, it too proposed to halt the spread of Protestantism, which the archbishop of Mexico City characterized in a pastoral letter of 1944 as "a wave of pacific conquest" financed by Protestant industrialists from the United States that could result in Mexicans' being "absolutely assimilated" into American culture within two generations. The archbishops of Puebla and Guadalajara issued similar pastoral letters directing the faithful to reject Protestant propaganda and to surpass their rivals in works of charity. Some dioceses passed out fliers to be affixed to the outside of houses with the words, "This home is Catholic. We reject Protestant propaganda." Other dioceses tried to offer more services to the poor. "If those in charge of Protestant propaganda in Mexico start a charitable institution," a Mexico City priest suggested, "Mexican Catholics should start one too, and, if possible, start a greater number of such institutions, following the Catholic Church's distinguished tradition in this area."[10]

Archbishop of Mexico City Luis María Martínez later emphasized that he was calling not for violence against non-Catholics but for "a crusade of teaching, of convincing, of love, and of peace."[11] But for some members of the clergy and of the laity who already harbored deep resentments against Protestants, this clarification came too late or simply was not heeded. During the 1940s and 1950s, in town after town, Catholic-Protestant conflict erupted. In Actipan de Morelos, Puebla, for instance, a group of men shouting "Long live

Sinarquismo and death to Protestantism" killed Protestant minister Leonardo Tamariz and wounded other Protestants. The Mexico City newspaper *El Popular* blamed the attacks in Actipan and others that occurred in Jalapa de Díaz, Oaxaca, Ojitlán, Oaxaca, and Cahuloti, Michoacán, on the archbishop of Mexico City's pastoral letter and on municipal authorities' unwillingness to protect Protestants.[12]

One way to look at the phenomenon of Catholic-Protestant conflict is through the life and activism of David Ruesga (1898–1960), the presiding bishop of the Iglesia de Dios en la República Mexicana (Church of God in the Mexican Republic) and for many years president of the Comité Nacional de Defensa Evangélica (CNDE; National Evangelical Defense Committee). After fighting with Villa in the revolution, Ruesga migrated to California, where he encountered the still glowing embers of the Azusa Street revival (birthplace of the modern Pentecostal movement). He converted to Pentecostal Christianity and returned to Mexico to start one of Mexico City's first Pentecostal churches, which grew to more than a thousand members by 1930. Despite numerous "church splits," Ruesga's Iglesia de Dios soon expanded into the farthest corners of the republic, enjoying special success in rural areas. It was precisely because of his denomination's rapid growth that he became the driving force behind the CNDE: the Iglesia de Dios's converts were being persecuted all over the country and needed some kind of protection.[13] By 1948 Ruesga was sending the Ministry of the Interior at least one complaint per week about attacks on Protestants, and he estimated that an average of one such attack occurred somewhere in the nation each day.[14] Although Ruesga's religious ministry and advocacy for religious freedom merit a study of their own, one of his letters will have to suffice here. A request that Ruesga made to the secretary of the interior for "direct and immediate intervention" highlighted two major reasons for the disillusionment that Protestants were feeling about the federal government in the 1940s.[15]

Ruesga first brought to the secretary's attention the many applications made by Protestant congregations for permission to open their churches for public worship services and asked that the secretary grant those requests. These applications were absolutely crucial to young, growing Protestant denominations, since all churches had to receive permission from the Ministry of the Interior before any religious services could take place inside them. If such permission were granted, the church building passed to the control of the federal government, since the Constitution specified that all church buildings belonged to the nation.[16] Protestants generally supported or at least tolerated these provisions of the Constitution, because they had served until 1940 primarily to weaken the Catholic Church. During the Ávila Camacho and Alemán administrations, however, Lindy Scott estimates that the Ministry of the Interior tabled "more than 1000" Protestant applications as part of an effort to placate the Catholic Church.[17] Whereas outright rejections would have given the Protestants recourse to the courts, mere inaction left them with few options. Confronted by the Ministry of the Interior's passivity, most Protestant congregations faced a no-win situation: if they chose to open their churches anyway, they risked losing their property outright and had no recourse if their opponents damaged or destroyed them; if they chose to continue honoring the law, they could not have public worship services of any kind.

Protestants found this predicament extremely frustrating. Having supported the revolution and the regime for thirty years, they were now being treated as second-class citizens, whereas the until recently rebellious Catholics were being treated with favor. To Ruesga, the Ministry of the Interior's practices seemed to deny the precepts of the Constitution itself, especially article 24, which said, "Each person is free to profess the religious beliefs that he chooses and to practice the ceremonies, devotions and actions of his respective creed, in church or in his home, as long as these actions do not constitute a crime or come under legal sanction." Granting permission to churches, argued Ruesga, was the unavoidable consequence of article 24, for if all Mexicans were free to believe as they wished and to practice the religious ceremonies that they wished, "for this guarantee to be effective, permission should be given for the opening of churches." To deny recognition to evangelical churches at a time when Catholic churches around the nation were open was to undermine the authority of the Constitution.[18] But now that the state and the Catholic Church were at peace, Protestants' minority status meant that they had little to offer to the Ávila Camacho and Alemán regimes, which were more interested in maintaining stability and in building the "business of government" than in larger ideological projects.

What Ruesga called "the tremendous acts of religious intolerance committed by clerical fanatics" posed an equally grave problem. Local authorities often wanted to help, he said, "but in spite of their desires to impart justice and to reestablish order in the area of liberty of conscience, they are unable to do so because they lack the power to establish respect for individual liberties." Ruesga believed that the best solution to this problem would be military intervention, but the secretary of defense had made clear that only the secretary of the interior could authorize the use of federal troops for such purposes. Ruesga asked for intervention in three towns in the state of México—Tabernillas in the municipio of Almoloya de Juárez, Santiago Yeche in the district of Ixtlahuaca, and Coatlinchán in the district of Texcoco—where Protestants had been attacked and killed and their churches and homes destroyed. "The evangelicals from these places are refugees in the City of Mexico, for in addition to having lost their modest possessions they have been threatened with death if they return and they are in danger of losing their plots of land, for many of them are ejidatarios."[19] The similarity of these events to the expulsion of Protestants from San Juan Chamula, Chiapas, in the 1970s and 1980s suggests that the latter events may have been exceptional in terms of scale but were part of a larger pattern of religious conflict in rural Mexico.

The problem for Protestants during the Ávila Camacho and Alemán administrations was not merely that the federal government and the different state governments lacked the political will to enforce the religious guarantees of the Constitution and to protect minority rights in rural villages. The deeper problem, as far as Protestants were concerned, was that their antagonists *knew* that the government had this attitude. For example, the reaction of Protestants in the state of México to anti-Protestant violence, especially in the town of San Andrés Timilpan, shows the deep fears and frustrations that government passivity in the face of continuing patterns of violence could generate. The scenario in San Andrés Timilpan was the following: on 25 May 1940, a group led by Catholic priest Arnulfo Hurtado destroyed the local Protestant church, burned the house of Anastasio Lucas, and forced more than two hundred Protestants to leave the village. Neither at that time nor later did federal or state authorities take action to prosecute any crimes or to restore order. In fact, when a Protestant girl was murdered on 13 July 1945, municipal authorities not only took no action but ordered her body removed from the local cemetery. In February 1946 the town's Protestants, desperate to return home after years in exile, arranged for an interview with the secretary of the interior of the state of México. When they asked for help in returning to their village and for the prosecution of those responsible for their plight, the secretary advised them not to return, citing their minority status.[20]

For Protestants in the state of México, this combination of violence and government inaction proved terrifying. Catholic opposition was bad enough, but government passivity intensified the problem, for it suggested to Protestants that, in the absence of state intervention, violence would only escalate. The desperation of Protestants in El Oro, México, was typical of many beleaguered Protestant groups during this period. In mid-1947 they complained to President Alemán that President Avila Camacho's declaration that he was a believer continued to haunt them: "We thought that the encouragement given to attacks and crimes against 'unbelievers' by a president's declaration of an established faith had ended. To cite a concrete example in this very State of Mexico, because of this declaration the brethren of San Andrés Timilpan had their Evangelical Church and their houses burned and some of them have paid with their lives for the unforgivable crime of being Evangelicals." Despite repeated requests over a period of five years, Protestants could not return to their village.[21] It seemed to the Protestants of El Oro that only Roman Catholics enjoyed true constitutional liberties.

It is interesting to note the importance these Protestants assigned to Ávila Camacho's "I am a believer" statement. To them it declared Catholicism "an established faith" and encouraged "attacks and crimes" against Protestants. Although Ávila Camacho probably intended neither to establish Catholicism nor to encourage attacks of any kind, the Protestants were not completely mistaken in interpreting the import of his words. They represented a sea change from Callista and Cardenista anti-Catholic rhetoric and signaled to the nation that the days of government-sponsored anti-Catholicism were gone. As such, and regardless of Ávila Camacho's intentions, the simple declaration emboldened many whose anti-Protestant attitudes had been kept in check by fear of government reprisals.

Hundreds of such incidents from the 1940s and 1950s can be found in the national archive in Mexico City. One writer cites 164 "violent acts" of this sort between 1945 and 1955, the most occurring in the states of Puebla (31) and México (39). Since these states border the Federal District, and since their inhabitants would therefore be more familiar with the federal government and more likely to appeal to it for protection, it seems reasonable to assume that other states had more such incidents that were not reported to the federal government. Documents in the Oaxaca state archive bolster this view, revealing that at least two hundred such conflicts took place in Oaxaca between 1948 and 1965 (files for years prior to 1948 were not available).[22]

The SIL Survives and Prospers

How did the SIL fare during an era when one Catholic writer identified Protestant missionaries as a manifestation of the "aggressive policies" of "vile Yankee imperialism"?[23] It expanded rapidly. Starting in 1935 with Cameron and Elvira Townsend's work in Tetelcingo, the organization grew to thirty-two workers in Mexico by the end of 1938, twenty-six of whom were working on thirteen different Indian languages.[24] In 1942 the SIL had forty-five translators working on twenty-two languages: Chinantec, Chol, Cuicateco, Huichol, Yucatec Maya, Mayo, Mazahua, Mazatec, Mixe, Mixtec, Nahuatl of Morelos, Nahuatl of Puebla, Tarahumara, Tarascan, Tlapaneco, Totonac, Tzeltal, Tzotzil, Yaqui, Zapotec, Zapotec del Valle, and Zoque.[25] In 1945 there were ninety-one translators working in thirty-nine languages: all of the above except Mayo and Tlapaneco, plus Amuzgo, Chontal of Oaxaca, Chontal of Tabasco, Cora, Guarijia, Huasteco, Huave, Huichol, Lacandón, Matlatzinco, Nahuatl of Guerrero, Nahuatl of the Isthmus, Otomi, Popoloca, Tepehua, Tojolabal, Trique, Zapotec of the Sierra, and Zapotec of the Isthmus.[26]

The simple answer to how the SIL entered these indigenous communities and stayed in them during a time of religious conflict is that they went in with as much authority from the federal government as they could muster. As Townsend wrote Cárdenas in 1942, "All the new recruits carry credentials of this Institute with seals from the SEP, the Departamento de Asuntos Indígenas, la Escuela Nacional de Antropología, and the Instituto Indigenista Inter-Americano. They also carry documentation from the Secretaría de Gobernación."[27] Officials in the Immigration Ministry seem to have offered a great amount of help as well. For instance, when linguists Hazel Spotts and Mildred Kiemele wanted to begin studying Mazahua in San Miguel Tenochtitlan, México, they first secured permission from the Immigration Ministry, which wrote to both the governor of the state and the municipal president explaining the women's mission and asking the officials to extend every courtesy to them.[28] During World War II, when foreigners were often viewed with suspicion, the Ministry of the Interior proved quite willing to write letters legitimating the presence of SIL linguists in indigenous communities.[29]

Much of the support the SIL received from the SEP, the INI, and the Ministry of the Interior must be credited to the SIL's success in winning the favor of individual Mexican officials in the 1940s and in staying in their good graces for the following thirty years. This success was not a fluke. The SIL won the favor of officials all over the country because friendship with officials was a major organizational priority. The organization's studious attempts to teach its personnel about the social conventions of Latin America resulted in numerous key allies in the Mexican government. After years of missionary work in Guatemala and Mexico, both Townsends, but especially Elvira, had developed great respect for local customs which they tried to pass on to their colleagues in the SIL. During the first years of Camp Wycliffe, Elvira taught a course on Latin American courtesy, which Cameron saw as one of the most important elements in training future missionary linguists.[30] Since she published her teaching in book form in 1941, we can examine her emphases in some detail.[31]

At the heart of Elvira's message is the call to her students to observe social conventions not merely out of obligation but with wholehearted emotional commitment. By warning Americans that they must be willing to set aside not only their "Hail-fellow, well-met" mannerisms but also the attitudes that underlie them, she sets up a fairly formidable challenge for her pupils. It will not be enough, she makes clear, to mime certain social conventions. Instead, visitors to Latin America must adopt the dignity that is for her the defining characteristic of Latin Americans.[32]

In practical terms, Elvira's advice sometimes amounts to little more than common sense (tip waiters and waitresses 10 percent or ask someone for the going rate), but often it displays real sensitivity to

cultural difference, as in her analysis of how those of inferior social status should relate to those of higher status. "The inferior person makes the approach to his superior," she clarifies. "Bear this in
mind especially in dealing with officialdom, that it is your place to
step up, always making the approach." This idea was counterintuitive
to most Americans, who assumed that "stepping up" or "making the
approach" was a faux pas, for in the United States they were accustomed to wait for the person of superior status to acknowledge them
before they dared to make any overture.[33] Insights like these are what
one might expect from such a book: they help the reader avoid social
mistakes and frustration by explaining practices and expectations
that he or she might not have noticed or understood otherwise.

But Elvira goes beyond the mere explanation of cultural practices.
She not only explains Latin American courtesy but also implies its
superiority. One can detect in Elvira's advice the chagrin that someone who had lived in Latin America for most of her adult life felt on
observing the social failings of her fellow Americans: her compatriots'
habit of looking around homes that they visit, letting their eyes light
upon books and papers, and peering into other rooms is "extremely
offensive" to their hosts; it is "most unbecoming" when travelers assume that restaurants or markets are unsanitary; boisterous or loud
conversation in a restaurant is "disturbing and annoying" to other
patrons; not allowing one's host to take one's umbrella, purse, or
other accoutrements manifests "rather embarrassing" distrust that
might wound a Latin American "forever"; turning down food is "hu-
miliating" to the cook and "deeply" offends the host; joking and loud
talk in a marketplace is "uncomplimentary and rude." Latin Americans, in fact, emerge from the pages of her book "far more cultured
than the foreigner" and possessing "a much finer sensibility."[34]

Elvira goes so far as to suggest that visitors to Latin America should
learn the history of their host countries and "be able to speak appre-
ciatively of the outstanding heroes of the country," viewing them
"from the standpoint of a patriotic national rather than from the
standpoint of American imperialists who favor political moves that
protect their efforts at selfish exploitation."[35] The essence of her philosophy is that visitors should not worry if they do not learn every
cultural practice, but they should let the "spirit of friendship" of Latin
America "master" them.[36] Like many other missionaries before her,
Elvira seems to have been "mastered" by her hosts' culture to the ex-

tent that she became critical of her own North American culture.[37] This is perhaps the key to the SIL's success in making friends. They put aside the usual American attitude of superiority and adopted, as well as they could, the culture and values of Mexico.

Linguistic Legitimacy

One of the first members of the SIL, Brainerd Legters, resigned in 1942 "at the request of Mr. W. C. Townsend together with Dr. K. L. Pike," because his "proposed evangelistic work" was "not compatible" with the organization's objectives.[38] Why would the son of the SIL's co-founder L. L. Legters leave the organization? In what sense was evangelistic work not compatible with the goals of the SIL? The answers to these questions and to the larger question of how the SIL managed to expand during a time when Protestants were being persecuted is that the SIL gained scientific legitimacy by emphasizing the linguistic side of its work and by severely restricting its evangelistic activity. "If our work isn't fit to publish in a scientific magazine, perhaps we should ask ourselves whether it is fit to publish as a Bible translation. I don't think it is too high a standard to set to say that each of us, by the time we finish and publish our New Testament, should have in hand in good shape the makings of a creditable, if not exhaustive, grammar, dictionary, book of texts," argued SIL Mexico deputy director Dick Pittman in 1942.[39]

At the SIL's annual meeting later in 1942, "the importance of publications" surfaced again with a resolution being adopted that all senior members be required to submit one scholarly article every six months.[40] In early 1943 Townsend expressed fears that the SIL's new magazine, *Translation,* designed for supporters at home, would attract unfavorable attention in Mexico. He hoped rather that the SIL could publish a purely scientific journal that would bolster the organization's reputation as an academic entity.[41] Clearly, the SIL's leaders were recognizing that, if they wanted to be taken seriously as a scientific organization, they had to *be* a scientific organization, a transformation that Legters and some other members found difficult to square with their missionary calling. However, the leaders of the SIL believed that, although critics in the government, in Catholic circles, and in indigenous communities knew of the SIL's religious goals, there was little of a concrete nature that could be pinned on them as long as they justified their existence with scientific production.[42] In terms of academic production, the strategy seems to have been more or less successful: in 1951 the SIL issued a bibliography that listed 381 published items written by 113 different SIL authors for thirty-four Mexican languages and in the general fields of linguistics and literacy.[43]

Part of the same dynamic was the drive to secure academic credentials for as many linguists as possible. The SIL's first doctorate went to an unlikely candidate. Before applying to the SIL, Ken Pike had been rejected from the China Inland Mission because of his unstable disposition, but he surpassed all expectations to become one of the leading figures in the field of linguistics during the 1950s and 1960s. At Camp Wycliffe in 1935 Pike easily might have been rejected again, but the young organization was in such need of personnel in its early years that he was allowed to stay. L. L. Legters, for instance, on seeing Pike sitting high in a tree at Camp Wycliffe (he was trying to overcome his fear of heights), thought, "Lord, couldn't you have sent us someone better than this?"[44] Quite soon, though, Pike proved to be a sort of "boy wonder" of linguistics, earning his doctorate in 1942 from the University of Michigan and publishing major works on phonetics, phonemics, tone languages, comparative linguistics, rhetoric, and African languages, even as he spent most of each year translating the Bible in San Miguel el Grande, Oaxaca, and teaching summer classes for the SIL.[45] At the University of Michigan he became an associate professor in 1948 and gained tenure in 1955, going on to become president of the Linguistic Society of America in 1961 and chair of his department in 1975.[46] During the 1940s Pike's linguistic prowess benefited the SIL in two ways: externally, it gave it credibility as a genuine scientific organization; internally, it provided SIL linguists with practically oriented theoretical material that directly aided their translation work. Pike also paved the way for nine other SIL linguists to earn advanced degrees in linguistics during the 1940s and 1950s, further legitimizing the SIL and helping its members deal with complicated linguistic issues.[47] As the director of the academic side of the SIL, beginning in 1941, Pike eased the administrative burden on Townsend, although at times the two argued "bitterly."[48]

Pike added more luster to the SIL's cause in 1951 by serving on a UNESCO commission that studied the issue of vernacular languages.

He and the other committee members came out strongly for the vernacular cause, concluding that "nothing in the structure of a language prevents it from being used as a vehicle of modern civilization" and that "every student should begin his studies in the mother tongue."[49] Since Mexican educator Jaime Torres Bodet, then serving as director of UNESCO, had endorsed the use of the vernacular in primary education at UNESCO's Fifth Assembly in 1950, and since appointees like Pike and Morris Swadesh were known advocates of vernacular literacy, the commission's conclusions were not overly surprising.[50] Still, the commission's findings bolstered the SIL's position as the chief advocate and enabler of vernacular literacy in Mexico.

The new academic credentials of the SIL's linguists and their ability to produce hundreds of scientific articles significantly aided the organization's official standing in Mexico. Now the friends that the SIL made in the government through practicing "Latin American courtesy" could point to the SIL's impressive linguistic achievements as a perfectly justifiable explanation of their presence in indigenous villages. Unlike Mexican Protestants and other American missionaries, the SIL had the official support of the Mexican government. Friendships with a host of officials and growing linguistic legitimacy meant that the SIL enjoyed advantages that other Protestants in Mexico could only dream about.

It should not be assumed, however, that government support could guarantee automatic access to a given community. In fact, many communities showed little regard for letters from Mexico City. Even those that accepted SIL linguists would often do little more than grudgingly tolerate their presence. The two indigenous communities examined in chapter 7, the Tzeltals of Chiapas and the Tarahumaras of Chihuahua, illustrate both the importance and the insufficiency of state connections to the SIL's work. Letters and personal visits from federal or state officials occasionally opened doors that otherwise might have been closed, but they often failed to accomplish much of anything.

There was also a contradictory element to the SIL's role as a representative of the state. As we shall see, the SIL did extend the reach of the state into indigenous communities, but its presence in these communities and the religious change it fostered could also lead to new kinds of administrative problems. In Chiapas, for example, the success of the SIL in fulfilling the dreams of its government patrons led not to a more dominant state but to a crisis of legitimacy. In practice, the processes of modernization, incorporation, and Mexicanization fostered by the SIL often worked against state goals such as peace, stability, and control.

6

Working for the Mexican State, Supported by the American Heartland

On 17 June 1953 federal troops entered Tepeji del Río, Hidalgo, to protect a small group of Protestants. Just as Ávila Camacho's statement that he was a believer had emboldened many Catholics, President Adolfo Ruiz Cortines's action had implications not just for one village in Hidalgo but for the whole republic. The federal government was willing, in some situations at least, to intervene to protect Protestants. The free hand that anti-Protestantism had enjoyed for twelve years was finally being checked.

Tepeji del Río's energetic priest, José C. Posadas, played a key role in making the town an inhospitable place for Protestants. Posadas seems to have flouted the law with impunity, organizing frequent outdoor processions and an annual pilgrimage to the Basilica of the Virgin of Guadalupe. In 1948 he started to pressure local authorities to take action against the town's evangelicals. In that year a group of twenty-five Protestants complained that their leader, Justinio López, had been imprisoned, supposedly to protect him from a group that wanted to lynch him. When fellow Protestants protested that neither he nor they wanted this kind of protection, the municipal president explained that he was trying to avoid problems with the priest and would only release the prisoner on the payment of a fifty-peso "fine" and on the condition that he and his family leave town immediately. The Ministry of the Interior's response to complaints about this incident was to insist that in general it had ordered "every kind of measure to guarantee strict compliance with the law" and that in this specific case it had directed local authorities to protect Protestants' rights. All it seems to have done, in fact, was to write to the state and local governments and to accept at face value their responses that everything was under control. The fate of Justinio López was not mentioned.[1]

In August 1952 Protestants affiliated with the Iglesia de Dios en la República Mexicana applied for federal recognition of their church building in Tepeji del Río, a prospect that the municipal president viewed as dangerous to public order because of Posadas's continued influence in the town. "The majority of the inhabitants of this town are Catholics and only an insignificant group of people are evangelicals," he told the Ministry of the Interior. "When this group appeared many relatively serious difficulties appeared at the same time and it is probable that establishing the evangelical church that they want would bring back those difficulties, with lamentable consequences." Without having received permission, the Protestants started using their church in December 1952. As the municipal president had predicted, the open expression of Protestant worship led to increasing tensions in Tepeji del Río during the first few months of 1953, including a fight on 9 June between Félix Servín, president of the local chapter of Acción Católica, and Toribio Rangel, a leader in the Iglesia de Dios congregation.[2]

One week later, after hearing Posadas fulminate that Tepeji del Río had room for only the Catholic religion, approximately nine hundred workers of La Josefina textile factory left their posts to march to the Protestant church, with the ostensible purpose of removing its sign. Another thousand people joined them as they marched to the church. This large group not only removed the sign but also utterly demolished the church building. Uncharacteristically, the Ministry of the Interior authorized the secretary of defense to send in federal troops. When a platoon from the Eighteenth Military Zone in the state capital of Pachuca arrived the next day, 17 June, they restored order and prevented bloodshed. They could not prevent the textile workers, however, from going on strike with the sole demand that La Josefina's five Protestants be fired. The community at large demanded that the town's forty evangelicals leave town or face their wrath. Unusually, again, the governor of Hidalgo, Quintín Rueda Villagrán, sent Gaudencio Morales, the director general of the Hidalgo Ministry of the Interior, to convince the strikers that their action was illegal and harmful to the state's economy.

Starting at 4 P.M., the representatives of the federal and state governments, the municipal president, and the commander of the seventy-fifth regiment of the *defensa rural* met with Catholic and Protestant leaders to negotiate a settlement of their problems. Six hours later, with most of the town still waiting outside the town hall, Morales suggested a three-point solution to the conflict: the five evangelical workers would be suspended until a commission made up of six representatives of the "different sectors" of the town negotiated a settlement with the textile union either to fire them or to keep them on the payroll; the "competent authorities" would resolve the "judicial aspects" of the case and would decide on the "housing situation" of the Protestants; and federal troops would remain in town to maintain the peace of the community and to protect the rights of the Protestants. The Catholic workers returned to work the next day.[3]

The documentary trail peters out at this point; the only subsequent document in the pertinent file, a complaint dated 17 October 1954 that Posadas was still leading processions and pilgrimages, mentions neither the fate of the five workers nor the "living situation" of the forty Protestants. Thus it is not clear how everything was resolved in Tepeji del Río.[4] What is clear is that the federal and state governments had finally responded to Protestant requests for military intervention, that such intervention probably saved Protestant lives, and that Protestants were deeply grateful for this government action. As Mexico's leading Protestant intellectual wrote at the time, "Seldom has official action to maintain the law and to insure constitutional rights to Protestants been more prompt and determined."[5] This intervention represented a policy change that played a role in the rapid growth of Protestantism during the Ruiz Cortines administration, when the number of Protestants, according to one scholar, may have tripled.[6]

At the same time, although the army had intervened in Tepeji del Río, it had done so to restore public order and to protect a textile business, not to apprehend those who had destroyed a Protestant church. Similarly, representatives of the governor of Hidalgo showed more concern for quelling unruly crowds than for minority rights. The state might intervene to save lives and restore order, but it was still far from being ready to offer the "guarantees" of religious freedom that Protestants longed for. It did not even seem ready to prosecute the most egregious crimes against Protestants. In fact, the action taken in Tepeji del Río was one of the only times that Ruiz Cortines used the army to protect Protestants. Its importance, like that of Ávila Camacho's "I am a believer" statement, was symbolic. Catholics who contemplated violence against Protestants could no longer take for granted that the federal and state governments would give them a free pass.[7]

As the situation for Protestants improved in the 1950s, the SIL took advantage of the more open environment to continue expanding and to ally itself even more closely with the Mexican state. The strengthened position of the SIL in the 1950s also was closely related to the development of a broad base of financial support in the American middle class.

Winning Over the National Indigenista Institute

As Henri Favre points out, indigenismo was always "closely linked to nationalism" and, in fact, might even be considered the "privileged form" of nationalism in Latin America.[8] Indigenismo's programs of incorporation and acculturation of the Indian therefore played a much more significant role in Mexican governmental policy than, say, the Bureau of Indian Affairs in the United States. Even when resources were lacking, the symbolic importance of indigenista policy, of doing *something* to integrate the Indian, was great. It was therefore serendipitous for the SIL that its goals, talents, and ideology meshed so well with indigenismo.

Shortly after taking the reins of the newly founded National Indigenista Institute in 1948, Alfonso Caso highlighted "the need for truly qualified men, sufficiently trained in Mexican or foreign universities, to lead study and work brigades that go to these [indigenous] communities and then propose ways of transforming them to the Federal Government."[9] The fact was that Mexican indigenistas (discussed in chapter 4) still did not have a good qualitative or quantitative grasp of the nature of the indigenous communities in the nation and needed all the help they could get. Since Caso believed that one of the most pressing issues was a study "of the population density of those who speak indigenous languages, as a foundation for future studies of communities that speak indigenous languages and the regions where they are found," there was a clear opening for the SIL.[10] UNESCO's 1950 affirmation of vernacular literacy and Ken Pike's growing reputation as a linguist made the SIL even more appealing.

Finally, for the same nationalistic reasons that we have mentioned, Caso also believed in vernacular education. Reading and writing indigenous languages was not an end in itself but part of a comprehensive program in which each step prepared the way for the next. Education in the vernacular was thus the beginning of a process that would end only when the indigenous students had been transformed into Mexicans.[11] Like many other Mexican nationalists, Caso believed that the school was the principal institution in the task of teaching citizenship. If the task of the schools was difficult in urban areas it was doubly hard in indigenous communities, where the students might not even speak Spanish or know that they lived in a nation called Mexico, much less harbor feelings of love for the *patria*. Vernacular education promised to act as a bridge to Spanish, which was in turn a bridge to true citizenship. Caso does not seem to have believed that indigenous languages were valuable in themselves or that every people had a right to education in its own language. Rather, he embraced vernacular education as the best means to the ends of Spanish language acquisition and Mexican patriotism.

It is thus no surprise that under Caso the INI worked very closely with the SIL. For example, in 1951 in Chiapas he used the SIL to provide Tzeltal and Tzotzil primers and to train the first groups of bilingual teachers at the INI's first Centro Coordinador Indigenista (CCI; Indigenous Coordinating Center). He could have no fundamental problem with the SIL's desire to change aspects of indigenous culture, for it coincided with his own dreams of transforming indigenous communities. While he was no Protestant, Protestantism had proved compatible with the practice of Western medicine and with a wide variety of scientific techniques that he hoped to see implemented in the villages. Was not the SIL's linguistic prowess proof of their modern, scientific outlook? Where later anthropologists would see in the SIL a personification of imperialism and ethnocentrism, Caso saw in the SIL much that was attractive and perhaps much that reminded him of his own goals and aspirations.[12]

In fact, for Gonzalo Aguirre Beltrán, the director of the INI's first center, in San Cristóbal de Las Casas, Chiapas, "the scientific contributions of the members of the SIL, already considerable, particularly those of Ken Pike, opened possibilities for literacy work, which formerly had been limited to only a few languages, among a greater and greater number of language groups." In Aguirre Beltrán's opinion, for the first time, Pike's practical yet theoretically rigorous "masterpieces" on phonetics and tones offered Mexico the ability to reduce its many tonal languages to writing.[13] Therefore, in its first few years the CCI worked closely with the SIL in what Aguirre Beltrán described to Caso as a vernacular literacy campaign that would serve as "a first step toward the goal of teaching Spanish."[14] The SIL's Marianna Slocum and Ken Weathers gave training classes for Tzeltal and Tzotzil and wrote primers that were used by the INI until 1975, when they were revised by another SIL linguist.[15] In fact, despite the CCI's desire to hire Mexican linguists to do the much-needed work in Tzeltal and Tzotzil areas, the only national linguists it managed to hire only stayed from 1954 to 1958, with minimal results. In 1979 the CCI still did not have its own linguists.[16]

The INI called on the SIL again in 1954 when it ran into problems with the tonal languages of Mazatec and Chinantec at its new CCI in Papaloapan, Oaxaca. The directors of that center, Isabel Arciniegas and Ricardo Pozas, found the problems of rendering tonal complexities in written form so daunting that they began advocating the old "direct method" of teaching Spanish. Since this policy contradicted the reigning theories of the educational and indigenista establishments, the INI organized a conference in 1956 in Temazcal, Oaxaca, to deal with the issues of the proper relationship between vernacular literacy and Spanish literacy. Despite a valiant fight by Pozas and Arciniegas, who were overwhelmingly outnumbered by supporters of vernacular literacy (and friends of the SIL) such as Ethel Wallis, Gonzalo Aguirre Beltrán, Julio de la Fuente, Alfonso Villa Rojas, Angélica Castro, and Juan Comas, INI chief Caso reacted to the issues raised by the conference by turning to the SIL's Sarah Gudschinsky and Eunice Pike for help.[17]

Gudschinsky and Pike's assignment to study the variant of Mazatec found in the small village of Soyaltepec, Oaxaca, quickly bore intellectual fruit. In two articles, "Native Reaction to Tones and Words in Mazatec" and "Toneme Representation in Mazatec Orthography," Gudschinsky argued that although the difficulties posed by tonal languages were extensive—not the least of which was the problem that native speakers were not necessarily conscious of meanings attached to tone—functional orthographies were possible.[18] She argued against the kind of orthography used in English, where letters have multiple sounds, and where tone, although used, is often not written, and for the use of additional characters not found in traditional Spanish orthography. Gudschinsky's suggestions seem to have convinced most indigenistas.[19] It was in many ways a moment of triumph: Mexico's foremost indigenistas had turned to the SIL for help, and the SIL had provided an intellectually rigorous response. The SIL was now the indisputable linguistic authority in Mexico.

Convenio with the Education Ministry

In addition to its alliance with the INI, the SIL had long sought to ally itself more closely with the SEP. Townsend's initial contact with Rafael Ramírez and subsequent tour of rural schools, his good relationship with Carlos Basauri, and President Cárdenas's arrangement for eight SIL linguists to receive salaries as rural teachers had demonstrated both the possibility of the SIL's working closely with the SEP and the importance of the SEP within the Mexican state.[20] Thus, when the Ávila Camacho administration had stopped paying salaries to SIL workers, Townsend almost immediately began arguing for a renewed relationship. In December 1941 Townsend had suggested that, if these salaries could not be restored, the SEP should find other ways of supporting the work of the SIL. "We hope to be able to put a great supply of data about the languages of fifty indigenous tribes of the nation at the disposal of those departments [the SEP and the Ministry of Labor] and of the University within ten years," proposed Townsend. "This information will not cost the Government one cent."[21] As the Ávila Camacho administration sought improved relations with the Roman Catholic Church, subsidizing Protestant missionaries simply was not high on its list of priorities. At the very end of his term, President Ávila Camacho did thank the SIL for its help in encouraging literacy, but that is as far as his support of the SIL went.[22] With the joining of the previously freestanding Department of Indigenous Affairs to the SEP in 1946 under the direction of the pro-SIL Gonzalo Aguirre Beltrán and the succession of President Miguel Alemán (1946–52), who was known to be married to a Presbyterian, the SIL had seemed to be on the verge of renewing its ties to the SEP.[23] "Circumstances," as Aguirre Beltrán says, delayed the alliance, for Alemán showed little interest in aiding either Protestants or Indians during most of his years in office. When an alliance did come, though, the SIL's fostering of vernacular literacy would be its most attractive feature to the SEP.

The pinnacle of the SIL's efforts to ally itself with the Mexican state occurred on 15 August 1951, when Cameron Townsend and Mariano Samayoa León, director general of the SEP's Dirección General de Asuntos Indígenas (DGAI, or Indigenous Affairs section), signed a *convenio* (agreement) that formalized the SIL's position in Mexico. In the preamble to the convenio, the DGAI and the SIL committed themselves to developing a "program of cooperation" on behalf of Mexico's indigenous peoples that would encompass linguistic and anthropological research and "all that signifies the betterment of these indigenous groups." The actual terms of the convenio, however, boiled down to more of a trade than a cooperative effort. The basic outline of the agreement was that the SIL would trade linguistics for legitimacy.[24]

The SIL's most important responsibilities were "an intensive linguistic study of each language" and comparative studies designed to classify the different indigenous languages. The SIL would provide interpreters to the DGAI, give rural teachers a basic introduction to linguistics, and train university students in more advanced linguistics. It would produce bilingual Spanish-vernacular primers "in order to facilitate the learning of the official language" and translate laws and other government publications into indigenous languages. With the DGAI it would publish a linguistics journal and organize linguistics conferences. Nonlinguistic responsibilities included anthropological studies of indigenous groups; the encouragement of sport, civic-mindedness, and cooperative service; and the "eradication of vice by all possible means."

The SEP's major responsibility was to arrange with the Ministry of the Interior for the SIL's linguists to enter and remain in the country. As "non-profit scientific researchers at the service of the state," members of the SIL would not have to pay any kind of immigration duty when they entered the country or any customs charges on their equipment. The SEP agreed to intervene with the Ministry of National Defense, so that the SIL could use airplanes and helicopters, and with the Ministry of Communications and Public Works, so that the SIL could acquire and employ radios, since this equipment would be "at the service of the Mexican Government." Finally, the SEP would provide the SIL with medicine for its clinics and would help it secure permission to use federal land for research centers.

The appeal of the convenio for the Mexican state came in the SIL's willingness to provide primers in indigenous languages "to facilitate the learning of reading and writing in Spanish for illiterate speakers of indigenous languages" and in its commitment to the "creation of bilingual primers with the goal of facilitating the learning of the official language." One SEP report characterized the convenio as an agreement in which the SIL joined "the campaign to teach Spanish and literacy to the indigenous population," a clear indication of the success of the SIL's long campaign to frame vernacular literacy as a bridge to Spanish.[25]

For the SIL, medicine and land were, of course, welcome additions to its work in Mexico, but the real benefit of the convenio came in terms of legitimacy. Having an agreement with one of Mexico's most important governmental entities provided a new kind of security and stability. Whereas previously the SIL had depended on favors dispensed by its friends and patrons on an ad hoc basis, it now had a firm legal basis for its presence in Mexico. Any critics or enemies would have to go through the SEP before they dislodged or even significantly damaged the SIL's position in Mexico. The convenio even gave tacit endorsement to the SIL's evangelistic activities: first, it framed the SIL's project quite broadly in terms of the "betterment" of indigenous people; second, if "betterment" did not have enough of a moral tone to it, the call for "the eradication of vice by all possible means" surely clarified the moralizing nature of the SIL's activities; and third, nestled among the SIL's duty to translate laws, advice about hygiene, and instructions for "tanning leather," was its responsibility to translate "books of high moral and patriotic value." Unless SIL linguists broke constitutional prohibitions on foreigners' acting as ministers of religion (i.e., taking official positions of leadership or engaging in any practice, such as officiating at communion or exercising disciplinary authority, from which other church members were excluded), their activities would be very hard to attack on legal grounds. By the terms of the convenio, SIL linguists had the right, in fact the obligation, to translate books of high moral value, under which category the Bible surely fell.

The Noble Work of Incorporation

It was not only in the area of linguistics that the SIL and indigenismo shared common goals. The SIL's underlying missionary raison d'être and Cameron Townsend's own vision for the cultural project of the SIL in Indian communities—"to study the situation in which he lives; endorse the good traits; exhort against the bad ones"—found its secular equivalent in the kind of cultural change advocated by many indigenistas.[26] Specifically, the indigenistas believed that they could improve indigenous culture by eliminating its negative aspects and preserving its positive aspects. The foremost proponent of this philosophy of cultural change was Mexico's first professional anthropologist, Manuel Gamio.

Gamio expressed his Mexican nationalism in his attempt to unify the nation by "Mexicanizing" its indigenous populations. Another aspect of his thought that made him a natural ally of the SIL was his belief in the superiority of Western culture.[27] While he did not believe that every aspect of Western culture was superior to every aspect of indigenous culture—he was quite willing to list the negative traits of the West and the positive traits of indigenous culture—Gamio did hold that Western culture was better, in the end, because it met human "needs and aspirations" more effectively through science. "Therefore," he argued, "public health, education, communication media, agriculture, industry and other cultural characteristics of modern, foreign origin are guided by scientific principles and methods, which does not take place in indigenous culture, which generally develops through experience and conventional ideas."[28] Convinced that Indians needed to be Mexicanized, he could thus sympathize with the SIL on two levels. First, he believed that substituting Western-style education, scientific agricultural techniques, modern medicine, and the Spanish language—all of which the SIL facilitated to one degree or another—for indigenous practices was one of the highest callings of the indigenista movement. Second, he believed that Western religion, such as Protestantism, was superior to indigenous religion.

In Gamio's mind, anthropology was a practical tool whose purpose was to gather information that would facilitate the incorporation of Mexico's indigenous population. Once gathered, anthropological data should be evaluated and then used to help indigenous communities adapt to the modern world. Indigenista agencies such as his Inter-American Indigenista Institute would attempt to "eliminate the obviously harmful or useless" customs, stimulate the positive ones, and introduce new ones "destined to satisfy aspirations and needs that formerly did not exist."[29] His investigations convinced him that the Seri ethnic group of the Pacific coast, for example, occupied the "lowest cultural level" and that they needed immediate protection and cultural improvement to survive. Similarly, the Tepehuan people of northern Mexico exhibited a "very low cultural level" because "characteristics of a prehispanic origin" predominated in their intellectual and material culture.[30] Helping such disadvantaged groups was not an imposition but rather a process of "satisfying the needs and biological, economic and cultural aspirations" of groups at the lowest level of cultural "evolution."[31]

Although not a believer himself, Gamio thought that, as the standard-bearers of the Western tradition, Protestantism and institutional Catholicism could play valuable roles in the process of cultural change. He believed that, as long as state teachers, Protestant missionaries, and Catholic priests treated indigenous customs with respect, a healthy "competition" among the "three moralizing elements" would benefit the Indians. Regardless of who won, the Indians would "advance." Protestantism could thus play an integral role in modernizing indigenous populations. Like institutional Catholicism, it could replace "superstition" with more "modern" beliefs. Protestantism could goad teachers and Catholic priests into renewed concern for the villagers, spurring them on to better works. Gamio also saw the potential for Protestants to play an important role in introducing another modernizing influence—scientific health practices—into these communities.[32] Ideally, all religion would pass away through the gradual substitution of "scientific knowledge and art in diverse manifestations." But this process could not happen overnight, because some indigenous groups existed at such a low cultural level that they were not ready for such a large cultural leap. In this context, he believed, "scientific and artistic substitutes should not be the same for the animist or fetishist Indian or the pagan Catholic campesino" as for the Roman Catholic or the "relatively more advanced Protestant who had ceased to worship idols."[33]

Gamio's musings showed that he was not only open to the arrival of an organization like the SIL but that he was consciously *hoping* for such an eventuality. When the SIL did come to Mexico he developed relationships with a number of key SIL figures, including Cameron Townsend, Ken Pike, and Ethel Wallis. This cooperation was most evident during the 1950s in the Mezquital Valley in the state of Hidalgo, where Gamio had developed ambitious plans to help the resident Otomis. Since the budget of the III was quite small and Gamio's dreams of integrating anthropological study, agricultural improvements, economic development, and cultural transformation were rather large, he was quite willing to work with the SIL.[34]

Part of Gamio's plan for cultural change in the Mezquital Valley was to present "theatrical works of a psychological character in which local Indians will be the actors," in a specially designed theater in Tasquillo, Hidalgo, financed by a UNESCO grant. Another of his ideas, also supported by UNESCO, was to introduce "the carpet industry with oriental techniques and regional decorations." Neither of these enterprises received much aid or interest from the Mexican state, reducing Gamio to desperate pleas for help.[35]

Faced with what he called a "reduced budget" that did not allow him to do even the minimum required by the international agreement that had founded the III, Gamio turned to the SIL for help. When he wrote a short drama called "El Coyote" for his drama project, he sent it to Ethel Wallis, who was working in Tasquillo, so that she could teach it to the local schoolteacher. He also depended upon her to oversee the weaving facilities and materials in Tetzú. When she returned to the United States in the summer of 1952 he begged Ken Pike to send her back to Mexico as soon as possible. Later he used the SIL's linguistic expertise to develop "seven booklets designed to aid in bettering living conditions" and in developing Otomi radio shows.[36] It is no wonder that Gamio referred to the SIL as "an extremely praiseworthy institution" that was engaged in the "noble work" of incorporating Indians into the national population.[37] For Gamio, the SIL's religious activities were nothing to be concerned about, while their linguistic work was of direct benefit to indigenous people. Most importantly, they were a modernizing force.[38]

Defending Mexico

One way the SIL made its partnership with the Mexican state more palatable to Mexican nationalists, who clearly felt odd about working so closely with American fundamentalists, was to defend Mexico and Latin America in print. Although this kind of writing does not appear to have influenced U.S. foreign policy, it succeeded on another level. By siding with Mexico and Latin America against the United States, Townsend and other SIL authors convinced Mexicans that they had their best interests at heart. Francisco Arellano Belloc, director of Petroleos Mexicanos, for instance, was convinced that Townsend represented "the good North American who tries to convey our way of life and of experiencing existence" to the politicians of North America.[39]

Although Townsend's most impassioned defense of Mexican interests took place in his 1938 tour of the United States in support of the
oil expropriation and in a booklet called *The Truth about Mexico's Oil*,
which resulted from that experience, it was far from the last, as one
author has charged.[40] His *Lázaro Cárdenas, Mexican Democrat*, finally
published in 1952, makes little sense except as a political document,
specifically, as a further defense of Cardenismo and a call for an ethical and enlightened American foreign policy toward Latin America.[41]
The theme of the book is simple: Cárdenas is the archetypal Mexican, and from the archetypal Mexican the United States has nothing
to fear. From the foreword, in which Frank Tannenbaum describes
Cárdenas as "deeply rooted in the Mexican soil," "part of the earth
itself," and "timeless," to its final description of the retired farmer-
general's commitment "to work, fight, and work again in obscurity
that Mexico might be democratic," the biography presents Cárdenas
as a secular saint who "combated vice, ignorance, selfishness and
prejudice."[42] Townsend concludes that, in the quest for a Western
Hemisphere free from "privilege, prejudice, exploitation, imperialism," Cárdenas's "principle of non-intervention" and "powerful influence for democracy" should serve as the model for North and South
American statesmen.[43]

In 1953, when Congressman Richard Simpson of Pennsylvania
threatened to damage several Latin American economies by imposing
high tariffs on zinc and other minerals, Townsend considered it "the
duty of all people who advocate inter-American harmony and prosperity" to convince the U.S. Congress to defeat the bill. To help in
this effort he proposed to distribute six hundred copies of his biography of Cárdenas to all the senators and representatives and to use
a lecture he was giving on the book at the Press Club as a "magnificent
opportunity" to attack the Simpson bill. He therefore requested a
sum of twelve hundred dollars for his "lobbying" efforts, or eighteen
hundred dollars if President Ruiz Cortines wanted another member
of the SIL to join him in his efforts.[44]

Townsend also used the Mexican press to criticize U.S. policy toward Latin America. In 1957 he and the director of the SIL's Mexico
branch, Ben Elson, publicly attacked the United States' raising of its
tariffs of zinc and lead and released a letter to Mexican newspapers
which claimed that the new U.S. policy was a "deviation from the
Good Neighbor Policy." It would anger all of Latin America and thus

serve as an "incalculable" aid to communism.[45] After the failed Bay of Pigs invasion in 1961, Townsend publicly censured President Kennedy for putting American economic interests in Cuba above the cause of justice. He gave the Mexican press a letter he had written to Kennedy which said, "It must be made clear, Mr. President, that our young men should not be sent to give their lives in defense of the interests of our investors there."[46] There is no evidence that Townsend's public and private political writings had any influence on American foreign policy. But that, of course, was not the point. By siding with Mexico and Latin America against the United States, Townsend won his way into the hearts of many a Mexican nationalist.

American Money

As important as the partnerships with the Mexican government were to the SIL's continued presence in Mexico, they were not enough. The relationships with key officials might be secure and the SIL's defense of Mexico in the press might be making them more secure, but those relationships did not pay anything. The SIL still had to support what was becoming a vast enterprise in Mexico. It succeeded: what started as a shoestring operation that had to use barrels instead of chairs at the first Camp Wycliffe in 1934 became a vast moneymaking machine over the years, taking in over $140 million per year in the late 1990s.[47] How did the SIL get all that money?

The answer proposed by later critics of the SIL is that wealthy industrialists, hoping to extend their financial empires into unexploited regions of the world, bankrolled the SIL as a means of pacifying indigenous people and introducing them to Western culture. The foremost proponents of this view, Gerard Colby and Charlotte Dennett, devote more than eight hundred pages to their attempt to link the SIL to Nelson Rockefeller's plans for the development and exploitation of the Amazon region. Despite the years that Colby and Dennett spent researching the SIL and their promise of "major revelations" dating back as far as 1979, their 1995 book *Thy Will Be Done: The Conquest of the Amazon: Nelson Rockefeller and Evangelism in the Age of Oil* is notable for the moderation of the claims it makes about the money the SIL received from various industrialists and their private foundations.[48] While the book gives us a good sense of the many wealthy evangelicals who contributed to the SIL, in the end the sums described are relatively small: the SIL simply could not have built up its multimillion-dollar budgets on these grants from industrialists and their foundations.[49]

The second alternative proposed by Colby and other critics of the SIL is that the organization received much of its funding from the U.S. government. Although there is an element of truth to this allegation, it once again can account for only a small portion of the SIL's funds. The SIL did receive grants from the United States Agency for International Development (USAID) for its work in various nations during the 1960s, as a groundbreaking denunciation of the SIL demonstrated in 1973. According to Laurie Hart, USAID gave the SIL more than two hundred thousand dollars for work in Vietnam in the late 1960s and also "authorized the use of a million dollars of surplus equipment."[50] The SIL bought surplus planes for its work in Peru and either bought or was given surplus equipment on a number of other occasions.[51] As Colby points out, the SIL also received fifteen hundred dollars and help in publishing a book from the Asia Foundation, which had ties to the CIA.[52] There is clearly a case to be made that accepting such grants from USAID and the Asia Foundation might have had some influence on the SIL's attitude toward the U.S. government, but it is quite another thing to charge that the SIL was actually in thrall to the State Department. The money involved was simply not enough to turn the SIL away from its primary task of translating the Bible, a task that had a constituency far more devoted and far more generous than either wealthy capitalists or the U.S. government.

Good evangelicals tithe; that is, they give one-tenth of their income to their church or to evangelical charities. Of course, not all evangelicals meet this standard, but a recent study found that, of those Americans who give away 10 percent or more of their income, 80 percent are evangelicals.[53] The SIL was, in fact, one of the evangelical organizations that pioneered new methods of fund-raising in the 1950s. In keeping with the "faith mission" tradition of Hudson Taylor's China Inland Mission, the SIL originally had not solicited any funds directly. The idea was that God would supply all the organization's needs by moving individuals to give to the organization in an almost miraculous way. This method worked well enough for the SIL's first decade and a half, but by the late 1940s Townsend's grand plans for expansion into the jungles of South America depended on the acquisition of big-ticket items, especially amphibious airplanes, that did not seem to arrive in the mail with the other donations. Despite misgivings from within the SIL, in 1949 Townsend began to organize appeals to raise the funds necessary for specific items and projects. The most successful such campaign involved city- or statewide solicitations for the planes needed in South America.

As Michael Hamilton relates, the SIL also managed to tap into the growing prosperity of evangelical families in the 1950s. At this time, a few evangelicals were pioneering the "faith promise" method of raising support, where fund-raisers would challenge church members to make pledges of future giving to missions above and beyond their normal tithe. Townsend eagerly adopted this more aggressive method in raising funds for airplanes. Also in the 1950s, the SIL began to require individual missionaries to raise their own support, allowing the organization to take on new personnel at a much faster rate by making every North American church a potential donor.[54]

Although these innovations might seem rather tame, in a practical sense their impact was immense. The idea of earmarking donors' future earnings and spreading the responsibility for fund-raising to each individual missionary meant that the web of donors financing the SIL expanded dramatically. Poor fundamentalists and evangelicals had always given to missions and other charities, but in the new system of fund-raising even working-class families could make significant contributions to the SIL by giving a modest amount on a monthly or quarterly basis. Since most missionaries had a network of friends and family members who were willing to support them, it was not impossible for would-be translators to raise their entire budget without ever approaching a stranger for money.

The dynamic of personal fund-raising that is the backbone of the SIL and of other evangelical mission organizations has never been well understood by critics of the SIL. Although it is true that the organization received gifts from wealthy industrialists, foundations, and the U.S. government, virtually all of its personnel costs were borne by a network that by 1994 consisted of two hundred thousand individuals and forty-five thousand evangelical churches that spanned the United States.[55] This type of financing depends much more on personal relationships than on corporate or government largesse. In fact, many small-scale donors will support individual missionaries for decades, giving thousands of dollars over the course of their lives. Thus, although a gift of eleven thousand dollars by the Pew family was a large one, it was surpassed over the years by a number of different teachers, truck drivers, and farmers who made monthly donations over the course of many decades. Faced with such committed giving, missionaries went out of their way to stay in touch, writing personal letters from overseas, sending out "prayer letters" on a regular basis, and visiting whenever possible. The practice of "furlough," in which missionaries returned to their home country for six months or a year after a five- to ten-year term of service, owed as much to the necessity to renew and revitalize relationships with donors as it did to its stated purpose of providing rest and training.

"While the Summer Institute was organized as an intrigue," David Stoll has stated, "it is clearly an evangelical intrigue."[56] A similar statement can be made about the organization's finances. While the SIL did, in fact, receive vast sums of money from North America, it received most of that money in small quantities from many thousands of evangelical and fundamentalist donors who were neither industrialists nor particularly wealthy. Far more than it served the interests of multinational corporations or the U.S. State Department, the SIL represented middle America, both in the sense of the translators' own identity and in the sense of their being sent out and supported by a large sector of the North American middle class.

By the end of the 1950s, then, the SIL had strong ties to the SEP, the INI, and the III. These ties depended on friendships with elite Mexican officials and were backed up by the SIL's growing reputation for linguistic prowess and its public defense of Mexican interests. At the same time, the organization could not have functioned in Mexico at all without the financial support of thousands of middle-class Americans. Although many have charged that the SIL was a tool of the U.S. government that was supported by American industrialists, in fact it was a tool of the Mexican government that was supported by the American middle class.

7

Good Soil and Rocky Places

Successes and Failures in the 1940s and 1950s

> A farmer went out to sow his seed. As he was scattering the seed, some fell along the path, and birds came and ate it up. Some fell on rocky places, where it did not have much soil. It sprang up quickly because the soil was shallow. But when the sun came up, the plants were scorched, and they withered because they had no root. Other seed grew among thorns, which grew up and choked the plants so that they did not bear grain. Still other seed fell on good soil. It came up, grew and produced a crop, multiplying thirty, sixty, or even a hundred times.
>
> —Mark 4:3–8 (New International Version)

The SIL made impressive alliances with the Mexican state in the 1950s, but how successful was it in the actual work of Bible translation and evangelism? To what degree did its connections to the INI and the SEP facilitate its acceptance in indigenous communities? Did its ties to the state attract or repel indigenous Mexicans? The answers to these questions depend heavily on local circumstances. The following two examples—the Tzeltals of Chiapas and the Tarahumaras of Chihuahua—highlight the ways in which the Mexican state could aid but not guarantee the SIL's entrance into and evangelism of indigenous communities.

These encounters of SIL linguists and various Tzeltal and Tarahumara communities serve as instances of what Gilbert Joseph has called "sites or contact zones where ideologies, technologies, capital flows, state forms, social identities, and material culture meet, and where multiple messages are conveyed."[1] In these encounters, the SIL linguists clearly had the advantage in power and resources, but they lacked local knowledge. At no point was their power complete. As will be seen, in both cases some indigenous people successfully resisted the purposes of the SIL and the state, while others worked closely with the SIL or even converted to Protestantism. It was not clear who had triumphed, for neither the state nor the SIL saw an altogether satisfactory result, nor did the indigenous communities manage to preserve the pre-SIL status quo. The results, in short, were partial and contested: written vernaculars in communities with many non-readers, and Protestantism firmly planted among some individuals yet entirely rejected by others.

Good Soil

Given their suspicions of outsiders and their integrated politico-religious system, the Tzeltals of Chiapas might have seemed unlikely candidates for conversion to Protestantism. Exploited by ladinos (mestizos and Hispanicized Indians) from the market city of San Cristóbal de Las Casas and the towns of Ocosingo and Chilón, the Tzeltals rebelled in 1712 and 1869 and staged smaller uprisings in 1911, 1914, 1917, and 1930. In general, they guarded their communities and their Mayan culture closely, trying to keep outside influences at a minimum. Each major Tzeltal town had its pantheon of brown-skinned *santos,* which could be found in the local church, dressed in the characteristic garb of the town. Although given the names of Roman Catholic saints such as Ildefonso or María, in practice these images functioned as deities with specific domains of expertise. For instance, Santo Tomás, the patron saint of Oxchuc, was renowned for his ability to bring rain. A succession of festivals not only secured the different saints' favor but also gave definition to the community itself.[2] Although separate religious and civil authorities existed, it was difficult to distinguish the religious from the political because the two were so inextricably intertwined.[3]

Despite these obstacles, in 1938 Bill Bentley arrived in the lowland Bachajón area of Tzeltal country, fresh from a summer at Camp Wycliffe. Although he visited many villages in the area, none allowed him to stay. Finally, after almost three years of living at a German-owned plantation, he used a letter of recommendation from the Department of Indigenous Affairs to convince the elders of a small village to grant him permission to stay. Although Bentley soon died of a heart attack, his fiancée, Marianna Slocum, decided that she would continue his work with the Tzeltals. When she and other SIL personnel arrived in Bachajón territory, however, letters from the SEP failed to convince the village elders to allow them to live in the village where Bentley had previously secured permission. "With an influential Mexican friend who has a plantation among the Bachajontecos, and with Ken and Juan, three weeks ago we made a trip into the region to ask them to renew the permission to us," wrote Slocum. "We talked with the Agente [local official] there, and with the Director of the Internado [government boarding school], showing them the letter from Perez H., with the result that they called the Indian leaders together to take counsel over the asunto [affair]. About forty of the Indians gathered on Sunday morning." The two main objections that the Bachajonteco leaders expressed were that the outsiders would take their land and destroy their religion. The agente and the director explained that the Americans' "sole object" was to learn their language, but the elders were unconvinced. "The letter from Perez H. had no effect on them at all—Mexico is far away and it's probably a lie—in fact, a recommendation that a small town official dashed off for us as we passed through en route to Bachajon had more effect, though still negligible," reported Slocum. The Bachajontecos had made up their minds: no outsiders would live in their town.[4]

Slocum and Ethel Wallis, a temporary partner from the SIL, lived for a time at the same German finca that had served as Bentley's base, but they felt that they did not have enough contact with the Tzeltals. Appeals to the governor of Chiapas for authorization to move into Bachajón territory produced no concrete results.[5] Eventually, Alfonso Villa Rojas, a Mexican anthropologist affiliated with the Carnegie Institution, offered to let Slocum use his house in Yochib, in highland Oxchuc Tzeltal country, for six months starting in June 1944. A large sign, "Centro de Estudios Etnológicos, dependiente de la Institución Carnegie de Washington," belied the house's small size and meager furnishings, but it did come with one large benefit: Villa Rojas's strong relationship with the local Oxchucs. Visitors came by the house often and, as soon as they learned that Slocum had medicine, asked for help with various ailments. Although Slocum made great progress in learning the language, medical work soon proved overwhelming, as more and more Oxchuc Tzeltals made their way to her house. The arrival of Florence Gerdel, a registered nurse who dedicated her energies to the medical work, freed Slocum to spend more time on translation. At the same time, when local shamans discovered the religious nature of Slocum's project they began to oppose her presence in Yochib.

They threatened and attacked the few people who had believed her message.[6]

By the end of 1946, Villa Rojas felt that Slocum should leave Yochib, since anti-Protestant feeling was growing not only there but also in Mexico City and other parts of the country. But when Manuel Castellanos, the head of the Department of Indigenous Affairs for the state of Chiapas, learned of Slocum's situation he intervened with the village authorities of Oxchuc. He convinced municipal president Isidro Ensin to sign a contract authorizing Slocum to remain in Villa Rojas's house for another three years. Slocum reported in the SIL newsletter: "We had quite an exciting time, with the Indian president of the region here with his silver-tipped bastón, the other local Indian authorities, the witch-doctor who owns the land (and blames the death of two of his children on a curse cast on them because of his having rented the land to outsiders), and the school-teacher who had tried to influence the Indians against 'mericanos.' In the presence of them all, the Indian Affairs official put down in writing that I was to be allowed to rent the land for three more years, and the contract was duly signed by thumb-prints." Gerdel's medical work attracted Tzeltals from throughout the region to her clinic, but it did not lead to many conversions, nor did it end the opposition in Yochib. When Tzeltals from the small village of Corralito expressed great interest in the religious side of Gerdel and Slocum's work and invited them to move to their town in the summer of 1950, the two women decided that they might find more success in a place where they were wanted.[7]

Corralito provided the perfect environment for Slocum and Gerdel's evangelistic work. Dozens, eventually hundreds, of people converted to Protestantism; enthusiastic young believers built a large church; when that was burned down by their opponents they quickly built a new one. Through Slocum the Corralito believers met ladino Protestants from the city of San Cristóbal de Las Casas and began the process of joining the Presbyterian Church. To be baptized in that church, explained a visiting ladino pastor, it would be necessary for couples to formalize their unions. When representatives of the would-be Presbyterians broached the topic with the town secretary, who had married only one couple in the previous year, he refused to cooperate with the 225 couples who requested to be married, so Slocum had to seek help from Mexico City. An official from the SEP came to town, rebuked local authorities for discriminating against Protestants, and arranged for a judge to come to town to marry the 225 couples. This judge conducted a mass wedding service on 8 August 1951 in which he stressed the permanence of marriage, warned against a number of common Tzeltal practices (such as child marriage), and stressed women's rights to children and property.[8]

It was in the early 1950s that Slocum's work began to come under attack from outside the Tzeltal community. Acción Católica circulated a flier about "false and adulterated" Bibles. "Watch out, Catholic," the flier warned, "for false prophets that are stirred up by opportunistic Protestant foreigners like 'La Marianna' and other gringos who live in Yashuquintelá and in the Lacandón jungle and sponsor the theft of land and attacks against Indians; they are perverting your soul, dividing your people, and doing a work of social destruction that is really an attack against the Nation."[9] A resident of Abasolo, Chiapas, denounced "the two American women two kilometers from here in Corralito who are producing a large amount of Protestant propaganda and have caused a division that more than once has led to verbal altercations and might soon lead to bloodshed."[10] Part of the problem was that Protestant converts no longer wanted to participate in or pay for festivals that used alcohol or to contribute to collections to bring priests to the village for masses, baptisms, or other rituals.[11] This attitude made perfect sense to them, but to the rest of the community it was a grave affront, for it formalized the growing rift in the village, undermined the politico-religious order, and made important traditional activities prohibitively expensive.

Although the SIL's presence in Tzeltal territory had been facilitated by branches of the federal and state governments, some government agencies had no idea who or what the SIL was. Thus, Gen. Agustín Mustieles reported in 1953 that the Oxchuc region was experiencing a religious conflict between Catholics and Protestants that had been "indoctrinated by two Mexican-American women, who have established evangelical churches in the area." He also mentioned their radio telephone, landing strip, American pilot, and airplane.[12] The Ministry of the Interior apparently knew little about the SIL, or at least about its activities among the Tzeltals, for it ordered the governor of Chiapas to conduct "a detailed investigation." His attorney general reported back to the Ministry of the Interior that there were indeed two women named Marianna Slocum and "Morrinson" working in Corralito and that they did indeed have an evangelical church, landing strip, and a plane, as well as "some victrolas that they lend to the Indians with records in Tzeltal, so that they can go to the small settlements to evangelize." There was also a similar property owned by one Guillermo Townsend in Yxoquintelá and another group of Americans in the Lacandón jungle, he reported.[13] Nobody mentioned the SIL or seems to have had any understanding that Slocum, Townsend, and the rest were part of a larger organization that was working closely with the federal government and, at least in theory, with the Ministry of the Interior itself.

Yet Slocum and Gerdel were having a profound influence on the highland Tzeltals. By the time the first Tzeltal New Testaments were distributed in 1956 the Corralito church had sent out their own "missionaries" to other Tzeltal towns and had founded twelve new churches for thousands of Protestant converts who lived within a day's journey of their village. With help from missionaries of the Reformed Church in America, the Corralito believers constructed a two-story health clinic where Gerdel not only treated the sick but also trained thirty-five Tzeltal men and women in the art of Western medicine, using Tzeltal language textbooks she had written. These practical nurses then set up and staffed fourteen clinics throughout the Tzeltal area that treated two thousand patients each month.[14]

The Tzeltal Protestants rejected or modified traditional rituals in accordance with their new beliefs. At planting time in April they chose not to give any money to Santo Tomás, the patron saint of Oxchuc, and not to participate in the rituals performed at sacred caves. Instead, groups of believers planted their fields together, then sang hymns and prayed for God's blessing on their crops. In marriage, the bride price was now paid in beef rather than in liquor, since the believers did not drink. Some respect was transferred from community elders to the national state, for, as a minority, Protestants had a natural interest in state protection. Slocum translated, in addition to the New Testament, the national anthem, the Mexican Constitution, and a handbook that explained how to vote in national elections into Tzeltal.[15] By 1965, when Slocum and Gerdel left Chiapas, there were seventy-two Tzeltal churches and more than six thousand believers. When they returned to visit in 1985 there were more than three hundred churches and forty-four thousand believers, evidence of the major role they and other SIL linguists had played in the shift of the center of gravity of Mexican Protestantism from northern to southern Mexico by the 1980s.[16]

Such an extensive change in Tzeltal religiosity had implications far beyond the confines of Tzeltal Protestantism. The institutional Roman Catholic Church, concerned about Protestant inroads, mobilized the lay evangelists of Acción Católica to re-evangelize the Tzeltals in the 1950s. The creed-based Roman Catholicism that Acción Católica brought, however, was just as disruptive of traditional Tzeltal religiosity as Protestantism had been and perhaps even more antagonistic toward Protestantism than the traditional religion. Thus, instead of firming up the Tzeltal religious system, Acción Católica divided communities even more. Now, in addition to religious traditionalists and Protestants, many villages had a third party committed to the institutional Roman Catholic Church.[17]

Because politics and religion had been so closely connected, the emergence of Protestantism and Acción Católica also had definite political ramifications. Whereas the political and religious hierarchies previously had functioned in tandem, in the 1950s they started to diverge. Since Protestants had no desire to hold religious posts but were quite willing to take civil positions, the civil side of the system rose in importance. In municipios like Oxchuc, where half of the population was Protestant by 1969, the religious hierarchy fell in prestige, for it was now more of a parochial concern than a path to leadership in the community as a whole.[18] Looking back in 1996, one former Tzeltal teacher suggested that Slocum and Gerdel's medical and evangelistic work had significantly altered the attitudes of the Tzeltal community: "The respect that there was for elders no longer exists. The traditional authorities have lost their prestige."[19] The fact was, though, that Slocum and Gerdel's work in Tzeltal country had clearly revitalized a moribund culture. The fall of the traditional authorities was not a cause of great sorrow to many Tzeltals, while the rise of vernacular literature and a new religion had created a vibrant new culture, different from the old but still boldly Tzeltal.[20]

Rocky Places

Of all the early recruits who came to Camp Wycliffe, none showed more promise than Eugene Nida. A Phi Beta Kappa linguistics major from UCLA and a member of Cameron Townsend's own Church of the Open Door, Nida combined evangelical zeal, linguistic knowledge, and academic potential in a way that made him just about the perfect missionary linguist. His assignment to the Tarahumara people in the fall of 1936 seemed to guarantee a quick and accurate translation of the New Testament into that language.

The Tarahumaras, also known as the Rarámuris, lived in widely dispersed settlements of one or two families throughout the mountains of the state of Chihuahua. Despite great efforts by the Jesuits (1607–1767) and the Franciscans (1767–1859), the Tarahumaras were less influenced by Hispanic culture than were any other indigenous people of northern Mexico, with the possible exception of the Seris of Sonora.[21] The Tarahumaras' main advantage in resisting the encroachments of outsiders was the extremely rocky, mountainous terrain in which they lived; when missionaries, miners, and merchants threatened their autonomy, the Tarahumaras simply moved deeper into the sierra. To make the most of a cold, inhospitable climate and rocky, abrupt terrain, they combined slash-and-burn agriculture with hunting, gathering, and small-scale animal husbandry.

When Jesuit missionaries returned to the Sierra Tarahumara in 1900, they found it quite difficult to overcome the syncretism that had flourished in their absence. Rather than the Trinity, the Tarahumaras worshipped Onurúame (Father Sun) and his wife Iyerúgame (Mother Moon), along with their son Sukristo (Jesus Christ) and their daughters the *sánti* (saints). Notwithstanding numerous tactics taken by the Jesuits, the Tarahumaras continued to accord their shamans, *tesgüino* (corn beer), peyote, and harvest rituals greater precedence than Catholic priests, sacraments, and holy days.[22]

Like the Catholic missionaries before him, Nida immediately faced the difficulty of the dispersed Tarahumara settlement pattern. He tried to establish contact with a group of Tarahumaras by basing himself on the grounds of a government boarding school. The director of the internado in Tonachic, Chihuahua, gave Nida "a fine whitewashed room in a new bungalow" and asked him to work as the school's carpenter and to teach carpentry to the students. Nida complained that his responsibilities left him with little time for language study and that the poor diet and cold weather were making his life miserable. Consequently, he was not overly upset when he had to give up his room at the end of November. Because of the difficult conditions in Tonachic and since he had not yet found anyone who consistently could help him to learn the language, he decided to move to another internado, in Sisoguichic, Chihuahua, but he stayed there for less than a month. By the end of the year he was back in California. The harsh conditions in the mountains had broken him physically and emotionally to such an extent that although he later traveled the world as a prestigious linguistic educator for the SIL and the American Bible Society, he never returned to the Tarahumaras as a translator.[23]

The SIL, though, did not give up on the Tarahumaras. At the end of Camp Wycliffe in 1940, Cameron Townsend assigned newlyweds Ken and Martha Hilton to Nida's old post.[24] Both Martha, the "uncomplaining and cheerful" daughter of a Minnesota mortician, and Ken, the more reserved son of a Kansas farmer, were hardworking, sincere Christians who, despite more remunerative opportunities, chose to attend St. Paul Bible Institute. Because times were hard and neither had much money, they decided to spend their honeymoon at Camp Wycliffe during the summer of 1940. They left for Mexico a few months later with only seventy-one dollars, hoping that somehow they would receive more. In January 1941, on the recommendation of a teacher they had met in Mexico City, the Hiltons began their work in the town of Guachochi. They were welcomed by the local teachers and given a one-room log cabin to live in, but because Guachochi seemed to be filling up with Spanish speakers, the Hiltons moved to a more remote location, Samachique, in 1942, and were again welcomed by the local teacher. There they started to make progress in learning the language and finished translating the Gospel of Mark in 1948, despite frequent interruptions by Tarahumaras requesting medical help. They converted their translation helper, Ramón López, and encouraged him to formalize his union with his partner, Matiana. When they agreed, the Hiltons gave a wedding banquet for the young couple, who were married by the municipal president of Guehuevo. López later became both a public school teacher and a lay evangelist, but other Tarahumaras seemed uninterested in the Hiltons' linguistic and religious work.[25]

Perhaps, Cameron Townsend suggested to the Hiltons, what they needed to jump-start their ministry among the Tarahumaras was a literacy campaign. With Townsend's help Ken arranged for a meeting with the governor of Chihuahua. The governor liked the idea enough to give Ken letters authorizing the campaign and encouraging local officials to cooperate with it. Literacy experts Ethel Wallis and Iris Mills Wares joined Ken in Guachochi for two months, but their efforts met with complete failure. The local schoolteacher, Candelario Viniegra, dismissed the governor's letter as having no validity in Tarahumara country and refused to help in any way. The Americans got their hopes up when thirty men came to an introductory meeting, only to see them dashed when no one returned for the next class. Despite repeated visits to different homes in the area, Hilton, Wallis, and Wares were not able to interest anyone in literacy much less to teach anybody how to read. They discovered later that a Catholic priest had warned people not to participate in the program.[26]

The Hiltons' family life during this period seems to have been extremely difficult. Son Roger had a difficult time living in Mexico and eventually went to live with relatives in the United States. Another son, Donnie, had Down's syndrome and was unable to talk or to function independently. After prayer, Ken and Martha decided to put him in the Good Shepherd Lutheran Home of the West, in California. The two other Hilton children, Roseanne and Richard, appear to have been much easier for their parents, but even they seem to have struggled to understand the sacrifices their parents were making to translate the New Testament into Tarahumara. Roseanne, for example, "cried bitterly" when she and her parents left Donnie at the Lutheran Home. "This I knew," she remembers, "my older brother was a stranger, it hurt to leave loved ones, and (in my childish thinking) I decided that missionaries should not have children."[27]

Paul and Ellen Carlson joined the Hiltons in 1952 to work on solving one of the major obstacles to the Hiltons' work, the Tarahumaras' widely dispersed pattern of settlement in an extremely mountainous area. Paul proposed to build a radio station in Samachique and to distribute to Tarahumaras throughout the region special radios tuned only to that station, at once creating a means of reaching thousands of people and preventing them from listening to other radio messages that he did not want them to hear. His plans, however, never came to fruition. When lightning destroyed his transmitter he gave up his project altogether. If the Tarahumaras were to be reached it would be through the SIL's traditional methods.[28]

The Hiltons published their Tarahumara New Testament in 1972. Despite decades of the Hiltons' hard work, physical hardship, and relational sacrifices, only a few people had learned how to read, and only Ramón López had become a committed Tarahumara Protestant. Not giving up, the Hiltons planned to record the New Testament on cassette tapes and to distribute tape players and tapes throughout the region, permitting even illiterate Tarahumaras to hear the message of the New Testament. Ken Hilton, though, began to develop lateral sclerosis in his left leg and soon could not move it at all. His condition effectively ended the Hiltons' ministry in Mexico, for he could no longer walk the steep mountain trails that were the only way to reach Tarahumara settlements. They returned to the United States with little to show for their decades of effort and loss. Only after the Hiltons had left Mexico did an appreciable number of Tarahumaras convert to Protestantism.[29]

Incorporation and Resistance

One can see how, in a large nation confronted with multiple social problems, a state that wanted to consolidate its power might make peace with its greatest rival. One can see also how, in a large nation possessing dozens of different ethnic groups, a state that wanted to consolidate its power might institute policies designed to "incorporate" its diverse ethnic populations. Although both policies must have seemed reasonable on their own terms, the combination of a modus vivendi with the Roman Catholic Church and institutionalized indigenismo put the Mexican state behind two rather contradictory policies. On the one hand, it was signaling its acceptance of Mexico's predominantly Catholic popular culture and was retreating from the anti-Catholic social engineering that had characterized the Callista and Cardenista regimes; on the other hand, it was sponsoring a movement that sought to transform indigenous culture, especially indigenous religion. Even when indigenismo was not explicitly pro-Protestant, it was almost always ready to modify indigenous religious practices and beliefs, which, if not exactly orthodox institutional Catholicism, still fell under the rubric of folk Catholicism.

The Ministry of the Interior serves as one of the best examples of the contradictions that characterized the state's approach to religion. While it played to Catholic interests during the 1940s by shelving Protestant requests for church recognition and by refusing to use federal troops to defend Protestants, it also upheld the SIL's right to enter indigenous communities. The Ministry of the Interior could only support the SIL in this way because of the SIL's connections to mainstream indigenismo. Although everybody who knew the SIL knew about its evangelistic agenda, especially if they ran across the continually proselytizing Cameron Townsend, the SIL's scientific identity and indigenista connections offered the Ministry of the Interior and other federal agencies a sort of plausible deniability. If pressed by Catholics, they could point to the SIL's indigenista connections and genuine linguistic accomplishments to justify its presence in indigenous communities. The SIL also served as a kind of bargaining chip against the Catholic Church. Just as religious restrictions from the Cristero era stayed on the books to keep the church honest, so too the presence of the SIL served to remind it of the state's eager Protestant allies.

There is little doubt that over the twenty or thirty years that SIL linguists spent in given communities they usually fulfilled at least some of the expectations of their indigenista allies. The Hiltons' lone convert, Ramón López, serves as a prime example. Through his contact with the Hiltons he not only adopted Protestantism but also learned to read, learned Spanish, invoked the state's authority in the area of marriage, entered the state educational system, and became a teacher. The same pattern was repeated on a much larger scale among the Tzeltals. Those who converted usually learned to read, attended school, interacted with mestizos, and accepted the state's authority in the matter of marriage. Among both the Tarahumaras and the Tzeltals, many who never converted did come to believe in the superiority of Western medicine through their contact with the SIL. Thus the SIL served the incorporative purposes of indigenismo. Through its work, Indians did indeed become Mexicans.[30]

At the same time, there is little doubt that the presence of SIL linguists often stirred up controversy and division. If such was not the case among the Tarahumaras, it was most probably due to the limited spiritual impact of the Hiltons' ministry. But when Protestantism took hold, as it did in Corralito, it led to just the kind of conflicts that the Mexican state wanted to avoid. Contemporary conflicts in the Chiapas highlands are not unrelated to the missionary activities of the SIL in the 1940s and 1950s. The exodus of forty-four thousand Tzeltals from traditional systems of control, for instance, signified a tectonic shift in local balances of power, one that caciques, Zapatista guerrillas, and others have sought to shift to their own advantages in recent decades.

Finally, it is important to recognize the limits that local resistance placed on state power. Bachajón refused entrance to Slocum and would not recognize the authority of various federal agencies. Yochib bowed to pressure from the state of Chiapas to allow Slocum to live there but barely tolerated her presence and persecuted her few converts. Only when a group of believers, converted not by Slocum but by a fellow Tzeltal, welcomed her to Corralito did her ministry really prosper. State power allowed her to establish a presence in an area where she otherwise would have had great difficulty, but the success of her work depended on its acceptance by a community of Protestants in a town where the state had not paved the way for her. Similarly, the Hiltons depended on support from public school teachers in establishing themselves in two different Tarahumara communities. This support did not extend to their religious work, however. It provided them with permission to live in Tarahumara country but did not translate into any real influence on Tarahumara culture.

The different responses to the SIL in the 1940s and 1950s are remarkably similar to what Jennie Purnell found in her study of agraristas and Cristeros in Michoacán in the 1920s—there was a wide variation in how rural communities responded to the state's agrarian reforms, depending on local history, tradition, and culture.[31] In a similar way, conversion to Protestantism by Mexican Indians cannot be categorized easily, for it could be seen as both resistance (to Catholicism and local caciques) and submission (to the state or North American culture).

To put the Tzeltal and Tarahumara stories in perspective, in 1962, of the eighty-one indigenous groups in which the SIL was working, seventy-three had one or more Protestant converts: Chol, Yucatec Maya, and Tzeltal groups each had more than five thousand; Mezquital Otomi, Southern Totonac, and Mazahua groups had at least a thousand; fifteen other groups had more than a hundred; eight more had between fifty-one and ninety-nine; twenty-two had ten to fifty; twenty-two had nine or fewer; five had none.[32] Thus, most SIL translation projects fell somewhere between the Slocum and Hilton experiences, with the majority falling nearer to the Hiltons' end of the spectrum.

The SIL's accomplishments might have seemed wider than they were deep, but evangelicals normally emphasized that, while it was their responsibility "to sow the seed," it was God's job to make it grow. To the SIL, therefore, the relationship with the state seemed like a good deal, despite the limited number of converts. Just the opportunity to present the Gospel to those who had not heard it before was success of a sort, although of course the lack of converts was a deep sorrow to many translators.[33]

As far as the Mexican state was concerned, its power simultaneously enabled and was extended by the SIL's wide dispersion throughout the indigenous communities of Mexico, yet the SIL's inability to enter certain communities or to accomplish much in others points to the limits of state power in the face of vigorous local resistance. If the Mexican state of the 1940s and 1950s had been stronger it could have placed the SIL wherever it wanted and enforced participation in its programs; but, of course, if it had been stronger it would not have needed the SIL at all.

8

Indians into Protestants in an Otomi Village

The violence began in a local drinking spot when a member of the Licona family paid too much attention to Virginia, the wife of patriarch José Tolentino. Long-simmering resentments and strong family allegiances soon pitted the Liconas against the Tolentinos in a drunken brawl that started a decade-and-a-half-long struggle for dominance in the village. The two factions spent the 1940s and early 1950s warring for control of the Otomi pueblo of San Antonio el Grande in the mountainous Sierra Oriente of the Mexican state of Hidalgo.[1] Although the Tolentino faction had ties to the allies of 1940 opposition presidential candidate Juan Andreu Almazán, and the Licona faction had ties to the ruling Mexican Revolutionary Party, the issues at stake in San Antonio were of a particularly local nature. Many of the reasons for the bloody feud remain obscure, but much of the blame must be assigned to José Tolentino, who had returned to the village after service in the Mexican army with an itch for power. His stint in the army had given him two tools that he would use to his advantage in the coming years: the Spanish language to form alliances with the mestizo world, and military skills to subdue his rivals.

Another motivation for the conflict may have been economic. Benigno Licona had been the first to introduce the cultivation of coffee to the town, whose previous cash crop had been sugarcane, and he had started selling the new crop to traders who bought it in town and transported it to Huehuetla, the head town of the municipio.[2] Turning cane into a marketable product was an arduous and time-consuming process. Afterward the grower had to transport it himself to Huehuetla for sale. The Liconas' switch to coffee gave them an economic advantage in the local economy and thereby challenged the Tolentinos in their quest for dominance.[3] Whatever the sources of the conflict, it soon became an all-consuming affair, not only for the approximately thirty-five combatants on each side but for the entire community.

The years of the fighting, referred to locally as "the wars," were times of extreme suffering in which women and children were not immune from the violence. So violent was the pueblo that most non-combatants would enter the village only during daylight and would spend the nights in caves and other hideaways, hushing their children for fear of giving away their hiding place. As the factions torched and plundered each other's fields, much of the pueblo faced starvation. Many families resorted to eating roots and other foods that they could scavenge from the mountainside. Meanwhile, those foolish enough to try to live in the village were killed for belonging to the wrong faction or for belonging to neither. Faced with such harsh conditions, many of San Antonio's residents left town and settled in neighboring villages. For example, José Neria, the town secretary, fled to Pantepec, Puebla. José Tolentino himself spent much of his time in Rincón, Puebla, or Santa María, Veracruz. The Tolentinos used a series of brutal assassinations that ultimately turned the tide of the war. After killing two Licona *jefes de armas* (military leaders), the Tolentinos took control of San Antonio and began quarreling among themselves over how to divide the lands they had seized.

The Tolentinos had finally conquered their rivals, but they too were tired of death and deprivation after more than a decade of fighting. When a drunken José Tolentino was knifed to death in the state of Puebla, the biggest barrier to peace was removed. His nephews came from Santa María and sold much of the family's land in San Antonio. In 1954 the remaining antagonists agreed to put an end to the conflict when a Captain Ramírez from Pachuca came to town to negotiate a truce.[4] Slowly, those who had left trickled back into town and began the hard work of replanting fields and rebuilding homes. "The town had been totally overgrown," they say today. "The vegetation had taken over the town." Although the war had ended, they still faced a period of hunger in which many people had to subsist on the roots of banana trees or work for meager wages in other pueblos.[5]

The Pueblo of San Antonio el Grande

The town for which the Liconas and Tolentinos fought, still little known to the outside world, is located in the Sierra Oriente of Hidalgo. The municipio of Huehuetla, where it is found, borders the state of Puebla on the east and the state of Veracruz on the north.[6] Because there was no road connecting San Antonio to the head town of the municipio, and no road connecting Huehuetla with other municipios, and because the area was extremely mountainous, until recently San Antonio's only contact with the outside world took place by means of treacherous footpaths.[7] Every year a few pilgrims would make the long trek to Tulancingo, Hidalgo, for the festival of its patron saint, and some hardy souls would walk eight hours to La Ceiba (today known as Villa Ávila Camacho), Veracruz, to see its plaza, but in general the people of San Antonio had contact only with neighboring towns such as Huehuetla and San Gregorio (both in Hidalgo) and Tlaxco (Puebla). As late as 1992 there was not one paved road in the forty-one towns of the municipio.[8] Because of this relative isolation, San Antonio remained almost entirely monolingual until primary education came in the 1960s. Before then anybody who had acquired the rudiments of Spanish by working outside the village had a very good chance of becoming the town's secretary.

Clearly, though, despite its difficult terrain and isolation, San Antonio was worth fighting for. Where other Otomis in the state of Hidalgo, for instance, eked out a meager existence in the dry, dusty Mezquital Valley, the Otomis of the Sierra Oriente enjoyed an excellent subtropical climate with plenty of rain. They could harvest their staple, corn, twice per year while simultaneously growing bananas, papayas, and a cash crop of sugarcane or coffee. The only problem was that because of the extremely mountainous terrain, flat, cultivable land was always in short supply. In fact, even the best land was too steep to plow and planting had to be done with a sharp, pointed stick. In the 1980s, as the population of the Sierra Oriente increased, many Otomis devoted their best land to coffee and actually had to buy maize imported from other areas.[9]

Here, as in other indigenous communities, the civil-religious hierarchy consisted of two parallel progressions of yearlong posts that male community members were expected to fulfill during their lifetime. In their twenties, young men started serving at the bottom positions, which included police duty and service to higher officers on the civic side and supervision of fiestas and cleaning of oratories on the religious side. After serving in these lower positions, men could become *padrinos, mayordomos, jueces,* and *secretarios.* Each padrino and his team of mayordomos had the responsibility to plan, finance, and lead the celebration of a fiesta corresponding to a specific saint or deity. The juez had the responsibility to administer justice and keep the peace in the pueblo, working in tandem with his secretarios and other aides. Men who passed through all these stations joined the elders, the highest position of authority in the village.[10] All men, regardless of whether they held positions in the hierarchy, were expected to fulfill a certain number of *faenas,* or communal obligations, such as digging drainage ditches, flattening paths, and repairing community buildings.[11] The religious portion of the hierarchy began to unravel in the 1960s, but the civil hierarchy still functions today.

In the traditional religion of San Antonio there are a number of important *yoguis* (deities): Moctezuma, the chief deity; Ojá, the name used by sixteenth-century Augustinian missionaries for the Christian God; Makamé, the Sacred Lady; Hmuth<u>o</u>, the Lord of the Mountain; Hmuthe, the Goddess of the Water; and Hmuspi, the God of Fire. Moctezuma and Ojá, although known and acknowledged, do not require ritual attention, but the other yoguis are more demanding. Led by the *bädis* (specialists in the traditional religion), devotees of the different yogui practice various rituals, travel to sacred sites in the mountains, and make offerings of chicken, bread, money, alcohol, and paper dolls. A *y<u>o</u>de* (shaman who can commune directly with the yoguis) has special power to heal and to divine the sources of curses placed upon members of the community.[12]

Difficulties in San Gregorio

While "the wars" had been raging in San Antonio, in the nearby village of San Gregorio, three American missionaries for the SIL—Katherine ("Katie") Voigtlander, Joyce Jenkins, and Vola Griste—had been working on the Eastern Otomi language. Jenkins and Griste had arrived in San Gregorio in 1943 after another SIL missionary (Bethel Bower) working on the Tepehua language in Huehuetla suggested to the SIL that local Otomis also needed the New Testament in their language.[13] The municipal president of Huehuetla suggested San Antonio as a site for their work, but when they passed through in 1940 they found the village deserted—due, they later found out, to the factional struggles mentioned above. On top of the next mountain they found San Gregorio, a smaller, more remote Otomi village, but one without the kind of violence found in San Antonio.

The SIL's normal method of translating the New Testament into indigenous languages started with the process of learning the language. The linguist-missionaries depended, especially in the beginning stages of their work, on help from local indigenous people. They simply could not learn the language they were hoping to translate without their cooperation. If there were already evangelical Christians in the town, they were often more than willing to help with the language learning process. Sometimes this help was freely offered by non-evangelicals curious about the strange foreigners living in their midst; sometimes it had to be paid for. Similarly, no evangelism could take place until the missionary had the ability to communicate effectively in the indigenous language. All SIL translators had to be students before they could be teachers.

This was definitely the case for the Americans in San Gregorio, as Katie Voigtlander, who joined Griste and Jenkins in 1948, relates. The linguists in San Gregorio started trying to pray with a group of boys that were interested without having understood the grammatical issue of exclusive and inclusive second-person forms. In Eastern Otomi, a speaker using the second person must indicate whether those being addressed are included in "we" or "us." Before Griste and Jenkins understood this distinction, they led prayers that sounded to native speakers like "God please forgive us [including God] because we [including God] are all sinners." After having their mistake pointed out to them, the linguists realized that they needed a much deeper understanding of the language before they could communicate theological ideas clearly.[14] As strongly as the missionaries desired to convert the people of San Gregorio, this was an impossibility for the first few years of their work for the simple reason that their limited grasp of the Otomi language prevented them from communicating complex ideas.

In San Gregorio, the American missionaries struggled to find anyone to help them learn the language. Local officials tolerated their presence in the village, perhaps because in addition to their linguistic activities they also provided some basic medical services to the village, but nobody had a great desire to spend more than a few minutes per day helping them learn the language. Teenage boys were interested in the exotic *zubis* (gringas), but they showed more initiative in trying to peek through the cracks in the walls of their house than in trying to offer linguistic assistance. When Voigtlander joined the team in 1948, Jenkins and Griste were frustrated by the slow pace at which they were learning the language. Whereas some SIL teams would have started actual translation work in their third year, as late as 1950 the linguists found themselves still struggling to understand the basics of the complex Eastern Otomi language, a tonal language that they now knew had thirteen vowels and no prepositions.[15] Not until much later did they realize that, in addition to the troubles that they had had in finding linguistic helpers, they were also dealing with one of the most difficult of Mexico's many indigenous languages.

Voigtlander, Jenkins, and Griste knew that to make real progress in learning and then translating Eastern Otomi, they needed to find better language helpers. Their one ray of hope was a group of young men from San Antonio el Grande who would occasionally come to San Gregorio. Unlike the residents of San Gregorio, these young men seemed to have no qualms about helping the American women learn their language. They would come to the women's house in San Gregorio, stay for hours, eat lunch with the linguists, and then talk with them for hours more before returning to San Antonio el Grande. For young men such as Eutimio San Vicente, Antonio San Vicente, Horacio Miranda, and Armando Cabellero, the free lunch that the Americans provided was surely a major part of the inducement for them to make the trek to San Gregorio.[16] Their home village was still suffering the dire effects of "the wars," and food remained in short supply. With their *milpas* (cornfields) still years away from full recovery, a free lunch of any sort was in itself a significant attraction.

But the food was not the only reason they came. As children who had grown up during "the wars," these young men had in their short lives suffered extraordinary hardships and seen friends and relatives murdered before their own eyes. Such experiences made them particularly receptive to new ideas and alternatives to traditional village life. Having experienced so much violence at the hands of their kinsmen and neighbors, they simply did not have the same distrust of outsiders that the people of San Gregorio demonstrated.[17] For the villagers of San Antonio, the enemy often had been a familiar one; the worst had come from nearby rather than from far away. Similarly, many of their friends and relatives had found refuge in Tepehua and mestizo towns, leading them to believe that some people from outside the village could be trusted.[18]

For these young men from San Antonio, the zubis of San Gregorio were providing not only free meals but also diversion from the harsh realities of life in San Antonio. As the zubis' Otomi skills gradually improved, the young men also began to understand that these foreign women had a startling, controversial religious message that they wanted to share. Where peaceful San Gregorio had little use for the zubis or for their controversial message, the young men of San Antonio found both the women and their message intriguing. When Voigtlander asked if she could come to live in San Antonio el Grande, they were enthusiastic. No doubt the increased proximity of their free meals figured in their decision, but the villagers' enthusiasm seems to have sprung from more than that. Coupled with the practical benefits and the appeal of the exotic, the young men of San Antonio also seem to have had a genuine spiritual hunger. They were ready to entertain ideas—evangelical theology and its wholesale rejection of much of Otomi religious tradition—that their contemporaries in San Gregorio would not even consider. Another reason for Voigtlander's attraction to San Antonio was a rumor she had heard about a man named Domingo Santiago, who had converted to Protestantism through the ministry of a traveling blanket salesman.[19] His brother Juan had met Voigtlander and invited her to come to the pueblo. When Domingo heard from his brother that American women in San Gregorio were translating the Bible and some hymns into Otomi, he was quite interested.[20]

In 1961, almost twenty years after the SIL's initial attempt to start working in the Eastern Otomi language, Voigtlander and a temporary partner from the SIL began working in San Antonio. Before sharing their religious message or trying to translate the Bible, they started their work by trying to interest people in literacy. They took some tables from Antonio Santiago's house, put their suitcases on top of the tables, and took out some stories they had written in San Gregorio. Voigtlander then read a story in Otomi. "All the people marveled that books could be read in Otomi," said one observer. Despite teasing from their friends, a number of young men decided that they would learn how to read and began studying with the linguists. When Voigtlander gave Fidencio Rosas, one of the best students, the Otomi Gospel of John in booklet form he carried it wherever he went. When his friends saw him reading it they asked if he would teach them to read during their lunch breaks.[21]

Consequently, even before they really understood what Protestantism was, a small group of young men was teaching themselves how to read and were poring over the Gospel of John. Voigtlander and her new partner, Artemisa Echegoyen, a Mexican Presbyterian, could not have asked for a more auspicious beginning. Although most of the village thought that the linguists were very lazy—anyone could see that they did no real labor, just sat at their desks all day—in fact they were working hard. They found their first translation helper in Juan Santiago, Domingo's brother, who had badly cut his hand and could not work in his fields. He was soon joined by other young men. Progress was much swifter than it had been in San Gregorio. Soon they were not only translating their first portions of the New Testament but also making their first converts. Using a preliminary translation of the Gospel of John, Voigtlander and Echegoyen started to re-awaken Domingo Santiago's Protestant faith. He soon opened his house to worship services and evangelistic meetings.[22]

Like the Santiago brothers, almost all of those interested in Voigtlander and Echegoyen's linguistic work and evangelistic message were young men. Not yet absorbed into the village's civil-religious hierarchy yet no longer under the control of their parents, these men in their upper teens and lower twenties were enjoying a period of life with an uncharacteristic degree of freedom. Although no decision to question the traditional Otomi belief system would leave them unscathed by village opinion, they had more freedom to investigate Protestantism than any other segment of the village. Macario Santiago Altamirano (cousin of Domingo Santiago), for instance, relates that despite his father's warnings he continued attending the meetings at Domingo's house. Whereas a younger child might have received a thrashing and an older man might have thought twice about risking his standing in the village, the twenty-two-year-old Macario found himself at that rare age where he had little to lose in choosing an untraditional way of life.[23] He was not alone in overcoming parental opposition. Fidencio Bacilio, for example, was locked out of the house when he started attending the Protestant services but eventually converted his father to the new religion. Domingo's willingness to open his home to these seekers provided them with a valuable asset, a space where they could investigate the new faith without interference.

During a time when Voigtlander and Echegoyen were away from San Antonio, Domingo began leading the Protestant meetings. Voigtlander and Echegoyen did not oppose Domingo's leadership role in the growing Christian community; in fact, they encouraged it. As far as they were concerned, the more responsibility was taken by the Otomi believers, the better. Voigtlander and Echegoyen had to shy away from activities that most missionaries would take for granted—preaching, public proclamation, assuming leadership positions in the new church that was forming—because, theoretically, they were not missionaries but linguists working in cooperation with the SEP who just happened to have shared their religious beliefs with a few friends. As one of the early Otomi pastors remembers, Voigtlander and Echegoyen made it clear that they could do no more than teach the Bible.[24] Although, from a practical point of view, it was obvious that the women exercised real leadership in the small Protestant community of San Antonio, not least of all because they had founded that community and because of their superior knowledge of the Christian faith, they tried to make a technical distinction between de facto authority and the formal leadership of the Protestant community.

Meanwhile, Voigtlander's knowledge of the language had improved enough that she began to make significant progress on the translation of the New Testament. "Bit by bit," she said, "we would explain to them what this verse or this passage was all about and then help them put it into their language. Checking a verse with many people often led to different suggestions from each person."[25] Because the translation needed to be as accurate, accessible, and clear as possible, Echegoyen and Voigtlander were put in the position of having to depend on the members of the community of San Antonio.[26] Despite their formal education and linguistic training, when it came to the Otomi language the two missionaries were neophytes while the people of San Antonio were masters.[27] This turning of the tables in the missionary/receptor relationship might have been expected to undermine the missionaries' effectiveness, but the reverse is actually the case. Voigtlander and Echegoyen's dependence on the community in their quest to produce a readable and accurate New Testament translation put them in contact with a wide range of people in situations that were not overtly evangelistic but which served to pique people's interest in the New Testament and in the Protestant religion. For instance, one of the men who worked with Voigtlander and Echegoyen checking the Gospel of John came from a family of shamans. When he came across the phrase "born by the spirit and by water," the linguists had a difficult time conveying the meaning to him, since one of the main deities in San Antonio was a water spirit. To him, the phrase meant "to be a worshiper of the water deity." "So we had to juggle the words around, to make it so that it wouldn't have anything to do with 'living by worshiping the water,'" related Voigtlander.[28]

Through such detailed discussions of the meaning of specific verses and how best to express them in Otomi, translation helpers could not help but pick up a fairly deep understanding of the New Testament. The translation process proved arduous yet rewarding for many of the Otomi men. "Sometimes it took a long time to translate one verse," remembered Agustín Arroyo Tolentino, "but for me it was marvelous to have been able to work on the translation because it is the Word of God. So when I read a verse I felt content because I could understand the word of God. I could understand what God wanted me to do."[29] For these unschooled men accustomed to manual labor, the new experience of prolonged "desk work" taxed their patience but also gave them the opportunity to interact closely with what they soon believed to be a direct communication from God in their own language.

The message of the New Testament proved both shocking and attractive. In one instance, the translation helpers read a passage from the fourth chapter of John in which Jesus' disciples came back from the town and offered Jesus food to eat and Jesus responded, "I have food to eat that you don't know anything about." "They were very impressed by that," suggested Voigtlander, "because they think they have to offer tamales, coffee, cigarettes, and money along the river, at the springs, and on mountain tops so that the deities won't get angry at them. They began telling each other, 'See, we don't have to feed the deities. We don't know what they eat.'"[30]

This incident reveals much about the impact of the Otomi New Testament. Clearly, its ideas posed a major challenge to the traditional Otomi belief system and would produce a significant religious division in the pueblo in the coming years, but before it brought many of these young men to the point of conversion to Protestantism, it first stimulated a kind of religious ferment *inside* their traditional belief system. The young men first applied Jesus' words to "deities," not to the Christian God, thus demonstrating the kind of creative thinking and reevaluation that often accompanies the translation of the Bible into the vernacular.[31] Similarly, another young man who listened attentively to Echegoyen's and Voigtlander's discussions of the New Testament never did convert to Protestantism but instead became a more committed member of the Roman Catholic Church. "I accepted God because in a dream God showed me that what Artemisa and Katie were saying was good and that he had created the world," he explained.[32] He combined traditional Otomi respect for dreams with the Protestant reliance on the Bible to become a lay leader in the Catholic Church.

The vernacular scriptures thus can be seen to promote an intellectual process based on both personal reflection and dialogue with other members of the community that frequently makes use of traditional indigenous religious resources such as dreams and visions. That this interaction can lead to a wide range of results in the religious sphere—conversion to Protestantism, new understandings of traditional religion, and increased Catholic devotion, to name just a few—suggests that common complaints about "forced conversions" and "cultural imperialism" may have missed the more complex nature of the conversion process that accompanies SIL's introduction of the vernacular scriptures.

Ready for a Change

One of the early Protestant converts remembers a meeting that took place soon after Voigtlander and Echegoyen had started working in San Antonio in 1961. Protestants and others interested in the new religion gathered together and pledged to live in peace and to work together to improve life in San Antonio. They saw the SIL linguists as integral to this process of rebuilding the village. "It is good that you came," they said to Voigtlander, "for we know that you are familiar with Pachuca and Mexico City. You know all the laws." "First," responded Voigtlander, "I am going to give you the law of our Lord. He tells us how to treat each other and how to stop fighting."[33]

Thus, from the perspectives of both the missionaries and the Otomis, even in the early days the religious mission was intertwined with the expansion of the Mexican state and with the larger phenomenon of the growth of evangelical Protestantism. The people of San Antonio were not so far off when they believed that the linguists "came with the authority of the government." This is not to say that Voigtlander and Echegoyen saw their primary purpose as expanding the reach of the state or that their converts did not find in Protestantism the answer to real spiritual yearnings. Rather, it points to the complexity and multi-leveled nature of their interaction. To the two missionaries, linking the community to the programs of the state was one way of serving the people of San Antonio, but offering the "law of the Lord" was even more important. Considering the recent era of violence, they had a real stake in the village's allegiance to law and order.

Consequently, the opposition created by subverting the traditional religion was countered by practical help to the community and by the generally exemplary behavior of their converts. The young men who converted withdrew from Otomi/Catholic religious rites, but they also almost entirely gave up alcohol, cigarettes, and womanizing. Their families benefited from increased stability and net family income; the results were most evident in the new cinder block homes—as opposed to homes traditionally made of balsa planks tied together with strips of bark—that many believers started to build. To this day, when asked how their religion has changed their lives, the Protestants of San Antonio routinely respond that they once used to waste their money on alcohol and sponsoring festivals but that then they saw the light and started building their cinder block homes. Many Protestants make a direct connection between the Otomi New Testament and the changes San Antonio has experienced. As one convert related, "When the people used to have their festivals many people sold their fields to pay their expenses, their house lots too, and because of this many people were poor. If a person is a mayordomo and he is poor he has to sell his fields or his house lot to meet expenses." On the other hand, "The people who had accepted the Word of God started to change, to work, to construct houses of cinder block and of corrugated metal. The pueblo started to change because the festivals stopped."[34]

Interestingly, this analysis is not limited to Protestants. One of the few remaining shamans describes the changes in a very similar way. "The beliefs of the people have come to an end because of the Gospel," he laments. "Before the Gospel arrived here many festivals were celebrated and there were many mayordomos and everything was very nice. But today not many festivals are celebrated because the majority of people are evangelicals." He too sees money as a key element of the equation. "Before, the festivals were very nice because bands came and because the festivals lasted fifteen or even twenty days," he remembered. "But when the Gospel arrived everything came to an end and although there are people today who want to celebrate the festivals, they cannot do so because it costs too much money."[35]

This might seem to be all the evidence that is needed to indict Voigtlander and Echegoyen for just the kind of division, destruction of indigenous culture, and creation of a capitalist mentality that social scientists have long blamed the SIL for. But as we have seen, these changes were embraced enthusiastically by a good portion of the community. Also, one of the early years of the missionaries in San Antonio also coincided with the term of a more "progressive" mayor who had himself rebelled against traditional religious obligations which he believed had impoverished the village. "In 1966 I was delegado," and "that was when the people started to quit sponsoring festivals because I did not force them to be mayordomos." Before he was delegado, his predecessors had forced the people to become mayordomos by putting a table in someone's house as a signal that that person had to be mayordomo. The new delegado, however, did not force them to become mayordomos because he had not done it himself.[36] That a man who had not served as mayordomo could be elected suggests that the religious side of San Antonio's civil-religious hierarchy had dropped significantly in importance.

All the new Protestants received a certain degree of harassment from some members of the community. Many believed that the converts were servants of the Devil, and the rumor circulated that when they met in the evenings they turned off the lights for sexual escapades.[37] When the converts met to study the Bible and sing hymns in the evenings, it was not uncommon for Panfilo Mendoza, Panfilo Naranjo, and Joaquín Naranjo to throw rocks onto the building where they met.[38] Domingo often was called "boxödi" (evil teacher) for his new role and once suffered a brutal beating.[39] On one occasion the new Protestants found a makeshift bomb waiting in their meeting hall (it did not explode). On another occasion one of the Protestants was jailed on trumped-up charges that he had stolen the clapper from the town bell tower. In response to these events, Voigtlander and Echegoyen explained to their converts that article 130 of the Mexican Constitution gave them the freedom to worship as they chose, but the women encouraged them not to do any preaching in the streets so as to avoid provoking their antagonists. In keeping with the Bible's admonitions to respect authority and the SIL's practice of working closely with the Mexican government, the missionaries also encouraged their converts to pray for, rather than resist, their leaders. "Whenever the judge changed each year, they always prayed for the future judge and invited us to pray too," remembered one convert. "They were always telling us that we should pray for all the government officials, the delegado, the juez, the municipal president, the governor and the government of Mexico because that is what it says in the Bible."[40]

The community as a whole did not turn against the linguists or their new converts, as had happened in other parts of the state of Hidalgo.[41] Part of the reason for San Antonio's resignation—there is no doubt that some local residents severely resented the intrusion of the linguists and the resulting religious change in their community— lies in the great disruption of "the wars" from which the village was still recovering. There was simply no political will to start another bloody conflict. At the same time, Voigtlander and Echegoyen's medical work filled a vital need in the community and undoubtedly saved a number of lives. Some of those who benefited from their medical attentions, which included free or inexpensive medicines and transportation to hospitals in Tulancingo and the state capital, Pachuca, converted to Protestantism, even the close relatives of a local shaman, while others did not convert but did become silent or vocal allies. Even the group that might have been most opposed to the missionaries, the bädis (specialists in the traditional religion), did not mount a sustained challenge. The bädis once summoned Voigtlander and Echegoyen to a meeting to blame them for destroying the local religion and culture. When the bädis began arguing among themselves, with some suggesting that the Protestant converts bore more responsibility than Voigtlander and Echegoyen for religious change in the village, the women were able to leave without further incident.[42]

The new converts also began to "translate" Protestantism into the Otomi culture of San Antonio, demonstrating their ownership of the new religion. They soon incorporated dreams and visions, understood by the new believers as messages from God himself, into their practice of Christianity. Voigtlander and Echegoyen, from conservative non-Pentecostal denominations, felt uncomfortable with this development, because it seemed to be undermining reliance on the New Testament, which they saw as much more trustworthy than dreams and visions. Although they would have preferred other expressions of faith, Voigtlander and Echegoyen had to admit that the Otomi believers' approach to the interpretation of dreams was profoundly Christian. For example, when one of the believers drowned and his distraught family made some spiritual inferences that Echegoyen could not support, a dream saved the day. The dead man's widow, already distraught because she had not found her husband's body, heard strange noises at night and was sure that her husband's soul was in torment because he had not been buried. The linguists did not know how to respond to spiritual concerns that they simply did not share. A few days later, though, the whole problem had been solved. The widow had a dream in which her husband, dressed in elegant white clothes, assured her that he was happy and that he was in a good place. She never heard the strange noises again.[43]

Introducing the State

If the linguists made some enemies in San Antonio by introducing the new religion, they made an even greater number of friends—Protestant converts and Catholics alike—by serving as mediators between the village and outside entities such as the federal government, the state government, and Protestant churches. Using contacts in Mexico City, Echegoyen's knowledge of Spanish, and their understanding of the functioning of the Western bureaucratic state, they helped the village acquire bilingual teachers from the federal government in 1963. As Echegoyen relates, "We had very good contacts in those days in the Education Department and we took our friends directly to the man who was in charge of the Indian work in the Education Department." When Echegoyen and representatives of San Antonio reported that their town lacked a school, the official told them that he would arrange for one. The linguists then helped to make the village a more hospitable place for the new teachers. For instance, the first teachers who were sent lacked supplies of all types, so the linguists bought them blankets and helped pay for the roof of a new school building.[44]

Echegoyen and Voigtlander helped the town petition for a road connecting San Antonio to Tulancingo in 1977 and helped secure electricity for the town in 1982.[45] Echegoyen's advocacy even balanced out the political strength of Huehuetla, the head town of the municipio, which was using bribery to divert the road away from San Antonio. Echegoyen called the construction company that was building the road and helped her friends from San Antonio explain what was happening.[46] Eventually the road did, in fact, go through San Antonio, which made more logistical sense. As Echegoyen pointed out to various officials, San Antonio was located on a ridge that provided access to other areas, whereas Huehuetla was located in a dead-end valley.

Because almost all of the Otomis were monolingual and ignorant about the city, they could be easily taken advantage of—a vulnerability the missionaries helped to mitigate. Much of what Echegoyen did was to provide contacts in Mexico City. In one instance, an employee of the electric company told the leaders of San Antonio that if they deposited money in a certain account they would get the electricity sooner than the two years that it would have taken otherwise. The San Antonio committee that was in charge of the electricity was suspicious of the man's request, so Echegoyen went with them all over Mexico City, trying to find the right office. She eventually established that such a payment would not speed the arrival of the electricity in any way.[47]

Division and Otomi Identity

The common charge of anthropologists that the SIL destroys culture and produces division in the indigenous societies in which it works would seem to apply, at least in part, to San Antonio El Grande. There is no doubt that the presence of Echegoyen and Voigtlander led to the acceptance and growth of Protestantism, which in turn undermined the credibility of the traditional Otomi religion and lessened the number of its adherents. After forty years of contact with the two linguists, the pueblo today has four Protestant churches, and less than half of its inhabitants practice the traditional Otomi rituals. Furthermore, the inroads of the modern state that the linguists facilitated—teachers, Western medicine, electricity, and the road connecting San Antonio to Tulancingo—have also weakened the traditional Otomi worldview. Although some residents of the town still visit the local shaman when sick or to gain release from a curse, many more depend on Western medicine. Television brings the Spanish language and images of Mexican material culture to numerous homes. Traveling salesmen, politicians, itinerant evangelists, beer suppliers, bureaucrats of the education system, and a host of other outsiders make use of the road to provide San Antonio with the products of consumer capitalism and the customs and ideas of mestizo society. So the anthropologists are right: Echegoyen and Voigtlander did divide San Antonio, and they did make inroads for capitalism and the national state into the formerly isolated Otomi culture.

Yet the anthropologists are only partially right. As de la Rosa and Campos Cabrera's 1992 study of San Antonio points out, "Up to the present day, relationships between Catholics, bädis and Protestants are common and good. Nobody avoids the members of other groups. There is some tension between the leaders of the Protestant churches, but in general this tension stays at the religious level, without affecting the other parts of life. . . . Protestants have peaceful relationships with non-Protestant family members; their work is valued in the community like that of any other person; and there are prestigious people who belong to or have belonged to a Protestant church, without their religion keeping them from holding civil and political positions."[48]

Besides the initial tensions in the early 1960s—rock throwing, the unexploded bomb, problems inside various families—San Antonio has seen little religious conflict. Protestants comply with their communal work obligations and participate on committees and in the local government. One Presbyterian from San Antonio, Tomás Flores, was elected as *presidente suplente* (substitute president) in 1993 and then became municipal president in 1994 when his running mate had to leave office. Protestants and Catholics in San Antonio buy and sell from each other, work together, and study together. In short, far from destroying the social fabric of San Antonio, the presence of Echegoyen and Voigtlander and the growth of Protestantism has coincided with a period of peace and prosperity in which the town is clearly less divided than it was in the period of factional warfare that preceded it.[49]

Another religious fault line now runs through the town. No longer does everyone see the Catholic and traditional Otomi religions as synonymous. As the town has received regular visits from priests based in Huehuetla over the last two decades, some inhabitants of San Antonio have embraced credal Roman Catholicism and have come to see traditional Otomi beliefs and practices, such as the adoration of the yoguis, as sub-Christian. Since the bädis still view themselves as Catholic and still assert their right to use the church building for certain rituals, a certain amount of tension has developed between the two groups.[50] In terms of theology, the Roman Catholics have more in common with the Protestants than they do with practitioners of traditional Otomi religion.

As far as ethnicity goes, in recent years some residents of the village have seemed less apt to embrace their Otomi identity, but this is a phenomenon with roots other than Protestant conversion. "One can see that the Otomi identity is rejected to some extent by some members of the community, but not on religious grounds," de la Rosa and Campos Cabrera point out. "This rejection generally occurs among the generation of youths that migrated to the city and, after living there for a time, either returned to town or visit occasionally. Presbyterians, Pentecostals, Catholics and bädis all demonstrate this phenomenon."[51]

Consequently, the interrelationships among religion, culture, and ethnic identity in San Antonio are quite complex, for rejection of Otomi identity can coincide with the continued practice of traditional Otomi religion, while conversion to Protestantism can exist comfortably with continued Otomi identity.[52] Protestants no longer worship the God of Fire and the Goddess of the Water and have lost this part of their heritage, but these same Protestants are by far the greatest proponents of the Otomi language in San Antonio. The use of the Otomi New Testament and Otomi hymns in the Presbyterian church and the Otomi preaching in the three Pentecostal churches sharply distinguish them from the Catholic church, which features a Spanish liturgy and Spanish preaching.[53] Protestantism in San Antonio has a definite Otomi cast, from its use of the vernacular to its compatibility with dreams and visions to its reliance on faith healing.

Is it possible to decide whether a bädi watching a *telenovela* (soap opera) or a Protestant reading his Otomi New Testament is "more Otomi"? The question is not really a useful one, but since some anthropologists believe that Protestantism has a deculturizing function, it needs to be emphasized that Protestants retain their Otomi identity as much as, if not more than, their Catholic peers. There is no fixed Otomi identity we can consult to decide who is more or less Otomi: none of the Otomis of today live or believe as their grandparents did; none of those grandparents lived in a culture like that before the Conquest.[54] It seems clear that Otomis can continue to be Otomis while interacting with, adopting, and adapting the various ideologies and products of modernity, including Protestantism. Unless anthropologists can make a convincing argument that Protestantism is exceptional, they will need to do better than presenting conversion to Protestantism as de facto evidence of deculturation.

The issue is not *whether* the SIL divides, but *how* it divides. San Antonio el Grande cannot stand for all the communities in which the SIL has worked in Mexico. It is but one example of that organization's work, but it does suggest that generalizations about "division," "cultural imperialism," and "ethnocide" obscure a more complicated story. The SIL's critics need to admit that its linguistic work has helped to preserve many indigenous languages. In the case of San Antonio, at least, there are no greater proponents of the Otomi language than its Presbyterians, and no outsiders, including the state and federal governments, who have done more to encourage the development of written Otomi than Voigtlander and Echegoyen.[55]

One More Conflict

In 1997, as it had fifty years earlier, San Antonio found itself embroiled in a local conflict with regional dimensions; this time, however, there was no bloodshed. Rumors swirled around the municipio of Huehuetla that, for the first time, the Institutional Revolutionary Party (PRI) was going to lose the municipal presidency. The rightist, Catholic-friendly National Action Party (PAN) and the leftist Labor Party were running candidates, and some said that either one could win. San Antonio, which as recently as 1991 had been perceived as a PRI stronghold, emerged as a hotbed of political dissidence, as Catholics disgruntled with the corruption of the PRI raised the banner of the PAN. Even worse for the PRI, San Antonio's most educated person, teacher and Presbyterian pastor Fidencio Bacilio, endorsed the Labor Party.

Faced with the unthinkable, PRIísta candidate José Rolando Sevilla Carranza actively courted the Protestants of San Antonio. He failed to sway pastor Bacilio, but he did win the allegiance of other key Protestant leaders. When election day came, those Protestant leaders came through for the PRI. The PRI carried San Antonio resoundingly, doing better there than anywhere else in the municipio. The Protestants not only had gained the gratitude of Sevilla Carranza but also had started to sense their own political potential. Just as Echegoyen and Voigtlander played a major role in bringing pluralism to San Antonio, their spiritual children will play a major role in deciding what direction a pluralist and democratic San Antonio el Grande will choose for its future.

9

Anthropology Takes a Radical Turn

In August 1961 a Cessna airplane carrying the governor of Chiapas, Leon Brindís, landed at a small airstrip in the isolated municipio of Ocosingo. The facility he was visiting was not a military base or a frontier settlement but an SIL training center where sixteen young Tzeltals were studying Spanish and were being instructed (in Tzeltal) in carpentry, math, mechanics, horticulture, writing, swimming, livestock care, health, sanitation, and geography. With the help of materials supplied by the SEP, the SIL was trying to help these young men "to improve their lives economically" and "to become more integrated into the national life of Mexico." "Our goal," Frank Robbins of the SIL explained to the secretary of education, "was not to offer formal or complete training, because a more complete or extended program might have resulted in alienating them from their respective communities. Instead, this course attempted to return these men to their communities prepared to initiate new ideas, under the supervision of the personnel of the SIL, which will have a deeper effect on these communities than training that did not take into account the interests of their communities. These young men," Robbins continued, "who know how to read and write their language and have left behind the old fears and superstitions, were ready to accept changes in their customs that could help them to better their lives and to progress within a national context."[1]

Thus, a quarter-century after Lázaro Cárdenas's momentous visit to the Townsends, linguistics, courtesy, and good relationships with government officials were bearing fruit in a second "Tetelcingo." Here was the SIL, working with the SEP, making Indians into Mexicans, and receiving a visit from the governor of Chiapas. What could be more emblematic of the SIL's success? Its linguistic prowess enabled it to offer training in an obscure indigenous language. Its agreement with the SEP enabled it to function as an auxiliary of the Mexican state. Its continued efforts at cultivating relationships with government officials (symbolized by Robbins's letter to the secretary of education) showed every sign of continuing to win influential friends, as they apparently already had done with the governor of Chiapas.

But no matter how much he might minimize it, Robbins also points to the possibility of some less-than-rosy developments. The gist of his letter is that the SIL has done all that is possible to reduce the risk of alienating its students from traditional Tzeltal culture or dividing their communities when they return. But in the face of the great changes that seem to have occurred in its pupils, it is hard to imagine how such problems could be avoided. In fact, sending bilingual, Protestant (or secularized) youths back to traditional Tzeltal communities with the goal of introducing changes proposed by the Mexican state and American missionaries was likely a recipe for alienation, conflict, or both. From the state's point of view, such conflict tended to diminish the advantages of using the SIL in the first place, for it simply substituted one problem for another. It offered contradictions from the SIL's standpoint as well, for neither community conflict nor the alienation of its converts served its evangelistic interests. The SIL would have to walk a very narrow path: on the one hand, it had to influence indigenous people enough to convert them and modernize them sufficiently to satisfy the Mexican state; on the other hand, it could not so alter its charges' worldviews that they no longer had any affinity for, or desire to relate to, their own communities—otherwise the decades-long process of Bible translation would influence no one except a few quickly acculturating individuals. Vernacular translations of the Bible were only effective evangelistically if their converts remained committed in some measure to their ethnic roots. If they fully appropriated mestizo culture, they would become alienated from their peers and would be unlikely to stay for very long in their indigenous communities. Put simply, if the SIL did not Mexicanize Indians it had no real use to the state, but if it Mexicanized them too much or too quickly it damaged its own religious purposes. After all, what good would its vernacular New Testaments do if everybody spoke Spanish? Still, to most observers, in the early 1960s the SIL seemed stronger than ever.

The Day of the Indian

In early April 1964 the SIL, the SEP, the INI, and the III sent out invitations to a joint celebration of the "American Day of the Indian" and an unveiling of the SIL's new headquarters in Mexico City. The more than one thousand guests who gathered in the Tlalpan neighborhood for the ceremony found themselves in quite select company.

President Adolfo López Mateos pulled the curtain from a plaque dedicated to Moisés Sáenz; INI director Alfonso Caso praised the SIL as "a group of men and women of good will, true friends, who are firmly committed to the material and spiritual development of the Indians of America"; Chilean ambassador and president of the executive council of the III Alberto Sepulveda Contreras and deputy director of the SEP Mario Aguilera Dorantes shared further kind words. The only hint that the SIL was more than a scientific entity (and not exactly a department of the Mexican state) came from longtime supporter Ramón Beteta, who lauded the SIL's efforts "to avoid the disintegration that modern life often causes in primitive groups by introducing them to the foundation of our civilization, which is Christian, through the translation of passages from the New Testament into indigenous languages."[2]

The Day of the Indian celebration pointed not only to the SIL's ability to mobilize its indigenista allies but also to the great strength of indigenismo in the early and mid-1960s. By 1962 the INI alone had opened 7 regional centers, 221 schools, and 68 medical clinics and had built or improved over a thousand kilometers of rural roads. There was no denying its ongoing and growing influence in indigenous communities around the nation. It was thus no surprise when in 1962 the Thirty-fifth Congress of Americanists officially recognized Mexico and the INI as paragons of indigenismo, or when in 1964 Mexico signed an agreement with the Organization of American States to train indigenistas from various Latin American nations at its center in San Cristóbal de Las Casas, Chiapas. As Mexico's secretary of foreign relations, Manuel Tello, boasted, the latter agreement pointed to his nation's preeminent position in the field of indigenismo: "The attention that the Mexican government has devoted to the solution of the indigenous problem, not only on a national level but also in the whole American region ever since the Congress of Pátzcuaro, is well known."[3] In 1968, twenty-eight years after the first Inter-American Indigenista Conference with indigenistas from all over Latin America again gathered in Pátzcuaro, Alfonso Caso's denunciation of racism and profession of faith in the gradual advance of indigenismo received a standing ovation.[4] To all appearances, Mexican indigenismo was prospering.

And to all appearances the SIL was reaping the fruits of its allegiances with the INI and the SEP. In 1965, as Mexico branch director

Ben Elson looked back on the previous six years, he could observe with pride that the SIL now had 266 members (12 with doctorates) working on 87 different languages in Mexico. The organization had developed a new strategy that involved periodic workshops held by special consultants in three new centers (Mitla, Oaxaca; Ixmiquilpan, Hidalgo; and Mexico City) that portended quicker translations. Secretary of Education Jaime Torres Bodet's personal intervention to secure land for the Mexico City headquarters only hinted at the strength of the SIL's relationships with important government officials. A special banquet for Cameron Townsend in 1960 had been a "success in terms of our total program and a special help in Government contact work," and the 1964 celebration of the Day of the Indian was "one of the most impressive of such ceremonies that Wycliffe has ever made." In fact, Elson reported, "Our friendships in Indian Affairs and at higher levels in Education have, I believe, never been better." Although the process of obtaining visas for linguists had become more complex because of changes in the law, "friends in Gobernación" eased any difficulties. All in all, the prospects for the organization looked bright. The one slight worry that Elson shared was in many ways evidence of the SIL's success in winning the confidence of Mexico's government. He hoped that the three new translation centers would not become "too isolated from tribal life." Linguistic analysis, no matter how impressive in an academic sense, could never substitute for the simple ability to speak a language well, which could only be achieved in the villages.[5] While the concern in the 1940s had been that linguists demonstrate their scientific accomplishments while simultaneously winning the friendship of influential Mexicans, in the 1960s the friendships seemed to have been firmly established and Elson was worrying that the SIL's linguists had, in effect, become *too* scientific.

Finally, the SIL's enhanced status and perceived role in spreading Spanish led to another major favor from the SEP: a land grant for a headquarters in the Tlalpan section of Mexico City. Secretary Torres Bodet secured land from President López Mateos with the stipulation that the SIL build a large center for the study of linguistics and indigenismo and return the land and the building to the Mexican government in thirty years. The new center was financed largely by a gift of five hundred thousand pesos from industrialist and politician Aarón Sáenz to honor the memory of his brother Moisés. Sáenz hoped the new linguistics center could print bilingual textbooks that, "without offending the natural sensitivity of the indigenous peoples," would encourage vernacular literacy as a bridge to Spanish. In this way, he hoped to contribute to the establishment of "a single national language."[6]

Internal Colonialism and Radical Anthropology

Unfortunately for the INI, the SEP, and the SIL, as impressive as Mexican indigenismo's achievements might have seemed, there were signs, even as the INI was receiving international acclaim, that in Mexico itself all was not well. Even before the Tlatelolco massacre of 2 October 1968 shattered the regime's legitimacy in the eyes of most intellectuals, a rising generation of anthropologists had begun to question the very foundations of indigenismo.[7] Sociologist Pablo González Casanova provided a theoretical impetus for this critical reexamination of anthropology in his elaboration of the neo-Marxian concept of "internal colonialism," the idea that cities such as Tlaxiaco, Oaxaca, and San Cristóbal de Las Casas, Chiapas, acted as regional metropolises that dominated internal "colonies" of indigenous peoples within Mexico.[8] The thesis had broad implications—if one followed its assertions to their logical conclusions, the Mexican state became a sort of occupying colonial power—that fostered a general attitude of suspicion toward even the most hallowed "revolutionary" institutions. Mexican anthropologists, who worked *with* indigenous people and, with few exceptions, *for* the state, found themselves and their discipline implicated by González Casanova's theory. Internal colonialism soon became a standard concept in Mexican anthropology, most obviously in the thought of Rodolfo Stavenhagen but also as the background to growing critiques of indigenismo by other young anthropologists and intellectuals.[9]

An intellectual current that involved both the social sciences and the Mexican state was destined, sooner or later, to involve the SIL. As Mexican anthropologists came to understood the nature and purpose of their discipline in new ways, they soon fomented a crisis for the SIL in Mexico. It might seem odd that internal changes in one academic field could endanger the position of a political actor as well entrenched as the SIL was by the mid-1960s, but it must be remembered that the SIL was closely connected to the Mexican indigenista establishment. Since indigenismo was not a pure science but a specific policy of the Mexican state (incorporating and Mexicanizing Indians), the SIL's favored position was vulnerable to changes in the political fortunes of the Mexican regime and of indigenismo itself.

As Tlatelolco and the social ferment of the 1960s put to rest the notion that the PRI was the true heir of the Mexican Revolution, they also opened up a myriad of alternative futures, many of which did not include traditional indigenismo or the SIL. In the realm of anthropology, the notion that most appealed to young visionaries was the idea of the pluralist or multiethnic society. In direct contrast to the earlier generation of indigenistas that had worked to Mexicanize the Indian, this generation of anthropologists dreamed of a Mexico in which ethnic particularities would be freely expressed, indigenous languages would be recognized by the state, and traditional indigenous communities would have a significant level of autonomy.[10]

These goals were not necessarily antithetical to the SIL's. In fact, if they had been the official policies of the Mexican state, the SIL would have adopted them quickly and without great pain. In the situation of intergenerational anthropological conflict, though, the SIL's ties to the older generation were more of a hindrance than a help. In the past the SIL had won the admiration of nationalistic indigenistas such as Manuel Gamio, Alfonso Caso, and Lázaro Cárdenas by praising Mexico and stressing Protestantism's ability to replace folk Catholicism. This stance proved much less impressive to the younger generation of anthropologists, which was decades removed from the Cristiada and saw American imperialism hard at work in Vietnam. The CIA's infamous deeds in Latin America in the 1950s and 1960s cast suspicion on all North Americans, especially social scientists and missionaries. Finally, even though the SIL would have welcomed an end to East-West tensions, the cold war tended to polarize political ideologies on both left and right. Where actual revolutionaries such as Cárdenas and Gamio had supported the SIL because, without agreeing with all of its policies or practices, they believed it was on the balance positive for Mexico, neo-Marxian anthropologists of the 1970s generally perceived the SIL in almost unremittingly negative terms.

The SIL of the 1960s was also not the SIL of the 1940s. Some of the organization's greatest triumphs—its growth, academic achievements, and completed linguistic and translation projects—had put it in the public eye in Mexico, the United States, and around the world far more than it had been in the 1930s and 1940s. The organization was devoting significant attention to publicizing itself, including television appearances in 1959 by Tariri, a former "head-hunter" from Ecuador who had converted to Christianity. An article on Tariri in *Reader's Digest*, a history of the SIL to mark its twenty-fifth anniversary, and a book telling "the breathtaking story of the Ecuadorian Indian girl who escaped from—and returned to—the world's most murderous tribe" gained the SIL further attention.[11] Cameron Townsend managed to convince the U.S. Senate to inaugurate a "Bible Translation Day" in 1966 and—a more difficult proposition—to convince the SIL to sponsor a pavilion eventually visited by more than a million people at the World's Fair in New York City in 1964.[12]

In 1959 a longtime SIL supporter, Secretary of Education Jaime Torres Bodet, arranged for the government to donate land for the new SIL headquarters in the Tlalpan section of Mexico City. George Cowan, the president of Wycliffe Bible Translators, might say, "As servants we seek to maintain a low profile," but with land worth three hundred thousand dollars, large buildings on the site, and frequent ceremonies like the one detailed earlier in this chapter, the headquarters gave the SIL a public, quasi-official presence in Mexico that could not help but attract attention. Cowan had to admit that such a center was "highly visible," but he hoped its Mexican-themed mural and its personnel's "genuine spirit of openness and humble service" would prevent it from becoming "an insurmountable barrier in our relations with the people."[13]

Although the leaders of the SIL's Mexico branch were skilled leaders who had learned their jobs from Townsend himself, they did not quite have the founder's stature. One of Townsend's best pupils in the area of government relations was Ben Elson, director of the SIL's Mexico branch during most of the 1960s. Not surprisingly, Elson emphasized Romans 13 as the foundation for a Christian philosophy of "politics and the political process" that consisted primarily of treating the government with respect and cooperating with it "in endeavors to do good for its citizens." Elson had learned from Townsend "to make whatever effort is necessary to maintain close relationship with the government," especially by calling frequently on government officials and by undertaking "as many cooperative endeavors with governmental agencies as possible."[14] Elson and his successor Frank Robbins maintained Townsend's example of building strong relationships with Mexican presidents and other high officials, but they probably would not have had the chutzpah to win over someone like Rafael Ramírez or Lázaro Cárdenas as Townsend had done. By the 1970s SIL leaders were warning the membership that certain of Townsend's policies—dual identity and the "Mexican patronato pattern" (an advisory board of influential nationals)—were "a priceless birthright" that would lead to "marvelous fruit, lasting throughout eternity," but, if ignored, to "tragic results."[15] The emphasis now was on duplication, not innovation.

This combination of a higher profile and a less dynamic leadership team coincided with what was by the 1960s a much larger and more diverse group of linguists. The organization's 1959 withdrawal from the conservative Interdenominational Foreign Missions Association due to its insistence that the SIL stop aiding Roman Catholic missionaries in South America signaled the SIL's move beyond fundamentalism.[16] Gradually more non-fundamentalists had joined the SIL and the training of those linguists had become more scientific, based on both the linguistic expertise of teachers like Ken Pike and the successes and failures of linguists in the field. The more than twenty-five hundred SIL members working on more than five hundred languages in the 1970s were required "to take advanced linguistic training, to attend periodic workshops, and to make the results of their linguistic research available in written form," and to take "classroom courses, readings, and workshops" in cultural anthropology.[17] One reform that the SIL did not make was to recruit or encourage Mexican members. SIL leaders recruited new linguists from Canada, Great Britain, and continental Europe but were afraid that Mexican Protestants, who had begun to inquire about membership, could not raise the required funds. Even if they did gain enough financial support, their "prayer letters" and visits to Mexican churches might attract unwanted attention to the religious side of the SIL's work. Artemisa Echegoyen (featured in chapter 8) and Maria Villalobos were two of the very few exceptions to this policy.

Thus, by the 1960s the SIL was a large, diverse, internationally recognized organization whose mostly American and almost exclusively non-Mexican members operated in several dozen remote locations in Mexico as well as in the halls of academe in Mexico and the United States. In short, Mexican social scientists would have had to try very hard *not* to notice the SIL. This prominence would have been a boon to the SIL if the social sciences had maintained the values and orientation of the 1940s and 1950s. Unfortunately for the SIL, the social sciences were radicalizing rapidly.

During the 1960s, at the National School of Anthropology and History in Mexico City, Daniel Cazés was alerting a generation of anthropologists to the bourgeoisie's use of their science as an instrument of domination, and fostering, in the words of an indigenista from a previous generation, an atmosphere in which "the insults and recriminations increased until arriving at their height in the anarchist-student movement of 1968."[18] In an influential symposium in the journal *Current Anthropology* in 1968, Cazés contended that anthropology in Mexico was an expression of the fact that "the mentality and interests of the ruling bourgeoisie in relation to the Indian groups is the same as that of imperialists in relation to their subject peoples." Since for Cazés the only solution to imperialist domination lay in "direct, revolutionary political action," Mexican anthropologists had to lay aside conservative agendas and give the people with whom they were working "the instruments of self-determination." As for foreign anthropologists, Cazés proposed "a permanent tribunal by which 'irresponsibility' may be condemned, suspicious research and applications unmasked and the principles of our scientific and humane responsibilities be established."[19]

Cazés's radical and critical words were by no means out of place in the *Current Anthropology* symposium, which was translated into Spanish and published in Mexico in *América Indígena* in 1969.[20] Gerald Berreman's article, for instance, opened with an epigraph that indicted traditional anthropology as an anti-revolutionary tool used by imperialist powers to subdue and pacify native peoples. The previous strategy for successful counterinsurgency had been to put ten soldiers in a country for every guerrilla in operation, but now the formula was "ten anthropologists for each guerrilla."[21] Even more inflammatory words came from Andre Gunder Frank, who endorsed the proposition that "virtually the whole of the 'free' world's social science is in effect one huge imperialist Camelot project." (In the infamous Project Camelot the U.S. Defense Department had employed social scientists directly.) Frank dismisses the other contributors to the symposium as "liberals" who "simply serve American imperialism better and more efficiently than the perhaps more outmoded children of an earlier imperialism." Anthropologists needed to follow the example of the guerrilla doctor Ernesto "Che" Guevara and "to use anthropology only so far as it is sufficient, while doing what is necessary to replace the nearly world-wide violent, exploitative, racist, alienative capitalist class system." In fact, the relationship between anthropology and counterinsurgency should be subverted. Anthropologists should reject their governments' plans and become actual revolutionary agents: "Then the counter-insurgency formula of ten anthropologists for each guerilla cited by Berreman will surely have to yield to a victorious popular insurgency formula of 10,000 guerillas with each anthropologist worthy of the name."[22] Thus, even as Mexico was winning international acclaim as the preeminent practitioner of indigenismo and social anthropology, indigenismo was quickly losing its luster while social anthropology's aims were turning almost 180 degrees.

A 1969 exchange between the dean of Mexican indigenistas and a young anthropologist illustrates the gulf between the two generations. The INI's director, Alfonso Caso, simply could not believe that the new attitudes would eventually carry the day. He made no effort to hide his disdain for the cultural relativism of the rising generation, which was to him a cruel exercise in intellectualism. It gave indigenous communities a kind of illusory dignity by protecting them from outside influences, but it failed them in the most basic areas of health and education. When young anthropologist Rudolf van Zantwijk criticized the subjectivism inherent in Caso's supposed ability to distinguish between the positive and negative aspects of indigenous cultures, Caso responded, "You are right; the criteria are subjective." He went on to explain that indigenismo was an official policy of the Mexican government and that like any other policy it was based on an "ethical foundation" and had a value system in which it distinguished between negative and positive.[23] He had little patience for those who asserted that belief in Western medical treatment was a "value judgment" that should not be imposed on non-Western peoples. Of course it was a value judgment, he argued, but withholding such a value judgment would put lives at risk.

The Omnipresent Central Intelligence Agency

If the popular press gave the crisis of indigenismo a middling amount of attention, and gave even less attention to connections to external and internal imperialism, there was one aspect of North American imperialism that did become a far more resonant issue in the newspapers of Mexico City. In 1967 *Excélsior* reported on a scandal developing in the United States in which various organizations, such as the National Student Association, admitted receiving funding from the Central Intelligence Agency.[24] To many on the Latin American left, this information confirmed what had long been suspected: the long reach of the CIA into Latin America through North American cultural and scientific organizations. As the same newspaper reported in April 1967, "It seems as if the interest of the CIA in cultural affairs is of two kinds: (a) the actual work of espionage in foreign countries, for which it employs students, members of the Peace Corps, *et cetera*, asking them for information or establishing relationships with them for this purpose, or (b) the attempt to neutralize independent movements of students, professors and intellectuals when it fails to transform them into pawns in its obsessive war against world communism."[25]

A year later the scandal only deepened. The United States' Rusk Commission, *El Día* noted, had established that at least thirty foreign organizations had received financing from the CIA. Fulbright scholars and U.S. Information Agency libraries, both common in Latin America, were under investigation.[26] By 1970 it was no exaggeration to say, "Whenever something occurs in some part of the world where North Americans have small or large interests—that is to say, practically everywhere—the CIA is mentioned." Even though the author of these words went to great pains to assert that the CIA was not as omnipresent or omniscient as some believed, the rest of his article painted a detailed picture of CIA operations all over the world: in Guatemala's coup of 1954, in Vietnam and Cambodia, in the attempted invasion of Cuba in 1961, in Iran, Korea, and Indonesia.[27] The intent may have been to demystify the CIA, but the result was a portrait of a violent, nefarious organization operating with impunity in Mexico's closest Latin American neighbors, Guatemala and Cuba. Consequently, at the moment when anthropologists were exposing their discipline as a child and a tool of imperialism, the U.S. Congress and journalists all over the world were conducting concurrent and reinforcing exposés of North American espionage and subversion. If the denunciations of anthropology could at times seem exaggerated—was the U.S. State Department really interested in the social hierarchies of remote villages?—revelations about the CIA, and especially about its channeling of funds overseas and its use of students and scientists, were gratifyingly specific. Here was explicit evidence of real imperialism.

The SIL knew of the ferment going on in the world of anthropology and took note of the allegations surrounding the CIA, but in the late 1960s and early 1970s it had great reason to hope that its position in Mexico might actually continue to improve. The policy of cultivating relationships with influential Mexicans seemed to have created an especially propitious situation. Even as one influential president of their Mexican advisory board, Ramón Beteta, died, he was replaced with perhaps an even more influential Mexican, former head of the UNESCO and ex-director of the SEP, Jaime Torres Bodet.[28] The new head of the SEP, Agustín Yañez, continued that ministry's close relationship with the SIL, while the SEP, the INI, and the III continued to celebrate the American Day of the Indian at the SIL's Mexico City center.[29] Most importantly, Luis Echeverría's election in 1970 put "a friend of the SIL for many years" in the presidency, while Gonzalo Aguirre Beltrán's appointment as director of the INI in the same year meant that the most important indigenista agency now belonged to a "longtime friend and member of the advisory board."[30]

Echeverría's acceptance of the SIL's invitation to be the honorary president of its advisory board and the SEP's continued dependence on the SIL as its virtual linguistics department gave the leaders of the Mexico branch great hope for the future.[31] "I want to emphasize that it seems to me that we have a more open door to work in coordination with the Secretary of Education and the INI than we have ever had before, perhaps, and there is the definite possibility of accomplishing concrete things," said SIL director of public relations Don Burgess in 1972. "The government really would like to have substantial amounts of literature in all of the areas where they work by the time Echeverria's term is up, and they have the money to do something about it."[32] With this kind of support from the Mexican government, there was talk of the SIL's finishing all of its work in Mexico by 1990, even though there were forty-two languages where projects had not yet even started.[33]

The seventh Inter-American Indigenista Conference in August 1972, offered much evidence to confirm the SIL's optimism. The Mexican government, according to its own report at the conference, had stimulated the economic growth of indigenous communities, restored lands on a grand scale, and created a model of indigenismo that stood as an example for the rest of Latin America.[34] Cameron Townsend, as a "special observer" of the Mexican delegation, received official recognition as the "benefactor of the linguistically isolated populations of America" for his role in providing monolingual Indians with "greater communication and integration with other peoples."[35] Mexican indigenismo once again had set the standard for Latin America, and once again its ally the SIL had displayed its own indigenista credentials.

But a small press conference held at the congress suggested that the great changes taking place in the field of anthropology were not totally absent from government-sponsored indigenismo. Margarita Nolasco, one of the Mexican delegates to the conference and a researcher at the INI, told reporters that she shared neither the optimism of the official statement about Mexico's accomplishments nor the generally self-congratulatory sentiments of the conference. In fact, Nolasco publicly denounced not only the "low scientific level" of the congress but also the specific government policies, which she believed failed to liberate indigenous people from conditions of oppression because they failed to take into account the "disequilibrium" between the highly developed national society and underdeveloped indigenous communities.[36] If a member of the official delegation to a major international conference was willing to attack Mexican indigenismo so directly, there could be little to prevent her from attacking the SIL. With revelations about the CIA coming out almost weekly, it was also likely that sooner or later someone would link those strange evangelical linguists from up north to the nefarious purposes of the Central Intelligence Agency.

Denounced!

Anthropology Turns against the SIL

In the late 1960s and early 1970s, committed, progressive anthropologists, having exposed the dubious origins of their discipline and its connections to Western imperialism, faced the daunting task of reformulating the rationale of their profession. Although they had rejected the imperialism and colonialism that tainted official indigenista policies of incorporation and integration, most were not quite ready to heed the cries of their most radical colleagues to work directly for revolution. It was one thing to denounce imperialism; it was quite another to join those ten thousand guerrillas in the mountains. What they needed was a new way of looking at their discipline that would enable them to remain both progressive (not sacrificing or compromising their political commitments) and anthropologists (not leaving the confines of the academy).

Perhaps the most influential voice in the struggle to reshape the discipline in the years around 1970 belonged to French ethnologist Robert Jaulin. After spending a good portion of the 1960s in the rain forests of the Amazon, Jaulin became convinced that it was his duty to oppose "ethnocide," which he defined as the "imposed and complete transformation of the everyday life" of an indigenous people. In the circumstances he had observed firsthand, ethnocide meant that the Bari people of the rain forest "had to dress like Europeans: to exchange their loin clothes for our ridiculous finery, which is totally unsuitable for the heat." They had to eat like Europeans, live in houses like Europeans, leave behind hunting and gathering, and enter the wage economy. Ultimately, the ethnocide of the Baris signified an exchange of their birthright of "gentleness and happiness" for the West's pottage of "pretence, drama and stupidity." Scandalized by the impact of indigenous peoples' incorporation into Western civilization, which he called "white history," Jaulin henceforth would devote himself to the protection of indigenous cultures against the ravages of the West.

At the same time, Jaulin recognized the scope of the opposition to his new plans. Very different groups of people—North American oil company employees, Catholic and Protestant missionaries, and South American colonists—could agree on at least one thing: indigenous civilization had no right to exist. When Jaulin attempted to denounce these destroyers of indigenous civilization he found himself in the midst of a global battle, fighting not merely against specific abuses but against an entire system, because "colonial acts" took place in larger contexts of domination. The battle for the indigenous peoples of the world therefore was simultaneously a battle for the soul of the West, for "the relationship of our civilization with these other civilizations is also the relationship of our civilization with itself." Jaulin's struggle thus had two prongs: the attempt to end ethnocide and the effort to remake the foundations of Western civilization.[1]

At the Congress of Americanists in 1968, in Germany, Jaulin called for an extended forum on ethnocide in the Americas. The French Society of Americanists agreed, and in February 1970 a group of mostly French social scientists gathered in Paris to discuss the situation of the indigenous peoples of North, Central, and South America. The presentations at the conference, according to Jaulin, were motivated "less as an explanation of ethnocide" than as "an expectant condemnation . . . of the machine that demeans us." Like a mirror image of imperialism's effect on indigenous cultures, the new anthropology also was devoted to cultural transformation—the transformation of the West itself. "Participation in white history is the process that the machine uses to perpetuate itself," argued Jaulin. "We must destroy the machine."[2]

Like Andre Gunder Frank's call to revolution, Jaulin's challenge to his colleagues probably asked for (or assumed) more commitment than they were ready to make. It is not clear from the conference proceedings, for instance, that Shirley Keith's qualified defense of the reservation system in the United States was a call for the "destruction of the machine" or that Jean Meyer's overview of the "Indian problem" in Mexico displayed any great animus toward the West.[3] Like Frank and Daniel Cazés, however, Jaulin did succeed in nudging his colleagues in his direction. Even if not all of them were ready to adopt the destruction of Western civilization as their raison d'être, many social scientists would join him in adopting a new understanding of their discipline that was based on a suspicious attitude toward Western culture.

Meanwhile, in Mexico, a group of young anthropologists based at the National School of Anthropology and History and led by Arturo Warman and Guillermo Bonfil Batalla were participating in the student movement of 1968. When their militancy cost them their positions, the faculty walked out to support them.[4] Influenced not only by the crisis of indigenismo and anthropology but also by their own experiences of the oppressive tendencies of the Mexican regime, in July 1970 Warman, Bonfil Batalla, and three other young anthropologists launched a broadside called *De eso que llaman antropología mexicana* ("About what they call Mexican anthropology"). The authors left few aspects of Mexican anthropology unscathed. According to Warman, anthropology was in general "a scientific aid to white expansion" and in its Mexican incarnation a bureaucratic, myopic servant of colonialism that was "incapable of complex analysis."[5] Other authors denounced the National School of Anthropology and History as "traditional and behind the times," the INI as a bulwark of "society's power structure and class organization," the National Institute of Anthropology and History (INAH) as possessing a "deformed, inflexible and old-fashioned" administrative structure, and the SIL as linked to "neocolonialist tendencies."[6] In an influential essay, Bonfil Batalla echoed the conclusions of the earlier French conference. "There is no way to redeem the Indian except by liberating our own society, ending the alienation of our culture," he contended. "This calls for anthropology's critical analysis of our sociocultural reality. This is our commitment."[7]

The Declaration of Barbados

Surprisingly enough, the World Council of Churches (WCC), the umbrella organization for "historical" (i.e., non-evangelical, non-Pentecostal) Protestant denominations, not only supplied Bonfil Batalla with a platform for his "critical analysis of sociocultural reality" but also published his findings in an influential volume.[8] In 1968 the WCC had resolved to educate itself and its member churches on racism through a "crash programme" of research, conferences, and reports on situations of racial oppression in different regions of the world. For its first conference, which would focus on South America, the WCC turned to the University of Berne's Georg Grünberg, a specialist in issues of genocide and ethnocide in Brazil.[9]

The group of "qualified anthropologists and ethnologists" who met in Bridgetown, Barbados, from 25 to 30 January 1971 painted a rather discouraging picture of the situation of the non-Andean Indians of South America.[10] National governments, international corporations, indigenista agencies, and religious missions were, at best, failing indigenous people miserably, and, at worst, actively and intentionally participating in campaigns of ethnocide and even genocide. Unlike at the Congress of Americanists in Lima in 1970, the SIL came in for its share of criticism. The Colombian government was apparently using the SIL to further its official policy of fostering acculturation by giving de facto authority over large swaths of land to nongovernmental organizations "who have the techniques or practical facilities for eliminating the problem as quickly as possible without making any further calls on the budget." Particularly worrisome was the possibility of the "amalgam of scientific research with para-proselytizing aims opening the door to the penetration of outside interests."[11] In Ecuador, the "collaboration between the Summer School [*sic*] of Linguistics and the Texaco company in the 'pacification' of the Aushiris" was part of a larger pattern in which missionary centers served as "focal points of internal colonization."[12] In Peru, due to its long-standing contract with the Ministry of Education, the SIL exercised so much influence that the bilingual education system did not employ a single Peruvian linguist or anthropologist. It was imbuing indigenous communities with "a spirit and values which are markedly individualistic and capitalist in the purest Weberian sense of the term."[13]

One of the most important documents that resulted from the conference was Bonfil Batalla's "The Indian and the Colonial Situation: The Context of Indigenist Policy in Latin America."[14] Bonfil Batalla's essay employed dependency theory to explain Latin America's relationship to the United States and Europe and used the concept of internal colonialism to depict the situation of the Indian in national society. He contended that the state-sponsored indigenismo of men such as Manuel Gamio and Gonzalo Aguirre Beltrán was destined for failure because it took account of neither Mexico's position in the world economy nor the Indian's situation in the domestic economy. The indigenistas were attempting to create a modern Mexican nation by attacking cultural pluralism, when the real problem was Mexico's "colonial structure." Bonfil Batalla proposed to turn indigenismo on its head in terms of both means and ends. Rather than Mexicanizing the Indian, the task for committed anthropologists was to destroy the "colonial bond" that kept Indians subjugated. Rather than a culturally unified Mexican nation, the proper goal was a situation of freedom and liberation in which "the numerous ethnic entities will emerge in all their vigour."[15]

Bonfil Batalla was also the "guiding force" behind the "Declaration of Barbados," which was signed by eleven of the participants.[16] Employing notions of dependency and internal colonialism, the declaration announced that the official Indian policies of Latin American states were "explicitly directed towards the destruction of aboriginal culture" in order "to consolidate the status of the existing social groups and classes." Anthropology and missions were both instruments of colonial domination, but they differed in that the former field of endeavor, although guilty of hypocrisy and timidity, at least recognized "the present painful situation of the Indian," while the latter was inherently "ethnocentric," "essentially discriminatory," and "hostile" to indigenous culture.[17]

The document expressed hope for both the future of Latin American states and the discipline of anthropology. Despite the Latin American states' gross dereliction of their responsibilities toward indigenous peoples in the past, the declaration called for the national governments of Latin America to take sole charge of the welfare of indigenous people and to appoint a suitable "national public authority responsible for relations with Indian groups" that could not delegate its powers to any other organization "at any time or under any circumstances." Anthropologists would take on the new assignment of "providing the colonized people with the data and interpretations both about themselves and their colonizers useful for their own fight for freedom" and denouncing genocide and ethnocide "by any and all means."[18]

The document showed no such optimism about the third agent in the indigenous equation, concluding that "the suspension of all missionary activity is the most appropriate policy for the good of Indian society and for the moral integrity of the churches involved." Knowing that this call was unlikely to be heeded, the declaration outlined ten "minimal obligations" in the areas of justice, equity, and respect for indigenous culture that missions must meet in order to avoid being held responsible for "crimes of ethnocide and connivance at genocide." Because the connection between the evangelical process and political domination was "intrinsic," because missions were fundamentally a "mechanism of colonialization, Europeanization and alienation," and because elements within the churches themselves were recognizing the "historical failure of the missionary task," the overwhelming implication was the futility of reform. Missions simply had no legitimate role among indigenous peoples.[19]

One reason why these social scientists might have had such a negative opinion of Protestant missionaries was that Latin American Protestantism showed clear signs of a political metamorphosis by the 1960s. Until then, Protestantism had a definite association with liberalism, not only in the minds of Protestants but also in the minds of Latin American intellectuals. In one example of this phenomenon, a "who's who" list of leading Latin American intellectuals (mostly not Protestants) contributed to the Protestant journal *La Nueva Democracia* (1920–63).[20] By the 1960s, however, Protestantism had split into two distinct political camps: one was still liberal and critical of U.S. imperialism, but the other was increasingly successful in urban areas, conservative, technologically savvy, and open to or supportive of U.S. foreign policy.[21] Any purveyor of reactionary politics would have been anathema to radical social scientists.

Until this point the SIL had remained fairly insulated from the growing critiques of anthropology and indigenismo. Although its ally, indigenismo, had suffered some serious wounds, the SIL itself had experienced no more than a few scratches. Missions had been linked by Jaulin and the "Declaration of Barbados" to colonialism and ethnocide, but direct references to the SIL had been rare. Protests were developing in Peru and Colombia, but Mexico still seemed to be friendly ground for the SIL. Nevertheless, Protestantism and missions were gaining a higher profile and attracting the attention of Mexican anthropologists. In 1970 the INAH's Museum of Anthropology began an exploratory survey of Protestantism in Mexico that produced an introduction to the major issues surrounding Protestantism in 1973. Included in the report was a chapter devoted to the "imperialist, pseudo-scientific agency known as the Summer Institute of Linguistics."[22] With Bonfil Batalla at the helm of the INAH (1972–76) and then of its research arm, the Center for Advanced Research

(1976–80), it is no surprise that Mexican anthropologists began to devote great attention to the SIL. The SIL's high profile as an ally of Mexican indigenismo, its deliberately ambiguous religious background, and its North American sources of funding would have invited increased scrutiny, even without the charges emerging from the Barbados conference. With the strongest voice from Barbados leading Mexico's anthropologists, however, it was only a matter of time before the spotlight turned to the SIL.

Focus on the SIL

Much new evidence came to light in December 1973 when the North American Congress on Latin America (NACLA) printed Laurie Hart's "Story of the Wycliffe Translators: Pacifying the Last Frontiers."[23] Since 1970, NACLA researchers had been attempting "to contribute to the development of revolutionary political forces" in the United States by conducting a "Church Research Project" designed to expose religion and religious institutions as "pillars of bourgeois ideology" and to demonstrate the ways in which religious people were advancing the "political and economic interests of the government and the corporations."[24] Hart's article caught the attention of anthropologists around the world. Virtually every major denunciation of the SIL in the coming years—and there would be many—would cite the article's evidence for claims against the SIL, as would an official report that eventually led to the end of the SIL's formal relationship with the Mexican state.[25]

The great strength of "Pacifying the Last Frontiers" was that it united a great deal of information about the SIL in one compact article. Unlike the case studies presented at Barbados or a denunciation of the SIL made by Colombian anthropologists in 1972, which could be dismissed by skeptics as anomalies, Hart was able to buttress her broad condemnation of the SIL with charts and statistics demonstrating its vast size (more than three thousand linguists), an overview of the organization's history, and a comprehensible theory of how the SIL fit into the global expansion of capitalism. For anthropologists alerted by the "Declaration of Barbados" to the problem of missions and for those already concerned about the SIL, Hart's article came at the perfect time.

What was the SIL? One could see from the text of Hart's article and the accompanying charts that the SIL was both an evangelical mission and a "global corporation" that worked in Brazil, Colombia, Guatemala, Vietnam, and a host of other nations where revolutionary movements were springing up—or had been violently repressed. What was the SIL's real purpose? "Generally," Hart argues, "the translators have the task of (a) insuring that indigenous consciousness not proceed beyond defense of the status quo and (b) moving it in the direction of peaceful submission to the incursions of civilization." How and why did the SIL do this? The SIL's ideology "derives from and also supports a specific political orientation," an orientation favoring the military and industrial interests of the United States.[26]

Hart's most damning evidence appears in a section of the article devoted to the SIL's role in Vietnam. First of all, although no direct link to the CIA has been established "yet," she demonstrates that the SIL has received at least three grants from the U.S. Agency for International Development (USAID) for work in that country. From the SIL's own *Translation* magazine, Hart could also see that the organization clearly favored the victory of the U.S.-sponsored South over the Communist North. She found hard evidence of the SIL's "imperialist and racist missionary objectives" in the following words from *Translation,* which are worth quoting at length, since they scandalized the Latin American left more than anything else in her article: "God uses military troops, but he has other methods also. . . . God turned the tables in Indonesia on the eve of a Marxist revolution, and the spiritual response of thousands turning to Christ has been tremendous. Cambodia put all missionaries out of their country in 1965, and it seemed that God's work there was finished. Suddenly—a coup d'état and a new responsiveness to missionary work."[27]

Although in evangelical circles these sentiments probably appeared unremarkable—theists as far back as the Pentateuch had affirmed the divine role in the rise and fall of earthly kingdoms without necessarily endorsing the human agents involved—to Hart and her readers the SIL seemed to be calling for the violent overthrow of progressive and revolutionary regimes.[28] Hart is right that the SIL favored non-Marxist governments, but, as can be seen in the quotation above, the major reason for this was that the SIL needed a certain amount of religious liberty to carry out its programs. The SIL valued "spiritual responsiveness" far more than right-wing politics and was prepared to work with governments of the left or the right, as its genesis in Cardenista Mexico demonstrated.[29]

Although Hart had established no definite link between the CIA and the SIL in Vietnam, she had raised the possibility that such a link did exist. When a new deluge of revelations about the CIA's use of anthropologists, students, and missionaries in Mexico came in 1974, those who had accepted Hart's account could scarcely avoid the inference that if the CIA was working in Mexico the SIL would be one of its likely fronts.[30] The fact that anthropologists in Colombia and Peru were denouncing the SIL for activities ranging from brainwashing Indians to gathering information for the CIA and that both countries were debating ending their contracts with the SIL gave even more weight to such suspicions.[31]

The fireworks really started, though, in September 1975, when Allegro Marzialle charged the SIL, the Mission Aviation Fellowship (another U.S.-based missionary organization), and social scientists from Harvard University with hiding behind supposedly religious or altruistic motives to carry out espionage in Chiapas. These missionaries, anthropologists, and pilots might deny being connected, Marzialle wrote, "but to local observers it is obvious that all these North American agents are well acquainted with one another, help each other, and work with a single plan."[32]

In October 1975 the first National Congress of Indigenous Peoples issued a document called the "Carta de las comunidades indígenas" ("Letter from the indigenous communities"), which suggested that the Mexican congress reform most of the institutions that dealt with indigenous people. The "Carta" was not a radical document, nor did it pay much attention to the SIL. Since most of its signatories were bilingual teachers dependent on the state for their salaries, it focused rather on giving indigenismo a more progressive slant, raising the budget for the INI, and creating a National Indigenous University. The one sentence that mentioned the SIL's now generally accepted ties to the CIA did so not in the context of the SIL's negative effects on indigenous communities but as a criticism of the "decline of anthropological training."[33]

The "Carta" faded quickly into obscurity, but another document that emerged from the congress, or at least from social scientists who were attending it, soon gained great prominence. On 8 October 1975, thirty-one anthropologists and sociologists signed the "Denuncia de Pátzcuaro," which was directed entirely at the SIL. The signatories, who included Margarita Nolasco and the INI's adjunct director, Salomón Nahmad, claimed that the SIL was a "pseudo-scientific agency linked with the CIA" that caused division in indigenous communities, devalued indigenous culture, and did medical experiments on unsuspecting Indians. The SIL's proselytism and "ideological penetration" were especially bothersome because they were being carried out with the support of the Mexican government. The only solution, argued the "Denuncia," was the immediate nullification of the convenio, suspension of the SIL's activities, and nationalization of its property.[34]

Nahmad's endorsement added great weight to the "Denuncia," for a high official at the nation's premier indigenista agency was now publicly breaking with the SIL. His signature also represented the effects of the growing barrage of negative publicity about the SIL. As director of indigenous education for the SEP, Nahmad had toured the SIL headquarters in 1971 and had maintained a cordial relationship with the SIL during the next few years, going so far as to address their annual meeting in 1973.[35] But gradually he had become convinced that the SIL was not what it said it was. Particularly influential in his change of opinion were the accusations about the SIL's role in Vietnam.[36] If a former friend was now committed to the SIL's demise, the tide truly had turned.

As plans were made for a second conference in Barbados, the SIL scrambled to defend itself. In accordance with its usual strategy, its major efforts went toward wooing influential Mexicans and by displaying its own pro-Mexican sentiments. Thus, Cameron Townsend launched the second edition of his biography of Lázaro Cárdenas, while the Mexico branch sought an influential new leader for its advisory board. Both plans seem to have been successful. A new edition of *Lázaro Cárdenas, Mexican Democrat* containing six new chapters garnered generally favorable reviews and won some positive publicity for the SIL.[37] And the new leader of the advisory board was none other than Amalia Solórzano, Cárdenas's widow. Now, attacking the SIL would mean attacking a living icon of the revolution.[38] The great man's son, Cuauhtémoc, was even invited to speak to the Mexico branch in September 1976. Although he did not seem entirely sure that the allegations against the SIL were false, he left declaring himself still a "friend of the SIL."[39]

The SIL was going to need all the friends it could muster, for the second Barbados conference, in July 1977, had a decidedly anti-SIL tendency, and more specifically an anti-SIL-in-Mexico tendency. Once again Guillermo Bonfil Batalla would play a leading role, but this time Mexico was also represented by two new researchers for the INAH, Miguel Alberto Bartolomé, who had left dirty war–era Argentina, and Stefano Varese, who had fled Peru after the downfall of the progressive Velasco government in 1975. Mexico was also represented by three indigenous leaders: Cirila Sánchez Mendoza of the Chatino communities, Natalio Hernández of the newly founded Alliance of Bilingual Indigenous Professionals, and Víctor de la Cruz, a Zapotec poet and intellectual with firsthand experience of the SIL's work in his hometown of Juchitán, Oaxaca. But perhaps most ominous for the SIL was the role to be played by Mexico's Anthropological Center for the Documentation of Latin America (ACDLA), which was in the process of forming a public archive on the activities of the SIL and had been asked to organize the conference.[40]

The information packet that ACDLA provided to the conference's thirty-five participants included two negative articles on the SIL, one by ACDLA's anti-SIL specialist Nemesio Rodríguez and one by Soren Hvalkof and Peter Aaby, Danish anthropologists who would soon publish their own influential denunciation of the SIL.[41] These articles, together with the knowledge and experience of the participants, led the conference to adopt a resolution called "The Colonialist Policy of the SIL," which was only slightly shorter than the conference's main document, "The Declaration of Barbados II." Where previous attacks on the SIL had assumed that its linguistics work was a smoke screen for its deeper purpose of ideological manipulation, the new statement presented the SIL's linguistics work as integral to its overall mission. Apparently, the SIL had two political objectives that involved linguistics itself. It wanted "to present a scenario of extreme dialectic and linguistic fragmentation, in order to demonstrate the implausibility of forming standardized linguistic communities, which are essential to the development of the political projects of liberation of the Indian peoples, and to foment the unhistorical, static and regressive idea that indigenous languages are incapable of absorbing the new collective experiences that confront oppressed peoples. In other words, they are denied the possibility of their own conceptual and linguistic interpretation of social dynamics and of nature."[42]

Through such policies of division and manipulation, carried out by its own corps of acculturated bilingual teachers and facilitated by "coercive evangelization," the SIL was starting "to control vast areas that constitute enclaves of strategic importance for imperialism's geo-political domination of the continent and for the eventual appropriation of natural resources." Despite apparent areas of agreement with the SIL—for instance, the statement's fundamental premise that "the vernacular language is a fundamental factor in the existence and in the liberation process of every people"—no room was left for compromise.[43]

The main reason for this blanket condemnation of the SIL, with its utter lack of hope for reforming it, may be found in the declaration's "main objective" for the struggle for liberation, which was "to achieve the unity of the Indian population," which would take place when indigenous communities in the Americas understood the true nature of their relationship to the state and society, which was one of physical and cultural domination. The second step, once indigenous people had been united, would be for them "to take control of the historical process and to end the era of colonization."[44] Thus, the SIL's principal fault was that its policies were seen to prevent the union of Indian populations, a charge based on the optimistic assumption that such populations could be united and that linguistic differences between, say, different Mixtec groups in Mexico were minor. It was not explained how the "fundamental" importance of the mother tongue—"a people that has lost its language has great difficulties in defining its identity and its historical project"—squared with the implied duty of linguists to unite indigenous populations.[45] Were they supposed to develop "master" languages that combined elements of different variants? Were they supposed to impose one variant on the speakers of other variants? Ironically, the participants in the second Barbados conference, enthused about a political vision and uninformed about the complexities of descriptive linguistics, were calling for a version of the "cultural domination" that they said they opposed. In this case at least, it was the SIL that was affirming the particularities of specific indigenous communities, while the anthropologists and indigenous representatives were calling for the leveling of such differences in the name of pan-Indian solidarity.[46]

Whatever the inconsistencies in hindsight of the second Barbados conference, its conclusions proved convincing and interesting enough in the succeeding months to generate three follow-up conferences in Mexico.[47] The combination of these four conferences and the resulting attacks in the press finally seem to have put the SIL on the defensive.[48] The organization stepped up its public relations efforts to almost a fever pitch, working all possible government contacts, wooing the new head of the Instituto Indigenista Interamericano, making contact with the president's sister (Alicia López Portillo), inaugurating the new Mexico-Cárdenas Museum at the Jungle Aviation and Radio Service headquarters in North Carolina, and meeting with critical anthropologists such as Nahmad and Félix Báez-Jorge.[49]

The SIL made every effort to train new branch members in government relations. "We have written to the new members of the branch," the public relations director explained, "informing them that we would like to have them accompany us to some of the offices as we make our calls in order for them to get a feeling for the kind of relationship that we have and the way in which we handle these contacts, even before they go to the villages." Even the cooks were told how to explain the SIL's linguistic mission to visitors. If anyone asked about receiving support from USAID, branch members needed to be perfectly honest about receiving "jeeps, mechanical equipment, and a helicopter" for the SIL's work in Mexico.[50]

Townsend, deeply concerned about the situation in Mexico and aware of the suspicion directed toward all missionaries because of the CIA's use of some, wrote to Presidents Ford and Carter, requesting that they not only end the policy of using missionaries to gather intelligence but also end the cold war itself.[51] Ford and Carter did not feel quite prepared to shut down the CIA or to announce the closing of the cold war, but friends did arrange for Townsend to receive Mexico's highest honor for foreigners, the Aztec Eagle, from Ambassador to the United States Hugo Margaín in June 1978.[52]

The Noose Tightens

Despite its many efforts, the SIL simply could not reach one group of people: the rising generation of anthropologists, some of whom now held positions of influence. The problem was less the evident disdain that Bonfil Batalla, Stavenhagen, Nahmad, and their colleagues felt for the SIL and more the nature of the changes they wanted to see take place in indigenismo. Basically, they wanted to transform the principles and activities of indigenismo so profoundly that it would no longer need the SIL. Taking seriously more than a decade of denunciations of colonialist anthropology, cultural imperialism, and North American espionage, they had come to a place where cooperating with the SIL was not really a possibility they could take seriously. Traditional SIL tactics of dinners, visits, letters, pro-Mexican articles, and even an Aztec Eagle had little chance to sway them. Anthropologists who were committed to ending colonialism, liberating indigenous peoples, and, as Bonfil Batalla had said at the first Barbados conference, seeing ethnic cultures "emerge in all their vigour" saw getting rid of the SIL as a necessary first step in a much larger process.

Nahmad, because of his positions as adjunct director of the INI, director of indigenous education for the SEP, and vice-president of the new Colegio de Etnólogos y Antropólogos Sociales (CEAS; College of Ethnologists and Social Anthropologists), played a particularly important role in both the development of the new indigenismo and the crusade to bring down the SIL.[53] Fueled with optimism by President José López Portillo's willingness to devote increased financial resources to indigenous causes, Nahmad set forth an ambitious plan to include vastly expanded numbers of indigenous youths in government programs by 1982. He proposed not just bilingual education but a new "bilingual, bicultural education" that would do away with paternalism and ethnocentrism once and for all. By "paying attention to the maternal culture of the students" in "both the content of the teaching and in methods of teaching," this new education would allow indigenous students "to understand their own cultural values and to participate in the articulation of those values in national society."[54]

Although this vision rejected the old indigenismo, it was not antinationalistic. It reconceptualized the nation and nationalism in a pluralist form that welcomed new ethnic contributions but rejected any interference from colonial and imperial powers, especially the United States. Thus, Nahmad came to believe that the SIL represented two dangerous trends that threatened his plans: on the one hand, the United States' use of social scientists to gather intelligence for the purposes of control and domination; on the other hand, its policy of fomenting Protestantism and other ideologies that fractured collective identities.[55] Even when missionaries provided seemingly helpful services, they still posed a threat to indigenous communities because they were inducing those communities to participate in a "systematic boycott" of official government programs, turning them away from their natural allies and toward imperialist oppressors.[56]

Meanwhile, Bonfil Batalla and Stavenhagen were attempting to create a corps of indigenous linguists that would make the SIL's services superfluous. In January 1978, Stavenhagen, head of the SEP's Popular Culture section, began a five-month program in the state of México designed "to help indigenous people to conserve their own cultural values" by teaching them enough linguistics to enable them "to set down in their own language and in writing the distinctive features of their culture."[57] Bonfil Batalla's Center for Advanced Research developed a more ambitious degree-level program to give indigenous teachers thorough training in linguistics and ethnology so that they could "promote the linguistic and ethnic development of their own communities." The program would not only provide technical skills but would also foster a process of "intellectual and even emotional decolonization" so that its students could recognize the "historical alternatives faced by indigenous peoples." Courses would be offered on such topics as "Indigenous Resistance" and "Theory and Practice of Self-Government," subjects the SIL would be unlikely to cover.[58]

On 26 January 1979, Nahmad requested that Secretary of Education Fernando Solana appoint a "committee of review" that would examine the SEP's convenio with the SIL and "try to cancel it or at least to reduce its scope."[59] Solana probably saw Nahmad's request as a good opportunity to dispense with the SEP's increasingly controversial ally, for he not only accepted the idea of an investigation but also appointed a commission formed of known foes of the SIL: Nahmad, Bonfil Batalla, Stavenhagen, and INI director Ignacio Ovalle. The CEAS soon got wind of the investigation in the SEP—Nahmad, after all, was vice-president of the CEAS, and Bonfil Batalla, Stavenhagen, and Ovalle were also involved in the organization—and informed Solana that it was going to conduct its own investigation of the SIL.[60]

While Nahmad and his colleagues studied the SIL, they issued a number of statements that suggested the direction in which their report was heading: Ovalle called for the SEP and the Ministry of the Interior to investigate whether the SIL should be expelled from the country; Nahmad implied that the SIL was to blame for Mexico's lack of linguists and referred to the SIL as a North American intelligence agency; and a newspaper reported Stavenhagen as saying that the SIL had contributed nothing to Mexican linguistics and that it was the one benefiting from the convenio.[61] Thus it was no surprise when the committee's "confidential memorandum," submitted to Solana on 19 June 1979, called for the immediate termination of the convenio.[62]

The memorandum's argument was clear, concise, practical, and, compared to the manifesto soon to be issued by the CEAS, balanced. It noted the divisive consequences of the SIL's presence in indigenous communities, faulted its compliance with the convenio, and suggested that the educational materials it had produced were of dubious quality. The memo admitted that the SIL had made some important contributions to the field of linguistics but lamented that few of its theoretical works had been translated into Spanish. Consequently, the convenio had benefited the SIL at the expense of the nation's indigenous people. "The SEP," concluded the report, "has fulfilled all the duties required of it by the convenio but the SIL has only fulfilled those that coincide with its interests and has failed to comply with those duties that are not important to its purposes, goals and projects."[63]

The memo also raised the possibility that the convenio could cause grave harm to the SEP's reputation. Members of the committee had heard reports from Gerald Zilg and Charlotte Dennett "of the *New York Times*" that their three-year investigation of the SIL had uncovered "a close relationship between this Institute and certain circles of economic power in the United States that require strategic information for the political control of the marginalized regions of the world and basic knowledge about the natural resources of these regions, including petroleum, minerals, and forest resources." Although the SIL had primarily religious, not geopolitical, objectives, these powerful groups had taken advantage of the "good faith" that characterized many of the SIL's linguists. When Zilg and Dennett's book appeared it would have an impact "similar to that of Watergate" and would compromise the SEP's image in the "public opinion of the nation and the world." Having heard this information, even the Cárdenas family was distancing itself from the SIL, the committee reported.[64]

Meanwhile, the situation heated up still further. The "Supreme Councils" of the Mazahuas, Otomis, Tlahuicas, and Matlazincas condemned the SIL in a joint statement called the "Declaración de Temoaya."[65] In August 1979, Nahmad sent a "technical commission" to investigate the SIL's properties in Chiapas. If that was not enough to let the SIL know that it was in deep trouble, by late August the press was reporting that a "memorandum written by a commission charged by the Secretary of Education with a preliminary analysis of the SIL" was circulating through "the different institutions where social scientists, linguists and teachers work."[66]

On 7 September 1979 the members of the CEAS gathered for a special assembly to consider the results of the investigation conducted by its own commission. The assembly approved the conclusion that the SIL was "an essentially missionary, political and ideological institution" that functioned as an aid to the expansion of capitalism through the "control, regulation, penetration, surveillance and repression" of indigenous peoples. The CEAS statement went further than the SEP's "confidential memorandum" in that it linked the SIL's project with the Mexican state's own project of control and domination. The SIL was one of many groups (including less committed anthropologists) working "at the service of imperialism and of the State." Therefore, the CEAS called not merely for an end to all contracts and relationships of the Mexican state with the SIL but also for the SIL's "immediate and definitive expulsion" from Mexico.[67]

Two weeks later, on 21 September, the SEP severed its relationship with the SIL.[68] Sensing that the next stage of the battle would be fought over the physical presence of its linguists in Mexico, and knowing that it now lacked the protective legitimacy conferred by the convenio, the SIL moved quickly to forestall one of the common charges against it, that it was engaged in subversive activities in Chiapas. It closed down its "Jungle Training Camp" in Yaxoquintelá, auctioned off the camp's equipment, and sold its house in San Cristóbal de Las Casas.[69] It also began a gradual withdrawal of all of its personnel from the state, so that it could say truthfully that its work there was done. When the common charge was made that, although the SIL claimed to work in a given community only until a New Testament, grammar, and dictionary were finished, many translation teams seemed to remain in indigenous communities indefinitely, the branch could point to Chiapas as evidence of its resolve to move on when it accomplished its goals.

Although the Ministry of the Interior never went so far as to revoke the visas of all SIL personnel, in late 1979 it made the decision to stop renewing SIL visas, which had almost the same effect. Gradually, as their visas expired, about 140 linguists and support personnel had to leave Mexico during the closing months of 1980. Most settled along the border, with a large contingent clustering around the new headquarters of the Mexico branch outside Tucson, Arizona.[70]

The eighth Inter-American Indigenista Conference in Mérida in November 1980, attended by Cameron Townsend and other SIL representatives, brought the SIL even more trouble. The SIL had long enjoyed cordial relations with the Instituto Indigenista Interamericano. In the 1950s, for instance, under the leadership of Manuel Gamio, the III had worked closely with the SIL's Ethel Wallis on projects involving the Otomis of the Mezquital Valley. Under Miguel León Portilla in the 1960s the III had used the SIL's Dow Robinson as a liaison for an III project involving the Nahuas of Puebla.[71] In Brasilia in 1972 at the previous III congress, as mentioned earlier in this chapter, Townsend had been honored by the III as a "Benefactor" of monolingual Indians. The tone in Mérida, however, was much different from what it had been in Brasilia in 1972. A "parallel forum" led by Nahmad, Bonfil Batalla, and Félix Báez-Jorge angrily denounced the SIL, while even the official delegations (except Chile, Brazil, Bolivia, Costa Rica, and Paraguay) adopted a resolution that all member nations should investigate the activities of the SIL. The final humiliation came when the congress passed a resolution to rescind the honor given to Townsend in Brasilia and the gathered delegates rose to their feet to applaud for seven minutes. Townsend retreated from the room in disgrace.[72]

Espionage, Imperialism, and Division

A chapter as full of denunciations as this one demands some attempt at assessing the validity of those charges, although the sheer variety of accusations against the SIL makes dealing with all of them impractical. Eliminating allegations that strain credulity, such as those about missile silos in Chiapas or uranium smuggling in Oaxaca, leaves a few major themes that come up again and again: linguistic ineptness, espionage, cultural imperialism, promotion of capitalism, and the division of communities. The short answer is a qualified "no" to the first two charges and a qualified "yes" to the latter three.

In the area of the SIL's linguistic competency, professional linguists will have to be the ones to judge, but it strains credulity to believe that the SIL is full of linguistic charlatans. The simple fact that their dictionaries and grammars are often the first and sometimes the *only* linguistic materials available in many Mesoamerican languages makes their contribution to the science of linguistics quite valuable. Many linguists who have no ideological sympathy with the SIL use these materials profitably; those who reject these materials because of the political orientation of those who produced them are displaying remarkable ideological purity but may be limiting their own knowledge to no great political effect.

It is also clear, though, that SIL linguists have as their primary goal the translation of the New Testament rather than the spreading or deepening of linguistic knowledge. Their theoretical contributions to linguistics, therefore, are of less value than their descriptive work. Ken Pike was the obvious exception to this generalization, but he was by no means the only serious linguist whom the SIL in Mexico produced. Eunice Pike, Joe Grimes, Doris Bartholomew, Velma Pickett, William Wonderly, Sarah Gudschinsky, David Tuggy, Steve Marlett, and Jim Watters have all made substantive contributions to the field. It may be true that the average SIL linguist lacked the theoretical sophistication of these more distinguished colleagues, but this in no way diminishes the value of their descriptive contributions.

In fact, most criticism of SIL linguistics quickly transformed into criticism of the SIL's destruction of indigenous culture. Obviously, the cultural impact of the SIL is an important issue, but equally obviously, it is a separate issue from whether they performed linguistic work adequately. The one area where the critics seemed to have good evidence of shoddy work was that of literacy materials. On both the theoretical and practical levels, the SIL's approach to literacy demonstrated serious flaws. Cameron Townsend, remember, had convinced Mexican linguists and indigenistas that literacy in the mother tongue would lead to Spanish language acquisition, but as Linda King points out, "there is no particular pedagogical or linguistic basis for assuming that the teaching of literacy in one language necessarily aids the learning of a foreign language, in this case Spanish." In a detailed study of SIL literacy materials, Gloria Bravo Ahuja concluded that SIL primers presented language in an "arbitrarily fragmented" and unscientific manner.[73]

As far as espionage is concerned, no one has ever produced good evidence linking the SIL to the CIA or any other intelligence agency. Three major denunciations of the SIL do not pretend otherwise.

Laurie Hart admits that "no covert association with U.S. intelligence or paramilitary organizations such as the CIA has yet been revealed." David Stoll contends, "For self-preservation if nothing else, the SIL evidently has tried to keep its distance from intelligence gathering and official violence." Gloria Pérez and Scott Robinson acknowledge that evidence of ties between the SIL and the CIA was "largely circumstantial."[74]

This does not mean that no member of the SIL ever served the CIA or passed on information. (One name often mentioned in this context is Larry Montgomery of the Peru branch.)[75] It would be surprising if an organization as large as the SIL had not been infiltrated by some U.S. intelligence agents. This puts the SIL in the same class as a number of other organizations whose good faith has been exploited by the CIA, but it does not make it into the kind of covert counterrevolutionary force often portrayed in the Latin American press.

The latter three allegations are, to my mind at least, much more interesting and will be dealt with at greater length in the book's conclusion. For now it should be sufficient to say that these three allegations seem to be valid, if partial, descriptions of the SIL's impact in many of the communities where it worked in Mexico. It needs to be said, though, that replacing indigenous "superstition" with more "modern" religion and opening formerly isolated communities to capitalism and to the state was to a large extent what Mexican elites hoped the SIL would do. As far as division is concerned, nobody in the Mexican government or the SIL saw dividing communities as a conscious goal, but both knew that division could be the by-product of Mexicanization and evangelization.

The merits of the above policies are clearly debatable. What needs to be emphasized here is that in allying itself so closely with the Mexican state, the SIL was not simply "submitting" to government power; it was allying itself with a specific political posture. In contrast to its own statements, such as Townsend's belief that his idiosyncratic interpretation of Romans 13 took the SIL "out of politics," embracing the indigenista policies of the Mexican regime put the SIL squarely in the middle of politics. Even in a democracy as moribund as Mexico's between 1935 and 1980, it would be disingenuous to insist that "submission" to the state and "honoring rulers" necessitated adopting the policies of the state as one's own. Townsend and his heirs led the SIL deep into the bosom of Mexican politics, a policy that paid political dividends for many years but which eventually had a definite political cost.

From the standpoint of Mexican anthropologists, it is easy to see why the SIL triggered such strong emotions. At a time when social scientists were not only trying to exorcise their colonialist ghosts but also attempting to distance themselves from Western civilization itself, Mexican anthropologists constantly confronted the presence of fundamentalist Christian missionaries from the United States working as the de facto linguistics department of the Mexican state. Even without allegations about the CIA and the advance of global capitalism, this would have been a hard pill to swallow.[76]

The conflict waged in Mexico between the SIL and its opponents during the late 1970s was in many ways an odd one. On the one hand, anthropologists, intellectuals, indigenous leaders, and other opponents of the SIL launched barrage after barrage of newspaper articles, academic papers, political speeches, and conference proceedings attacking every aspect of the SIL's practices and policies. On the other hand, the SIL scarcely made any public statements at all. Gonzalo Báez-Camargo and Gonzalo Aguirre Beltrán wrote a few newspaper columns, but in general the SIL's defense effort occurred in dining rooms, offices, and other private meeting places. For all the SIL's opponents' sympathy for revolutionaries in Vietnam, for all their inspiration in Andre Gunder Frank's call for each anthropologist to lead ten thousand guerrillas, their actual campaign against the SIL took the form of a partisan smear campaign. In short, the putative radicals achieved their objective by means of political tactics that were not uncommon in the Western liberal democracies for which they professed disdain.

The SIL, on the other hand, despite its long protestations of being above politics, displayed an enviable grasp of the realities of power in twentieth-century Mexico. In January 1981, only a few weeks after the painful III conference in Mérida, Townsend and SIL Mexico branch leaders Bob Goerz, Ben Elson, and John Alsop met with President López Portillo in his private office at Los Pinos. Before getting down to business, Townsend thanked the president for awarding him the Aztec Eagle in 1978: "Then I told him that we needed a solution to our problems so that our people who had had to leave Mexico could return. I explained to him how we want to give an alphabet to every linguistic group, how we want to analyze the grammar of their languages, how we want to form dictionaries for linguistic science. But above all we want to give them the Bible. We feel that each group has a right to that spiritual treasure. The President seemed to be in accord and told us that we do not need to worry, that things will be taken care of. We came out of his office rejoicing!"

Then the group met with the president's personal secretary to iron out the details. "He was just as attentive as the President had been. It was fabulous. He wanted to know what the problems were. He told Goerz, who was handling things, to describe the special treatment the government had given us in the past, and he would see that everything was reinstated so that we could go ahead with our program until every one of the 150 languages of Mexico has been reached."[77]

The details of exactly what López Portillo did for the SIL are not yet available in the archives, but the results are clear: the SIL was permitted to stay in Mexico and its linguists were slowly allowed to return to the country, so that by the 1990s it seemed to be operating at levels similar to those of 1979. The anthropologists who thought they had won the war with the SIL realized that they had only won one battle and that, despite everything, the SIL was still operating in Mexico, now without any contractual obligations to restrain its evangelistic activities. Hearings in the Mexican Senate in 1983, an investigative committee in 1984, continual denunciations by anthropologists and indigenous leaders shocked to find that the SIL was still in their country—nothing could dislodge the SIL from Mexico. The time and energy that the SIL had devoted to friendships and allegiances over the previous fifty years had paid rich dividends.

Conclusion

In the fall of 1999 the municipal president of Mitla, Oaxaca, spoke in Zapotec to a group of about one hundred people. He blushed and stammered a bit as he spoke, as if he had not spoken the language for years, then regained his composure as he switched to Spanish. Clearly he wanted to establish that he was not only an educated Spanish-speaking municipal president but also an indigenous leader still in touch with his roots. After he sat down, a number of young men and women took their turns at the front of the room. They too spoke indigenous languages before switching to Spanish, but their words in the vernacular languages often rang out with more clarity and confidence than their fluent Spanish.

The worst fears of the SIL's opponents had been realized, for this scene took place not at an INI conference or a political convention but at an SIL-sponsored conference on linguistics for SIL-affiliated indigenous translators at an SIL-owned linguistics center in Mexico. At the close of the twentieth century the SIL was still working in Mexico and intertwining religion, politics, and science. Although it had surrendered its Mexico City headquarters ten years earlier, the SIL continued to fill its busy translation centers in Ixmiquilpan, Hidalgo, and Mitla, Oaxaca, with North American and European linguists and their indigenous assistants. If the number of translators operating in Mexico was reduced from its height in the 1970s, this was more a function of past successes (completed language projects) and new translation strategies than of opposition from the Mexican state.

Although 140 linguists had left the country in the early 1980s due to the aforementioned visa problems, there had never been any blanket prohibition on the SIL's presence or work in Mexico. In 1983 and 1984, hearings on the SIL in the Mexican Senate and the rumor that President José López Portillo had ordered the expulsion of all SIL linguists led many anthropologists to believe that the SIL's days in Mexico were numbered. But as Cameron Townsend's statement at the end of the previous chapter indicates, any such hope was wishful thinking. Some linguists did leave Mexico for good, but these were mostly those who had finished or nearly finished their translation work. Virtually all the translators from Chiapas, for instance, left Mexico having completed New Testaments in their respective languages. Other linguists left for a few years, then returned when the situation had cooled off in the late 1980s and early 1990s. Katherine Voigtlander, for example, spent most of the 1980s working on various tasks for the SIL in the United States, including the creation of the Museum of the Alphabet in Waxhaw, North Carolina, before returning to Hidalgo in 1990. Some linguists never had to leave Mexico at all.

In general, it seems that the SIL tried to lower its profile by encouraging linguists to do as much work as they could in the United States, by moving the headquarters of the Mexico branch across the border to Arizona, and by developing a new, less obtrusive strategy of Bible translation that significantly reduced the SIL's impact on indigenous communities. Basically, translators started spending much less time in indigenous villages: they spent two or three years there to learn the language, then moved to cities or large towns for the rest of their work. Rather than spending decades of their lives in indigenous villages, translators began to invite their indigenous assistants to come to urban areas to work there on the translation of the New Testament. The new strategy meant that in the 1990s SIL linguists were much less likely to be major influences on indigenous communities, but it also meant that they had come much closer to validating one of the criticisms leveled at them: that they were outsiders who really did not understand indigenous culture yet were meddling with it in a way destined to change it profoundly.

Rather than reviewing what has been said in the previous chapters, this conclusion will take up some of the larger issues raised by the SIL's years in Mexico. Specifically, it examines missionaries and social scientists as political actors. In the same way that SIL linguists did not, and could not, function in a purely religious realm, Mexican social scientists did not, and could not, simply study indigenous peoples and write esoteric papers for the academy. At times, concern for indigenous people brought the SIL and social scientists together as allies in a common project; at other times, concern for indigenous people led the SIL and social scientists in very different directions.

The SIL did not arrive in Mexico and immediately start "sharing the Word." From Cameron Townsend's first days in the country during the height of anticlericalism in the 1930s until the SIL's own days of crisis in the late 1970s and early 1980s, Townsend and the SIL found themselves immersed in concerns far beyond those of more traditional evangelical missions. Since the SIL worked as both a Christian missionary organization and a scientific arm of the Mexican state, it functioned simultaneously in the realms of religion, science, and politics. Although church-state conflict has been a common theme in Mexican history, as has the related struggle between reason and science against religion and "superstition," the SIL's union of Protestantism, personalistic politics, and linguistics made it one of the few avowedly religious institutions extensively involved in both politics and science.[1]

This commitment to three contested fields of human endeavor might seem to have needlessly complicated the SIL's primarily religious mission, but it had some definite advantages. Because the SIL was not simply a mission but also a scientific organization with political connections, it surmounted or bypassed barriers that blocked the expansion of other religious organizations. Linguistics and political connections opened doors that remained closed to others. John Dale, for instance, was a North American missionary who began trying to start a mission to Indians in Mexico at almost exactly the same time as Cameron Townsend. Fifty years later, Dale's Mexican Indian Mission employed a handful of missionaries and worked in only one area of Mexico, whereas Townsend's organization had become one of the largest mission agencies in the world. In general, linguistics and personal politics served the SIL's religious mission, opening doors that would have been closed to a purely religious entity. At the same time, though, the SIL's religious identity was not entirely superfluous to its appeal to Mexican politicians and indigenistas, especially in its early years in Mexico, since for Cárdenas and others Protestantism was vastly preferable to Catholicism.

In the 1930s the desire of the Callista and Cardenista regimes to wrest rural Mexico from the clutches of "fanaticism" made both the SIL's linguistic skills and its religious project attractive to the Mexican state. A decade later, by making the religious aspect of the SIL's work more controversial, the rapprochement between church and state pushed the SIL to emphasize the scientific side of its work. Despite, and to a certain extent because of, the religious conflict of the 1940s and 1950s, the SIL worked closely with the state, as indicated by the 1951 convenio with the SEP, which enabled the SIL to function as Mexico's virtual linguistics department for almost thirty years. In the 1960s and 1970s, new anthropological understandings of the value of indigenous culture and religion and of the oppressiveness of the West cast doubt on both the SIL's scientific achievements and on the ethics of inducing indigenous peoples to change their religion. Nevertheless, the SIL managed to remain in Mexico because of its ongoing cultivation of relationships with political elites.

In terms of Mexican history, the SIL represents just the sort of religious intrusion into the political realm that Mexican liberals in the nineteenth century and their revolutionary heirs in the twentieth had devoted great attention to preventing. The Constitution of 1857, the reform laws of the Restored Republic (1867–76), and the Constitution of 1917 progressively stripped property, economic privilege, and political rights from religious institutions, with the Roman Catholic Church as the obvious target. In theory, limits on church wealth and power derived from liberalism's valuation of reason over tradition. Liberals who took their liberalism seriously believed that reliance on authority or revelation led to superstition and fanaticism and that a modern state therefore needed educated citizens who could make rational decisions free of priestly influence. In practice many nineteenth-century liberals simply adopted anticlericalism as a handy badge of ideological legitimacy that often had the added benefit of increasing their own economic opportunities by making church lands available for purchase. Still, notions of the backwardness of religion and of the necessity of diminishing its role in society continued to appeal to many on the left side of the political spectrum, through the Porfiriato and into the revolution.

The situation had changed dramatically by the end of the 1960s. Many intellectuals had come to believe that indigenous religions and the many varieties of folk Catholicism were authentic expressions of native culture that therefore deserved not only to be preserved but to be protected from external criticism of any sort. Although Protestantism in general came under attack for its impact on indigenous cultures and its connections to the United States, the SIL received a disproportionate share of criticism. For the first time, its scientific credentials proved a liability, for it was the SIL's official relationship with the SEP that brought the organization to the attention of young anthropologists such as Salomón Nahmad and Margarita Nolasco. It was now taken for granted that investigators working "at the service of the state" should abstain from any sort of religious proselytism. Similarly, the SIL/Wycliffe dual identity served only to confirm the anthropologists' worst suspicions, for why would any legitimate organization have to resort to such an obfuscation of its real purposes?

If the story of the SIL adds anything to the scholarly literature on state formation and imperial encounters, it is surely that religion can and does play a major role in both. In terms of one scholar's formulation of a "field of force" between state hegemonic processes and popular cultures of resistance, it seems clear that religion can stoke the fires of resistance or it can serve the interests of the state. Similarly, the story of the SIL seems to confirm the idea presented by Jennie Purnell in her study of Michoacán peasants that a simple categorization of peasants as "religious" or "non-religious" is not helpful, for almost all Mexican peasants were religious.[2] The real question in terms of state formation is *how*, not *whether*, religion functions. I hope that chapters 7 and 8 have made clear that the Protestantism associated with the SIL was both voluntarily accepted and voluntarily rejected, that it was at once a tool of the state and a welcome addition to some indigenous communities, that it was, in short, a contested terrain between the state and popular culture.

In a similar vein, religion can serve as a significant element of the "postcolonial" encounter in Latin America. Neither a pure mystifier nor a pure liberator, foreign religion, in this case Protestantism, was evaluated, digested, and adapted or rejected, in whole or in part, according to the needs, concerns, and dispositions of different indigenous communities. As both anecdotes and statistics demonstrate, indigenous people of Mexico responded to the SIL and its religion in a spectrum of ways that defy easy categorization.

One of contemporary Mexico's most controversial issues, the expulsion of thousands of religious and political dissidents from the Tzotzil community of San Juan Chamula in the state of Chiapas, offers a good opportunity to assess both the legacy of the SIL and how scholars and other observers have treated that legacy over the past thirty years. The expulsions from the municipio of San Juan Chamula demonstrate the ways in which the work of SIL linguists could continue to have an impact on an indigenous community long after they had returned to the United States. At the same time, the vastly different

significance that scholars have given to the SIL's role in San Juan
Chamula illuminates the ways in which scholars have struggled to
make sense of the larger issue of religious intersections with the
realms of political economy and science.

The Gospel in San Juan Chamula

Although SIL linguists Ken and Elaine Jacobs hoped to translate
the New Testament into the Tzotzil language of San Juan Chamula,
Chiapas, they were refused permission to live in San Juan Chamula.
They had to begin learning Chamulan Tzotzil in the market city of
San Cristóbal de Las Casas in 1954, at first through the help of two
Chamulan men, Domingo Hernández and Miguel Gómez Hernández.
Over the course of the next decade, as they helped the Jacobs translate
the New Testament, both men converted to Protestantism and then
shared their faith with friends and family members. While there were
still only two Chamulan evangelicals in 1964, in the course of the next
two decades Chamulan Protestantism experienced rapid growth, expanding to 35 people in 1965, 120 by 1969, 1,000 by 1976, and 4,000
by 1983.[3]

The rapid spread of Protestantism among the Chamulas is all the
more remarkable considering that it occurred in the midst of violent
campaigns of persecution. Starting in 1966 and continuing until the
present day, authorities in San Juan Chamula have attempted to rid
their municipio of Protestants and other "dissidents" by any means
necessary. For example, for the years from 1976 to 1983 Mexico's National Commission on Human Rights listed the following events in
the municipio:

15 August 1976: 600 evangelicals are expelled from various
neighborhoods.

22 August 1976: Numerous families are jailed, beaten and expelled from the Joltzemen neighborhood.

23 August 1976: Numerous families from Zactzú are jailed,
beaten and expelled.

12 September 1976: A house is burned and numerous people
are expelled.

18 November 1976: 18 people who had returned to the municipio are beaten and expelled.

30 November 1976: Nicolás Pérez Coltosh of the Chiotic neighborhood, apparently an evangelical, is assassinated; seven suspects are detained but all are soon released.

9 November 1977: 19 families from the Nichén neighborhood are expelled.

9 November 1977: Ten families from the Milpoleta neighborhood are expelled.

25 November 1978: 80 evangelicals are expelled from various neighborhoods.

16 December 1978: 75 people are expelled from five neighborhoods.

4 March 1980: 34 families are jailed, beaten and expelled from the Muquem neighborhood.

24 July 1981 Miguel "Cashlan" Gómez Hernández [the Jacobs' first convert and the first preacher in Chamula] is murdered; his nose, lips, and an ear are cut off; his eyes are gouged out and his scalp is pulled off before he is hanged.[4]

Most of the "expulsados" gathered in new Chamulan colonias formed in the 1970s and 1980s on the outskirts of San Cristóbal de Las Casas.[5] Despite repeated attempts to return to San Juan Chamula, several thousand Chamulan Protestants remained in the different refugee neighborhoods in 2005.

The intensity of the persecution of the Chamulan Protestants flows from a number of different factors. First of all, San Juan Chamula has a large population, a high population density, and a limited amount of cultivable land.[6] Even without the growth of Protestantism there would have been a great strain on the municipio's natural resources and hence pressure for emigration from the community. San Juan Chamula's proximity to the ladino market town of San Cristóbal de Las Casas meant that it needed, even more than most indigenous communities, to practice constant vigilance in order to preserve its distinctive traditions against the constant onslaught of ladinos and ladino culture.[7] Chamulan leaders therefore demanded rigid obedience to tradition, seeing in such resistance to change the only guarantee of continued autonomy for their community and for themselves. The system devised by Chamulan elders was both closed and centralized. Outsiders such as doctors, priests, and teachers could visit the municipio only with the elders' approval and could never spend the night there for any reason. From the *cabecera* (head town) the elders watched vigilantly over every aspect of life in the municipio and monopolized communication, transportation, and commerce with the outside world.[8]

As Jan Rus has shown, there was more than a little self-interest in such policies, for much of "tradition" consisted of drinking *posh* (liquor), whose sale was monopolized by the elders in collusion with the PRI (in return for delivering the municipio's vote to that party). In fact, by the 1950s the elders had transformed "tradition" into a vehicle that perpetuated their interests at the expense of most Chamulas. Such exploitation was not an ancient Chamulan custom but was rather the end result of a complex process starting in the late 1930s in which the state had succeeded in subverting native government through the creation of a class of educated, politically astute indigenous leaders.[9]

Thus, in a situation where religious and cultural traditions had been hijacked by self-serving caciques, religious change of any kind threatened not just a way of life but the political and economic interests of San Juan Chamula's most powerful families. Protestants, who rejected alcohol of any kind, refused posts in the cargo system, and formed alliances with ladino co-religionists from San Cristóbal and beyond, represented the greatest danger to "tradition." Protestants were not alone—entrepreneurs, Catholics who developed ties to the institutional church, and political dissidents who affiliated with parties other than the PRI also threatened the caciques' system of control— but Protestants were the largest single group of those classified as "enemies of tradition." When efforts at intimidation failed to convince the converts to renounce their new religion, mass expulsion became the Chamulan elders' policy of choice in dealing with the spread of Protestantism. Expulsions simultaneously rid the community of the Protestant troublemakers, offered other would-be dissidents a stark example of what would happen to them if they departed from "tradition," and opened the expulsados' agricultural land for expropriation by Chamulan elites.

One might expect that intellectuals would have taken up the cause of the expulsados. After all, here was clear and copious evidence of the human misery caused by the PRI's co-optation of indigenous communities. In actuality, it was the SIL and Protestant sects, not the PRI, that at first received most of the blame for the situation. In 1978

Salomón Nahmad, for instance, mentioned the situation in San Juan Chamula as a prime example of how Protestant missions manipulated indigenous communities in order to cause division.[10] In the same year, one newspaper columnist identified the two thousand refugees from the conflict in San Juan Chamula as evidence of the "great sociological penetration" of "foreign political agents."[11] The CEAS blamed the SIL for causing the "explosive situations in the Chiapas highlands," even as it condemned the SIL for counseling submission to the Chamulan caciques rather than resistance or vengeance.[12] In an interview with the influential magazine *Proceso*, the president of the CEAS, Andrés Fábregas, characterized the SIL's advice to Chamulan Protestants not to resist their oppressors as an example of the "effective destruction of genuinely popular leadership."[13]

Scholars writing in the 1990s and since have taken a much different approach to the expulsions from San Juan Chamula than their predecessors did in the 1970s. In the more recent accounts the SIL's role is much diminished. Far from being the leading cause of the expulsions, the SIL is now hardly mentioned. For example, Jan Rus, who had co-written a scathing indictment of the SIL's work in Chiapas with Robert Wasserstrom in 1981, hardly mentioned the organization when he wrote an article about the "subversion of native government in highland Chiapas" in 1994. In 1981 the SIL had figured as a major actor that exploited "the dissolution of community ties" in San Juan Chamula for its own purposes and had created "a kind of third party, an organization of non-combatants that expected fundamental change to occur only in heaven," but in 1994 Rus's venom was reserved for the caciques alone.[14]

In recent works, Thomas Benjamin and Lynn Stephen examine the cultural ferment that occurred in the Mayan communities of Chiapas during the period from 1970 to 1992, without even mentioning the SIL.[15] This omission is especially striking because Benjamin and Stephen emphasize the contemporary Mayas' use of vernacular writing to reappropriate their history. Since the SIL worked on eight different variants of Tzotzil and Tzeltal (in addition to other Mayan languages), creating alphabets and producing the first written materials in most of those languages, it seems quite likely that the SIL had something to do with the apparent renaissance of indigenous writing.[16] At the very least, even in cases where indigenous communities might have developed new alphabets, the SIL's work served as a spur to indigenous linguists. Benjamin seems to believe that Protestantism has played only a superficial role in modern Chiapas, for his only reference to evangelicals is to dissidents "labeled as Protestants" or "branded as evangelical Protestants."[17] Stephen pays Protestantism and the SIL even less attention, despite the fact that she devotes more than one hundred pages to precisely the area of Chiapas where the SIL was most active. Benjamin believes that the Tzeltal translation of the book of Exodus produced by progressive Catholics from 1972 to 1974 was "the first book of the Bible translated into Tzeltal," whereas Marianna Slocum had translated the entire New Testament into Tzeltal by 1956. Stephen also highlights the importance of this Tzeltal translation without any reference to the earlier and much more extensive translation work done by the SIL.[18] The fact was that by 1974, *thousands* of Tzeltals had been reading their own language for years, some for decades.[19] Omitting the SIL means that Benjamin and Stephen tell only half of the story and distort the part of the story that they do tell.

Thus, whereas anthropologists once saw the SIL as the chief villain in the Chamulan story, today some scholars have virtually removed the SIL from the equation. Because in the 1970s cultural preservation trumped other concerns, it made sense to lay blame for the Chamulan situation at the door of the major agent of cultural change, the SIL, even though it was evident that Chamulan Protestants were being cruelly persecuted for a voluntary change of religion. The idea was that if the SIL had not meddled in Chamulan affairs, the expulsions never would have been necessary in the first place. Yet to scholars nearer to the close of the century the SIL seemed hardly worth mentioning because expulsions of non-Protestants indicated that religion and cultural change were not the only issues at stake in San Juan Chamula and because the rise of Zapatista guerrillas in the Chiapas highlands had made clear that indigenous people themselves were rejecting the PRI-controlled caciques.

Both approaches to understanding the situation in San Juan Chamula distort the role of the SIL: the first one overemphasizes the importance of religion, while the second underemphasizes it. Both approaches are symptomatic of the difficulties that scholars (many of them not personally religious) encounter when they try to incorporate religion into their studies of political and social phenomena. All too often we find otherwise perceptive thinkers falling into the trap of black-and-white thinking and blanket generalizations when it comes to the matter of religion. Thus, the indigenista prejudice against indigenous "superstition" was replaced in the 1970s by the assumption that indigenous religion lay beyond the realm of criticism. Indigenista support for Protestantism was replaced in the 1970s by a new certitude of its reactionary nature, then in the 1990s by an apparent belief in its irrelevance.

A more nuanced approach to the expulsions from San Juan Chamula would integrate an examination of the roles played by the SIL and Chamulan Protestants with an analysis of the religious, cultural, economic, and political situation in which they and other actors were struggling. It seems clear that, were such an investigation undertaken, it would lead neither to the kind of statements about the SIL's exclusive culpability issued in the 1970s nor to the kind of explanations prevalent in the 1990s in which the SIL is almost invisible. Both attitudes toward the SIL are not so much fallacious as unbalanced: there is a sense in which the Jacobs' translation and evangelization did cause the expulsions by leading to the conversion of two Chamulas who in turn evangelized their friends and families, fracturing the religious unity of their municipio; and there is also validity to later interpretations which suggest that dissidence was inevitable because of the essentially exploitative nature of the Chamulan political and economic order. But either understanding is reductive if it is asserted as the last word or the overarching explanation.

The fact is that the SIL played an important but limited role in the expulsions. As many social scientists and historians now admit, Chamulan society in the 1960s was ossified, exploitative, and directed toward the benefit of the few at the expense of the many. The fact that, in the midst of scarcity and poverty, Chamulan elders had both diverted traditional Chamulan spirituality toward their own enrichment and stifled economic and agricultural innovation on ostensibly religious grounds made Chamula ripe for religious discord. By claiming their domination of the municipio as a kind of religious and cultural preservation project, the elders succeeded for decades in suppressing dissent, but they also laid the groundwork for those who would eventually oppose them. As it became increasingly difficult to identify truth, justice, and freedom with the traditional religion of

San Juan Chamula, it could come as no great surprise when significant numbers of Chamulas turned to the SIL and to Protestantism in the 1960s and 1970s.[20]

Where, in a freer society, the decadence of Chamulan religion might have spurred a process of internal religious reform, this was simply not an option in San Juan Chamula. Similarly, overpopulation and a shortage of land necessitated economic and agricultural change: people simply had to find new and better ways of supporting themselves, or they would starve. Condemning economic and agricultural innovators as "heretics" cowed some into submission, but it also pushed innovators to seek nontraditional religious justifications for their activities. The SIL, then, did indeed influence religious and cultural changes in San Juan Chamula, but it would be hard to argue that it played a more important or more villainous role than the Chamulan elders, or for that matter, than their allies in the PRI.[21]

At the same time, we should not fall into the trap of ignoring the SIL's role, acting as if the ongoing expulsions and tensions in San Juan Chamula are the function of purely secular factors, as if religion were merely a smoke screen for other matters. The fact that religion sometimes *did* function as a smoke screen indicates not that it was always a smoke screen but that such an explanation for domination maintained some ability to justify otherwise obviously inequitable actions. Those scholars seeking to publicize the fate of oppressed indigenous people in Chiapas need to pay more attention to Protestants as an early group of dissidents who opened up political space for the secular dissidents who followed them.

Ken and Elaine Jacobs need to be included in the history of San Juan Chamula, but their impact should be neither exaggerated nor minimized. They never lived in the municipio, yet they exercised great influence over some Chamulas, who in turn influenced others. They developed the Chamula Tzotzil alphabet, produced the first written materials in that language, taught many Chamulas to read and write in their language, translated the New Testament into Chamula, and converted the first Chamulan Protestants. Since most Chamulan converts came to the new religion through friends and family members rather than through direct contact with the linguists, it would seem difficult to argue that the Jacobs somehow imposed Protestantism on unwilling converts. Similarly, since thousands of Chamulas were expelled from the municipio for converting to Protestantism, it would

seem difficult to study Chamulan politics without paying great attention to the dynamics of religious dissidence. As with the larger history
of the SIL in Mexico, the story of the SIL's impact on San Juan Chamula is best understood not as the machinations of an all-powerful,
malevolent destroyer of indigenous culture or as the religious gloss
on a political process. Rather, the SIL played an important but not
determinative role in the crisis of the Chamulan sociopolitical system
in the 1960s and 1970s. Although neither the Jacobs nor their converts were thinking primarily about political or economic matters, the
long-term effect of mass conversions was to expose the illegitimacy
of the domination exercised by the Chamulan elders. The economic
result of mass expulsions was that many Chamulas began to support
themselves through small-scale commerce and urban forms of wage
labor in San Cristóbal de Las Casas, a dramatic break with the traditional Chamulan agricultural lifestyle.[22]

The SIL's Legacy in Mexico

There are reasonable grounds for criticism of the SIL, but as the preceding account of the Chamulas and the previous chapters have demonstrated, these grounds are not those upon which most detractors
have based their arguments against the institution. Although the
charges against the SIL have been many, perhaps the most persistent
and damaging have been those concerning its role as an agent of
imperialism and a sower of division in indigenous villages.

Far from being an anti-Mexican tool of North American imperialism, the SIL has been determinedly pro-Mexican during its entire
history in that nation. Cameron Townsend publicly criticized U.S. foreign policy toward Mexico on a number of occasions, yet he never
publicly criticized Mexican policies of any kind. He and his colleagues
went out of their way to cooperate with the Mexican government,
never going where they had not received permission to go, always seeking to encourage indigenous people to participate in state-sponsored
educational programs, often facilitating further incursions of the
state into indigenous communities through roads, electricity, and social services.

A more valid criticism of the SIL would be that it was too willing
to cooperate with programs of the Mexican state that did not serve
the best interests of indigenous people and not critical enough in its

dealings with a regime not known for its commitment to human rights. Basically, the SIL's early years in an environment inhospitable to religion of any sort led it to adopt an extremely submissive posture toward the Mexican state and its elite allies and a policy of almost blanket support for state policies and actions. But what had been a tactical solution to an immediate problem soon assumed enshrined status as *the* way to operate in Mexico and as a doctrine to teach to converts.

Townsend's sharp criticism of the U.S. government and of the behavior of its capitalist allies suggests, however, that even in terms of the SIL's own philosophy, there might have been some room for the criticism of authority. It is unfortunate that SIL policies hardened to the extent that, in situations of grave injustice, old and worn tactics from a different time and different situation trumped the more nuanced application of biblical principles. The policy of avoiding all criticism of authority, moreover, was at variance with the SIL's own history, for some of Townsend's most crucial successes had come from his willingness to render helpful advice to the U.S. State Department. When Chamulan authorities, for instance, grossly abused their power, it is hard to see how appealing to state and national authorities for justice would have violated biblical injunctions to submit. After all, was the SIL itself being "unsubmissive" when it appealed to higher authorities to gain access to certain villages?

Still, it must be mentioned that the SIL's general posture of submission to Mexican authorities compares quite favorably with that of other North American entities operating in Mexico. The oil companies, for instance, seem to have believed that large bank accounts and U.S. passports made them exempt from obedience to Mexican authorities. It must also be pointed out that until the Tlatelolco massacre of 1968 many progressive intellectuals in both Mexico and the United States had no great qualms about working with the PRI, which was still regarded as embodying, at least to a limited extent, some of the sacred ideals of the revolution.

The charge that the SIL divided indigenous communities and the closely related accusation that it destroyed indigenous cultures are partially true. It would be absurd to argue that the conversion of any significant group of indigenous people to Protestantism would not both divide a village and destroy significant aspects of its culture. Consequently, when the unity of indigenous communities and the preservation of indigenous culture were taken as unqualified "goods," there could be no doubt that the SIL was an utterly reprehensible organization. It was completely logical that those who asserted the primacy of unity and tradition passionately opposed the SIL, for its missionary project was the antithesis of their value system.

The fact is, though, that such values were based on false and inconsistent assumptions. First of all, the notion that there ever was any kind of unified, closed indigenous community for the SIL to fracture is highly suspect in itself. Before the SIL arrived on the scene, indigenous villages had both their own internal divisions and significant contacts with the outside world. The SIL thus did not "create" division in the sense of splintering an organic whole, nor did it ever function as indigenous communities' sole contact with the outside world. Second, the myth of cultural innocence (the idea that indigenous societies maintained some kind of primeval moral purity) simply does not do justice to the complexity of any society. Indigenous communities had their own problems before the arrival of the SIL, problems that in some cases benefited from the SIL's presence. Alcoholism, for instance, generally declines when large numbers of people convert to Protestantism.

The Mexican anthropologists who were so critical of the SIL's role in indigenous communities had their own set of "divisive" and "destructive" policies. To take just one example, access to Western medicine is one opportunity that few anthropologists would have denied to indigenous communities. Yet Western medicine, by its very nature, undermined traditional views of healing, disease, and causality. In doing so it eventually challenged the authority of traditional healers and introduced division, as some community members upheld the traditional ways while others embraced the new. The real argument, then, was not between those who wanted to protect indigenous people from all outside influence and those who wanted to alter every aspect of their lives, but between two partial but competing agendas for cultural change.

In contrast to what many anthropologists claimed, the SIL did display a fair amount of respect for indigenous cultures, not in the sense that it affirmed every aspect of those cultures, but in the sense that it proposed alternatives without forcing anyone to accept them. At the same time, the translation of the New Testament into an indigenous language usually has as a by-product the creation of a written language.[23] Although many indigenous communities never adopt vernacular literacy at all and many others view vernacular literacy as a predominantly Protestant phenomenon, all have the choice of taking up the written language as a tool that can be employed as they see fit. The recent flourishing of vernacular writing in Chiapas, despite some changes in orthographies, owes much to the early efforts of the SIL. The written word, like other tools, can be used in any number of ways. The fact that many current writers of Tzeltal and Tzotzil espouse causes that the SIL would never endorse indicates the voluntaristic nature of the SIL's project: it proposed both a religious message and a certain technology of knowledge, both or either of which indigenous communities were free to accept or reject.

A more apt critique of the SIL, and one to which both the SIL and its critics might be willing to listen, is that it inconsistently applied its own policies. There is no biblical requirement that Christians *must* work hand in hand with secular governments, nor is church-state cooperation permitted by the Mexican Constitution. Consequently, the decision to collaborate closely with the Mexican state was both a choice and a genuinely political action that put the SIL in the middle of religious politics, indigenista politics, and linguistic politics. Similarly, the cultivation of friendships with Mexican elites was always a political act—otherwise Townsend and company could just as well have devoted their time and resources to befriending merchants and clerks. At the same time that it was actively involved in Mexican and international politics, however, the SIL tried to define itself as a purely apolitical organization and to teach its converts to withdraw from the political realm in a way that did not square with its own behavior.

The compatibility of the SIL's project with indigenista thought led to close cooperation with the SEP, the INI, and the III during the 1940s, 1950s, and 1960s. The incompatibility of the SIL's project with the cultural protection and preservation advocated by the next generation of anthropologists led to conflict and crisis in the 1970s and early 1980s. Part of the reason why the decade from 1986 to 1995 was much quieter for the SIL than the previous ten years had been was that the social sciences, once again, were undergoing major changes in their understandings of culture.

Rejecting all vestiges of paternalism and internal colonialism, progressive social scientists emphasized that their relationship with indigenous communities should be one of support, not leadership.

"This requires the decentralization of ethnological, linguistic, histori-cal and cultural research," the SIL's old nemesis Solomón Nahmad now pointed out, "so that the indigenous pueblos themselves can carry out their own research and rescue their own ethnic and regional cultures with the help of their own intellectuals and scientists."[24] At the heart of this new approach was the realization that indigenous people had the right and the ability to make their own choices, to plot their courses into the twenty-first century.

No one represents the implications of the new developments for Protestantism and the SIL better than Guillermo Bonfil Batalla, the guiding force behind the "Declaration of Barbados" in 1971, a lead-ing participant at the second Barbados conference, in 1977, and one of the organizers of the "parallel forum" that denounced the SIL at the III conference in Mérida in 1980. Previously, Bonfil Batalla had advocated political change for indigenous peoples but viewed reli-gious change as evidence of domination and exploitation. Political mobilization was an authentic expression of indigenous autonomy; re-ligious conversion was an imposition of alien and destructive values. Thus, Bonfil Batalla had no qualms about championing revolutionary indigenous political movements at the same time he was attacking the SIL for altering the religious status quo.[25] For him there was no con-tradiction between supporting one kind of change and opposing an-other: Indians must remake their own societies, free from undesired colonialist influences.

In the half-decade before his death in 1991, though, Bonfil Batalla seems to have developed more confidence in the vitality of indigenous culture. Mesoamerican patterns of thought and practice, he believed, constituted a "deep" and abiding cultural foundation, not only for Mexico's Indians but for its mestizos as well. Rather than focusing on negative influences, he expressed hope for the development of hy-brid, dynamic indigenous cultures. "There is no reason," he con-tended, "for the Mayas not to keep being Mayas in the context of an industrial society. The English were English before the industrial revolution and continued being English after it. The same should hap-pen with the indigenous peoples of Mexico."[26] Indigenous culture, he implied, did not need to fear the loss of some immutable essence; it had the strength and dynamism to adapt to changing situations.

In his influential best-seller, *México Profundo: Reclaiming a Civiliza-tion*, Bonfil Batalla even applied this understanding to Protestantism.

"The imposition of a new religion in itself does not necessarily imply a change in ethnic identity or a rupture in the cultural and historical continuity, as is irrefutably demonstrated by the 'spiritual conquest' of Mesoamerica." He still had no love for the SIL, but he was not so worried as he once had been about the effects of its work. In 1971, his "Declaration of Barbados" had expressed nothing but dismay about the strife and division caused by missionaries; in 1987 he was more intrigued than angered by the new settlements being formed in the jungles of Chiapas as Protestants broke off from their home villages. "Contrary to the obvious wishes of the pastors and missionaries," he suggested, these Protestant villages "could become a new framework for the continuity of Mesoamerican civilization . . . if their members appropriate the new religion and insert it with their own modifications into the matrix of their own culture, as happened centuries ago with Catholicism."[27]

To demonstrate the vitality of indigenous culture, Bonfil Batalla points to the sixteenth century, when "indoctrinated" and "fanaticized" indigenous youths destroyed idols and denounced their own parents for "heresy." At the time, many observers probably assumed that they were witnessing the end of Mesoamerican civilization, but this was by no means the case. In the same way, he suggests, contemporary indigenous people can accept Protestantism without giving up their indigenous identities.[28]

This new intellectual climate, more open to religious change as a genuine expression of indigenous self-determination, greatly reduced the number of attacks on the SIL. It was not so much that social scientists' views of the SIL had changed; Nahmad, for instance, still viewed the organization with suspicion in 1999.[29] It was more that anthropologists and sociologists had come to greater confidence in the ability of indigenous communities to direct their own destinies. If the pluralist, multilingual, multicultural Mexico that Bonfil Batalla, Nahmad, and others envisioned was to be true to itself, there had to be room for evangelical indigenous communities. Protestantism, obviously, was not what progressive intellectuals hoped to see in the pueblos; at the same time, it seemed increasingly to be something they were willing to live with. If a truck-driving PRIísta shaman can be Otomí, why can't a Pentecostal? Would anyone argue that left-wing political parties should be kept out of indigenous villages because it might "rend the fabric" of the PRI's control of local politics? Of course not. On the political level, almost every serious advocate of indigenous people in Mexico *wants* division in the pueblos.

The new emphasis on indigenous agency harmonizes well with the ways that different communities responded to the SIL. Some villages rejected the SIL altogether. Many villages tolerated the presence of linguists for years and even decades, accepting medical aid and other practical help but never demonstrating more than a slight interest in their religious message. In other villages, a few individuals converted to Protestantism and learned to read their own language, but the community as a whole rejected the new religion and saw no need to adopt mother tongue literacy. In a small minority of cases, villagers enthusiastically adopted both Protestantism and vernacular literacy. In these villages, such as Corralito, San Juan Chamula, and, to a lesser extent, San Antonio el Grande, the SIL literally changed the course of history. For the Tzeltals affected by Marianna Slocum and Florence Gerdel, the Chamulas influenced by Ken and Elaine Jacobs, and the Otomis affected by Katherine Voigtlander and Artemisa Echegoyen, the coming of the SIL marked the beginning of a new era. To some, of course, the new era was a time of tragedy and loss, but to others it was a time of rebirth and renewal. Even its detractors must now admit that, in these villages at least, the SIL was not merely an instrument of division and destruction. For these indigenous groups, conversion to Protestantism and the adoption of vernacular literacy served as part of what sociologist Jean Pierre Bastián calls the process of ethnic "recomposition." Rather than erasing all cultural distinctions, the kind of religious change fostered by the SIL can function "as a way of reaffirming and modernizing ethnic identity."[30] As indigenous people weave new patterns in the richly textured, continuously evolving ethnic tapestry that is Mexico, some, at least, have found inspiration in the Protestantism and vernacular literacy bequeathed to them by the SIL.

Notes

Abbreviations

AGN	Archivo General de la Nación, Mexico City
APLC	Archivo Particular Lázaro Cárdenas, AGN
ARC	Ramo Adolfo Ruiz Cortines, AGN
CTA	Cameron Townsend Archive, Jungle Aviation and Radio Service Headquarters, Waxhaw, North Carolina
DGG	Dirección General de Gobierno, AGN
INAH	Instituto Nacional de Antropología e Historia, Archivo Histórico, Mexico City
INI	Instituto Nacional Indigenista, Archivo Histórico, Mexico City
LC	Ramo Lázaro Cárdenas del Rio, AGN
MAC	Ramo Manuel Ávila Camacho, AGN
MAV	Ramo Miguel Alemán Velasco, AGN
MG	Archivo Manuel Gamio, INAH
NACP	National Archives, College Park, Maryland
PMA	Records of the Pioneer Mission Agency, Divinity School Library, Yale University
RG	Record Group
SNS	Personal Archive of Salomón Nahmad Sitton, to be donated to the Centro de Investigacione y Estudios Superiores en Antropología Social, Oaxaca
SRE	Secretaría de Relaciones Exteriores, Archivo Histórico, Mexico City

Introduction

1. Miller, *Mexico around Me*, 287–94. This episode is discussed in John Britton, *Revolution in Ideology: Images of the Mexican Revolution in the United States* (Lexington: University Press of Kentucky, 1995).

2. "A los interesados en la política del lenguaje," in Olivera et al., *Indigenismo y lingüística,* 187.

3. "SIL 2002 Annual Report," http://www.sil.org/sil/annualreport/2002report.pdf.

4. Marsden, *Understanding Fundamentalism and Evangelicalism,* 57.

5. Marsden, "Fundamentalism and American Evangelicalism," 25. It is hardly surprising, therefore, that fundamentalists would devote great amounts of energy to Bible translation.

6. Carpenter, *Revive Us Again,* 6, 9–10.

7. Niebuhr, "Fundamentalism," 525–27, cited in Carpenter, *Revive Us Again,* 13.

8. Carpenter, *Revive Us Again,* 9–10.

9. Ibid., 16–17.

10. Ibid., 82.

11. Garrard-Burnett, *Protestantism in Guatemala,* 53, 69.

12. Steven, *Doorway to the World,* back cover.

13. The SIL represents the extreme of a more general phenomenon in which missionaries serve as agents of cultural exchange who taught many Americans "everything they knew" about other nations and who often "functioned as critics of the homeland itself." Bays and Wacker, "Introduction," 8.

14. Colby and Dennett, *Thy Will Be Done.* The best book on the SIL is Stoll, *Fishers of Men.* Hvalkof and Aaby's collection *Is God an American?* is somewhat uneven but includes some excellent articles.

15. My own work in the Cameron Townsend Archive revealed no connection whatsoever between the two men.

16. For an evangelical scholar disturbed by Colby and Dennett's work, see Anderson's review of *Thy Will Be Done.*

17. Slocum and Watkins, *The Good Seed;* Steven, *They Dared to Be Different.* Other books by SIL personnel or friends about Mexico include Hefley and Hefley, *Uncle Cam;* R. Scott, *Jungle Harvest;* Clark, *Not Silenced by Darkness;* Hilton, *They Were Considered Faithful;* Steven, *Manuel;* and Steven, *Doorway to the World.*

18. J. M. Hart, *Empire and Revolution,* 3.

Chapter 1

1. Svelmoe, "A New Vision for Missions," 167.

2. Hefley and Hefley, *Uncle Cam,* 62–75.

3. Elvira Townsend, prayer letter, December 1932, doc. 01671, CTA; Cameron Townsend, "A long prayer meeting at Keswick," n.d., doc. 01743, CTA; Addison Raws, "Born in prayer," n.d., doc. 01744, CTA. Fundamentalists were not the only Americans drawn to Mexico at this time. As Helen Delpar details in *The Enormous Vogue of Things Mexican,* intellectuals, artists, travelers and "political pilgrims" from the north saw much that was attractive in the politics and culture of Mexico in this period.

4. L. L. Legters to Pioneer Mission Agency, 1 September 1933, doc. 01737, CTA; L. L. Legters to Cameron Townsend, 29 August 1933, doc.

01739, CTA; Moisés Sáenz to Cameron Townsend, 18 October 1933, doc. 01736, CTA.

5. Even Legters, who did not plan to work in Mexico himself, "resigned as a clergyman" before entering the country. Cameron Townsend to Executive Council of Central American Mission, 7 November 1933, doc. 01733, CTA; Cameron Townsend to Mr. and Mrs. Lewis Gall, 11 November 1933, doc. 01729, CTA.

6. Cameron Townsend to Bill Nyman and Etta Nyman, 8 April 1934, doc. 01882, CTA.

7. This distinction between Protestant and Catholic views of clerical identity (and of sacred spaces) probably also figures as a secondary reason for the former group's greater tolerance of clerical restrictions and church closures: Protestantism could function quite well without clerics or church buildings.

8. Cameron Townsend to Elvira Townsend, 13 December 1933, doc. 01717, CTA.

9. Cameron Townsend to Elvira Townsend, 20 December 1933, doc. 01716, CTA.

10. C. Townsend, "You're Back Again, Uncle Cam," 33; C. Townsend, "Go with Them," 35.

11. It is also possible that Ramírez, Moisés Sáenz's friend and ally, was influenced by that educator's endorsement of Townsend. See Gonzalo Aguirre Beltrán, "Introducción," in Ramírez, *La escuela rural Mexicana*, 5–47.

12. Cameron Townsend, diary, 28 December 1933, doc. 01791, CTA.

13. In fact, he witnessed to Ramírez and his wife for many years, eventually converting the latter and possibly the former. C. Townsend, "Go with Them," 35; C. Townsend, "You're Back Again, Uncle Cam," 33.

14. Cameron Townsend to Elvira Townsend, 20 December 1933, doc. 01716, CTA.

15. For the relationship between fundamentalism and science, see George M. Marsden, "The Evangelical Love Affair with Enlightenment Science," in Marsden, *Understanding Fundamentalism and Evangelicalism*, 120–52; Hefley and Hefley, *Uncle Cam*, 82–88; "Summer Training Camp for Pioneer Missionaries," 1934, pamphlet, doc. 01868, CTA.

16. Hefley and Hefley, *Uncle Cam*, 83.

17. Cameron Townsend to R. R. Gregory, 12 July 1935, doc. 01933, CTA.

18. Cameron Townsend to Bill and Etta Nyman, 8 April 1934, doc. 01882, CTA.

19. C. Townsend, "Mexico's Program of Rural Education"; see also Cameron Townsend, "Mexican Peasants Eagerly Accept Socialistic Program," *Dallas News*, 9 December 1934; the first of the three articles was apparently published in March 1934, but I have not seen a copy of it.

20. Rafael Ramírez to Cameron Townsend, 15 March, 4 June 1934, docs. 01886, 01870, CTA.

21. Pike quoted in Steven, *Doorway to the World*, 40.

22. C. Townsend, "We're in the People Business," 56.

23. Pike quoted in Steven, *Doorway to the World*, 40.

24. Genaro Vásquez to Lázaro Cárdenas, 4 March 1936, exp. 545.3/145, LC.

25. Cameron Townsend to L. L. Legters, 11 October 1935, doc. 01920, CTA.

26. Cameron Townsend to Josephus Daniels, 18 December 1935, doc. 01911, CTA; Cameron Townsend to L. L. Legters, 14 November 1935, doc. 01917, CTA; Cameron Townsend to A. M. Vandever, 8 October 1935, doc. 01921, CTA. From this point on it seems that Townsend's ideas and innovations assumed more and more importance as the more traditional missionary strategies of Legters slowly waned. Legters died in 1940.

27. C. Townsend, *Lecciones sencillas para aprender a leer;* Cameron Townsend to L. L. Legters, 14 November 1935, doc. 01917, CTA.

28. Genaro Vásquez to Lázaro Cárdenas, 4 March 1936, exp. 545.3/145, LC; Genaro Vásquez to Autoridades Civiles y Militares de la República, 18 December 1935, doc. 01907, CTA; Genaro Vásquez to Autoridades Civiles y Militares de la República, 18 December 1935, doc. 01909, CTA; Genaro Vásquez to Graciano Sánchez, 15 April 1936, doc. 02075, CTA.

29. Cameron Townsend to Josephus Daniels, 18 December 1935, doc. 01911, CTA.

30. Ibid.; Hefley and Hefley, *Uncle Cam,* 94.

31. Hefley and Hefley, *Uncle Cam,* 94.

32. L. L. Legters to Cameron Townsend, 11 November 1935, doc. 01916, CTA; Steven, *Doorway to the World,* 75, 82, 120.

33. Cameron Townsend to Lázaro Cárdenas, 29 January 1936, exp. 710.1/1598, LC.

34. Cameron Townsend to Lázaro Cárdenas, 11 March 1936, exp. 710.1/1598, LC.

35. Cameron Townsend to Lázaro Cárdenas, 7 April 1936, exp. 710.1/1598, LC.

36. Cameron Townsend to Lázaro Cárdenas, June 1936, exp. 710.1/1598, LC.

37. Cameron Townsend, "Commoner, Not Communist, Is Cárdenas," *Ashville Citizen-Times,* 21 June 1936; Cameron Townsend, "Commoner, Not Communist, Is Cárdenas," *Tulsa Daily World,* 21 June 1936.

38. Cameron Townsend to Luis I. Rodríguez [personal secretary to President Cárdenas], 27 August 1936, exp. 710.1/1598, LC.

39. Lázaro Cárdenas to Cameron Townsend, 28 March 1936, exp. 710.1/1598, LC.

40. Cameron Townsend to Lázaro Cárdenas, June 1936, exp. 710.1/1598, LC.

41. Luis I. Rodríguez to Cameron Townsend, 20 July 1936, exp. 710.1/1598, LC.

42. Cameron Townsend to Lázaro Cárdenas, June 1936, exp. 710.1/1598, LC

43. Luis I. Rodríguez to Cameron Townsend, 2 June 1936, exp. 710.1/1598, LC.

44. Mariano Silva y Aceves to Cameron Townsend [about the request that

the National University sponsor SIL linguists], 10 February 1936, doc. 01957, CTA; Cameron Townsend to L. L. Legters [about the request that the Department of Labor pay ten SIL workers], 11 October 1935, doc. 01921, CTA; Cameron Townsend to L. L. Legters [about the request that the "Indian bureau" of the SEP give jobs to SIL linguists], 14 November 1935, doc. 01917, CTA.

45. Cameron Townsend to Luis I. Rodríguez, 27 August 1936, exp. 710.1/1598, LC.

46. Cameron Townsend, prayer letter, 15 October 1936, doc. 901974, CTA. Missionaries send such letters to financial and spiritual supporters to keep them informed of their activities and to ask for prayer.

47. Townsend believed that later Cárdenas did convert. Cameron Townsend to H. T. Marroquín, 25 July 1939, doc. 02453, CTA.

48. Lázaro Cárdenas quoted in Luís L. León, "Al margen de la campaña cárdenista," *El Nacional,* 28 June 1934.

49. C. Townsend, "Cartillas lingüísticas," 48.

50. Ibid.

51. Cameron Townsend to Lázaro Cárdenas, June 1936, exp. 710.1/1598, LC; Lázaro Cárdenas to Secretario de Educación, 27 January 1936, exp. 609/221, LC.

52. Gabino Vásquez, Jefe de Departamento Agrario, to Antonio Villareal, delegate of Departamento Agrario, exp. 508.1/216, LC.

53. Javier Uranga, 5 March 1938, exp. 508.1/216, LC.

54. Cameron Townsend to Lázaro Cárdenas, 4 January 1939, exp. 710.1/1598, LC.

55. Piquinto Martínez et al. to Lázaro Cárdenas, 29 March 1935, exp. 503.11/33, LC; Alfonso Peña to Lázaro Cárdenas, 23 March 1936, exp. 503.11/33, LC.

56. See Paul Friedrich's *The Princes of Naranja* for the classic account of post-revolutionary agrarian caciques.

57. Javier Uranga to Lázaro Cárdenas, 28 February, 2 March 1938, exp. 710.1/1598, LC; Cameron Townsend to Elvira Townsend, 9 August 1937, doc. 02136, CTA; Manuel Genis Guevara to Francisco Carrillo, 2 September 1937, doc. 02259, CTA.

58. Javier Uranga to Lázaro Cárdenas, 2 March 1938, exp. 710.1/1598, LC; Elena Trejo to Cameron Townsend, 3 August 1937, doc. 02175, CTA; Elena Trejo to "folks," 3 August 1937, doc. 02235, CTA; Javier Uranga to Lázaro Cárdenas, 6 December 1937, exp. 503.11/33, LC.

59. Javier Uranga to Lázaro Cárdenas, 26 January 1938, exp. 503.11/33, LC.

60. Javier Uranga to Lázaro Cárdenas, 10 April 1940, exp. 503.11/33, LC.

61. Cameron Townsend to Pioneer Mission Agency, 8 September 1937, doc. 02102, CTA.

62. C. Townsend, "I Saw a Lamb," 45.

63. Cameron Townsend to Lázaro Cárdenas, 26 December 1936, exp. 710.1/1598, LC.

64. C. Townsend, "I Saw a Lamb," 45.
65. Cameron Townsend to Pioneer Mission Agency, 8 September 1937.
66. Elvira Townsend to Wycliffites, 26 October 1943, doc. 03466, CTA.
67. C. Townsend, "Keep Those Sailors on Board," 160.

Chapter 2

1. Colby and Dennett imply that Townsend ingratiated himself with Cárdenas but then turned his back on all liberal and revolutionary causes after 1940. *Thy Will Be Done*, 102.
2. Pérez-Enríquez, *Expulsiones indígenas*, 216.
3. Regional and local analyses would prove particularly helpful in clarifying the situation, since anti-religious policies varied at the whim of governors and local authorities. The situation in Tabasco, often regarded as exceptional, may have been more representative than has been thought. Sonora and Veracruz, at least, suffered similar degrees of extreme anticlericalism. The best analyses to date of the religious situation in the 1930s (Negrete, *Relaciones*; Blancarte, "Aspectos internacionales del conflicto religioso") focus on Mexico City and the state of México, in the first case, and on the international situation, in the second. Reich, *Mexico's Hidden Revolution*, stresses Catholic efforts at accommodation but misses, I believe, the hierarchy's willingness to experiment with various methods of resistance, especially the international pressure detailed by Blancarte.
4. Krauze, *Mexico*, 406, 421.
5. *Diario Oficial*, 8 January 1931; Mecham, *Church and State in Latin America*, 476–78, 499; John Cornyn, "2200 Churches in Vera Cruz to Be Closed," *Chicago Daily Tribune*, 19 June 1931; "Vera Cruz Dismisses All Catholic Teachers," *New York Times*, 11 August 1931; "Attack Vatican in Mexican Suit," *New York World Telegram*, 29 June 1931; "El radicalismo antireligioso en Mérida, Yuc.," *La Prensa* (Mexico City), 14 September 1931.
6. Reich, *Mexico's Hidden Revolution*, 36.
7. Cornyn, "2200 Churches in Vera Cruz to Be Closed."
8. See also papal encyclical *Iniquis Afflictique* (1926).
9. Negrete, *Relaciones*, 78, 336.
10. Ibid., 78, 79, 145; Alberto María Carreño, "Memorandum," 17 November 1934, film M1370, roll 41, doc. 812.404/1349, RG 59, NACP.
11. Negrete, *Relaciones*, 79, 161, 173.
12. Reich, *Mexico's Hidden Revolution*, 41.
13. Josephus Daniels to Secretary of State, 18 December 1934, film M1370, roll 41, doc. 812.404/1388, RG 59, NACP.
14. Baldwin, *Protestants and the Mexican Revolution*, 24, 35, 57.
15. Bastian, *Los disidentes*, 303.
16. "In contradiction to the accusations of their critics, Protestants, who were liberal and nationalist, opposed it [United States intervention] in various ways." Mondragón, "Protestantismo, Panamericanismo, e Identidad Nacional," 317.

17. Read, *Latin American Church Growth*, 342–44.

18. Báez-Camargo, *Is There Religious Persecution in Mexico?* 1–15.

19. Guy Ray to Secretary of State, 8 November 1934, film M1370, roll 41, doc. 812.404/1321, RG 59, NACP.

20. Bastian, *Los disidentes;* Bastian, *Protestantismo y sociedad en México*, 198; L. Scott, *Salt of the Earth*, 43; "Epilogo," in Espejel López and Ruiz Guerra, *El protestantismo en México*, 206; National Conference of Jews and Christians, "Interfaith declaration on the religious situation in Mexico," 1935, and Henry F. Brown to National Conference of Jews and Christians, 1935, exp. 547/31, LC.

21. Mexican American Cultural Relations Association to Franklin D. Roosevelt, 21 November 1935, exp. 547/31, LC; Samuel Guy Inman to Lázaro Cárdenas, 19 December 1934, exp. 547/12, LC. During the Obregón and Calles regimes, Andrés Osuna had played a similar role, speaking to Protestant leaders in "over 150 places" in the United States to explain that their churches had nothing to fear in Mexico. Daniels, *Shirt-Sleeve Diplomat*, 156–57.

22. Fernando González Roa to Secretaría de Relaciones Exteriores, 12 December 1934, and Pablo Campos Ortiz to Secretaría de Relaciones Exteriores, April 6, 1935, exp. III-304-1, SRE.

23. Francisco Castillo Nájera, address to Academy of World Economics, 21 May 1936, exp. III-327-13, SRE.

24. Francisco Castillo Nájera quoting Lázaro Cárdenas in address to Academy of World Economics, 21 May 1936, exp. III-327-13, SRE.

25. Mexico had flirted with the Soviet Union during the 1920s, but it turned toward the United States at the end of the decade. Spenser, *El triángulo imposible*.

26. Josephus Daniels to Sumner Welles, 23 April 1936, Sumner Welles Collection, Franklin D. Roosevelt Presidential Library, Hyde Park, New York.

27. Daniels, *Shirt-Sleeve Diplomat*, 143.

28. "En el Templo Jesús será celebrado mañana una misa conforme al rito ortodoxo," *Excélsior*, 30 May 1936; A. Lara, "Rural Organizations"; Millett, "Protestant Role," 373.

29. Moisés Sáenz to Lázaro Cárdenas, 14 September 1935, exp. 533.4/1, LC.

30. "Church in Mexico Asks for Prayers of Catholic World," *Montreal Gazette*, 4 February 1936; "El congreso de prelados trata serio problema," *La Prensa*, 18 February 1936; "No habrá oposición del gobierno federal para la reapertura de templos católicos," *Excélsior*, 18 February 1936.

31. "Consiste su objetivo en la realización del necesario ajuste social y económico," *El Nacional*, 5 March 1936; Cárdenas quote from "La cuestión religiosa no es problema para el Gobierno," *La Prensa*, 6 March 1936; "Cardenas Opposes Mexican Fanatics," *New York Times*, 6 March 1936.

32. "One Mexican State Relaxes Church Law," *New York Times*, 12 March 1936.

33. "Ban on Mexican Catholics Removed by Congress," *New York World Telegram*, 26 March 1936; "Mexican Catholics See Easing of Laws," *New York*

World Telegram, 30 March 1936; "Reapertura de unos templos," *Excélsior*, 27 April 1936; quotes are from "Ambassador Daniels Goes to Mass in Mexico, D.F.," *New York Times*, 13 April 1936; "Forty Churches Open in Mexican Capital," *New York Times*, 6 April 1936; "Garantías al clero en el E. de Sonora," *La Prensa*, 14 April 1936.

Chapter 3

1. Lázaro Cárdenas to Francisco Castillo Nájera, 8 February 1939, exp. 39-10-2, SRE.

2. Francisco Castillo Nájera to Lázaro Cárdenas, 15 June 1939, exp. 39-10-2, SRE.

3. Francisco Castillo Nájera to Lázaro Cárdenas, 8 August 1939, exp. 39-10-2, SRE.

4. William Svelmoe explains how Townsend became Cárdenas's "Man in America" in "The General and the Gringo."

5. Cameron Townsend to Lázaro Cárdenas, 25 May 1937, exp. 710.1/1598, LC; Ramón Beteta to Cameron Townsend, 27 September 1937, doc. 02168, CTA; Cameron Townsend to Elvira Townsend, 19 August, 24 August 1937, docs. 02126, 02122, CTA; Steven, *Doorway to the World*, 91.

6. Cameron Townsend to "Evangelical Missionaries of Mexico," 22 December 1937, doc. 02079, CTA.

7. The first letter that Townsend wrote with the pen invited Cárdenas to get to know his "best friend" (Jesus Christ). As far as the money was concerned, Elvira wrote back saying they would use it instead to build ten houses for the Indians. Cameron Townsend to Lázaro Cárdenas, 28 February 1938, roll 19-1, APLC; Cameron Townsend to [his father] Will Townsend, 6 March 1938, doc. 02309, CTA.

8. Britton, *Revolution and Ideology*, 131, 154, 195.

9. Cameron Townsend to Lázaro Cárdenas, 20 September 1937, exp. 710.1/1598, LC; Cameron Townsend to Lázaro Cárdenas, 20 March 1938, roll 19-1, APLC.

10. Cameron Townsend to Lázaro Cárdenas, 30 October 1937, exp. 710.1/1598, LC.

11. Hefley and Hefley, *Uncle Cam*, 107.

12. Elvira Townsend to Guelph Hummel and Karl Hummel, 31 March 1938, doc. 02308, CTA. The Hefleys state that the idea for the trip came from Cameron (*Uncle Cam*, 106–7).

13. Elvira Townsend to Guelph Hummel and Karl Hummel, 31 March 1938.

14. Steven, *Doorway to the World*, 101–9; letter of introduction for Cameron Townsend to see Franklin Roosevelt, from Josephus Daniels to McIntyre [Roosevelt's personal secretary], 4 April 1935, doc. 02315, CTA.

15. Cameron Townsend to Miguel Arteaga [personal secretary to Cárdenas], 16 April, 2 May 1938, roll 19-1, APLC.

16. Cameron Townsend to Miguel Arteaga, 9 May 1938, roll 19-1, APLC.

17. Cameron Townsend, "The Petroleum Situation in Mexico," *Dallas Times-Herald*, 8 May 1938.

18. Cameron Townsend to Lázaro Cárdenas, 14 October 1938, 710.1/ 1598, LC; Lázaro Cárdenas to Cameron Townsend, 9 August 1938, roll 19-1, APLC.

19. Cameron Townsend to Miguel Arteaga, 16 April 1938, roll 19-1, APLC; Cameron Townsend to H. T. Marroquín, 15 September 1938, doc. 02284, CTA. Townsend also wrote a booklet about the expropriation, called *The Truth about Mexico's Oil*.

20. He did win the long-lasting appreciation of Cárdenas, though. In 1946 Cárdenas said of Townsend, "With his work in the United States he served my government in an important way during the campaign waged by the foreign companies." Cárdenas, *Obras: Apuntes, 1913–1940*, 201.

21. Cameron Townsend to Cordell Hull, 10 September 1938, roll 19-1, APLC; Cameron Townsend to editor of *New York Times*, 18 January 1939, roll 19-1, APLC; Cameron Townsend to Lázaro Cárdenas, 18 October 1938, roll 19-1, APLC.

22. Cameron Townsend to Rafael Ramírez, 15 November 1938, doc. 02278, CTA.

23. Cameron Townsend to Max Lathrop, 27 January 1939, doc. 02478, CTA.

24. Steven, *Doorway to the World*, 116.

25. John Twentyman to Cameron Townsend, 30 November 1936, doc. 02002, CTA.

26. Cameron Townsend to Karl Hummel, 12 February 1937, doc. 02158, CTA; Cameron Townsend to Pioneer Mission Agency, 8 September 1937, doc. 02102, CTA; Cameron Townsend to Brainerd Legters, 9 April 1940, doc. 02612, CTA.

27. Cameron Townsend, "Answer to critics of our policy of cooperating with governments and scientific organizations," 29 November 1939, doc. 02436, CTA.

28. Cameron Townsend to fellow workers, 4 December 1939, doc. 02432, CTA.

29. Delpar, *The Enormous Vogue of Things Mexican;* Anhalt, *A Gathering of Fugitives*.

30. Richard Pittman, "Why Are You Two?" in Pittman et al., *The Wycliffe Sapphire*, 9.

31. Kenneth Pike to Kenneth Latourette, 23 January 1956, PMA.

32. Cameron Townsend to Ken Pike and Eugene Nida, 20 February 1937, doc. 02157, CTA.

33. Cameron Townsend to Pioneer Mission Agency, 8 September 1937, doc. 02102, CTA.

34. Cameron Townsend to William Townsend, 6 March 1938, doc. 02309, CTA.

35. Elvira Townsend to Guelph and Karl Hummel, 31 March 1938, doc. 02308, CTA.

36. Cameron Townsend to H. Marroquín, 25 July 1939, doc. 02453, CTA; in *Lázaro Cárdenas, Mexican Democrat,* Townsend tempered this conviction but still harbored hopes that Cárdenas was a Christian: "Personally, he is not a Roman Catholic, nor a Protestant, nor an atheist. As a Freemason he has declared his belief in the Supreme Being, and it may be that he goes farther than that in his personal faith" (369).

37. Cameron Townsend to Lázaro Cárdenas, 1943, doc. 03450, CTA.

38. C. Townsend, "Answer to critics."

39. Cameron Townsend to Brainerd Legters, 9 April 1940, doc. 02612, CTA; Romans 13:1, King James Version.

40. Cameron Townsend to "folks," 25 November 1941, doc. 02716, CTA.

41. Cameron Townsend to fellow workers in Mexico, 14 November 1941, doc. 02715, CTA.

42. Romans 13:1–7: "Let every soul be subject unto the higher powers. For there is no power but of God: the powers that be are ordained by God. Whosoever therefore resisteth the power, resisteth the ordinance of God: and they that resist shall receive to themselves damnation. For rulers are not a terror to good works, but to evil. Wilt thou then not be afraid of the power? Do that which is good, and thou shalt have praise of the same: for he is the minister of God to thee for good. But if thou do that which is evil, be afraid; for he beareth not the sword in vain. For he is the minister of God, a revenger to execute wrath upon him that doeth evil. Wherefore ye must needs be subject, not only for wrath, but also for conscience sake. For this cause pay ye tribute also: for they are God's ministers, attending continually upon this very thing. Render therefore to all their dues: tribute to whom tribute is due; custom to whom custom; fear to whom fear; honour to whom honour." Another similar text is 1 Peter 2:13–17, which says, in the King James Version, "Submit yourself to every ordinance of man for the Lord's sake: whether to the king, as supreme; or to governors, as unto them that are sent by him for the punishment of evildoers, and for the praise of them that do well. For so is the will of God, that with well doing ye may put to silence the ignorance of foolish men: as free, and not using your liberty for a cloak of maliciousness, but as the servants of God. Honour all men. Love the brotherhood. Fear God. Honour the king."

43. Pittman, "O King, Live Forever," 3.

44. Ibid., 4.

45. C. Townsend, "Let Your Light Shine," 51.

46. Ibid.

47. C. Townsend, "Honor to Whom Honor Is Due," 86–87.

48. J. M. Hart, *Empire and Revolution,* 399.

Chapter 4

1. Pablo González Casanova, "El indio y nosotros," *El Universal,* 29 November 1935.

2. Lázaro Cárdenas quoted in "Discurso del Señor General Cárdenas," *El Universal*, 26 September 1936.

3. As Claudio Lomnitz points out, one of the three key principles of Mexican nationalism was "defense against foreigners." It is possible to use one group of apparently altruistic foreigners to defend the nation against other, more rapacious foreigners, but this stratagem is a dangerous one, for it invokes the early national period when anti-American *escoseses* and anti-British *yorquinos* emphasized their anti-foreign sentiments but clearly simply wanted to get their hands on the state. *Deep Mexico, Silent Mexico*, 31, 32.

4. These indigenistas were not alone in viewing language this way. As James Scott notes, "a unique language represents a formidable obstacle to state knowledge, let alone colonialization, control, manipulation, instruction or propaganda." *Seeing Like a State*, 72.

5. Antonio Sánchez Torres, "El problema lingüístico de México," *Gráfico* (Mexico City), 3 December 1936.

6. The examples of Switzerland, Belgium, and other multilingual modern nations apparently were not considered.

7. Aguirre Beltrán, *Lenguas vernáculas*, 342; for Moisés Sáenz's Protestant influence on educational theory see Bastian, *Protestantismo y sociedad en México*, 155–67.

8. "El interés por la lingüística," *El Nacional*, 4 July 1933.

9. "Psicoanálisis en el estudio de la lengua," *El Nacional*, 23 January 1937.

10. Cameron Townsend to Secretario de Educación Pública, 24 December 1941, doc. 02697, CTA; Cameron Townsend to Josephus Daniels, 18 December 1935, doc. 01911, CTA; Mariano Silva y Aceves to Cameron Townsend, 10 February 1936, doc. 01957, CTA; Cameron Townsend to Pioneer Mission Agency, 8 September 1937, doc. 02102, CTA; Cameron Townsend to Karl Hummel, 12 February 1937, doc. 02158, CTA.

11. "Psicoanálisis en el estudio de la lengua"; "El ciclo de conferencias lingüísticas," *El Nacional*, 21 January 1937; "Curso lingüístico en la Universidad," *Excélsior*, 19 January 1937.

12. Cameron Townsend to Karl Hummel, 12 February 1937.

13. Cameron Townsend to Pioneer Mission Agency, 8 September 1937.

14. Silva y Aceves, "Las cartillas lingüísticas"; see also C. Townsend, "Cuestionario lingüístico," 2.

15. C. Townsend, "Cartillas lingüísticas," 2.

16. Jorge A. Vivo, "México y el indio," *El Nacional*, 13 May 1937.

17. Torres, "El problema lingüístico de México." In 1975 Joseph Grimes estimated that the actual number of languages in Mexico was 205. Aguirre Beltrán, *Lenguas vernáculas*, 323.

18. Sierra, *Obras completas*, 7:113, quoted in Aguirre Beltrán, *Lenguas vernáculas*, 136.

19. Lombardo Toledano, "Nacionalidades oprimidas," 107.

20. "Que se les enseñe español a los indios, pero que se les conserve su propio idioma," *El Nacional*, 31 May 1934.

21. Aguirre Beltrán, *Lenguas vernáculas,* 343.

22. Cameron Townsend and Elvira Townsend to Pioneer Mission Agency, September 1939, doc. 02443, CTA; Cameron Townsend to fellow workers, 4 March 1940, doc. 02617, CTA.

23. Moisés Sáenz to Secretaría de Relaciones Exteriores, 20 November 1936, exp. III-1244-9, SRE. The words in italics are underlined and printed in red in the original.

24. Sáenz, *México integro,* 156.

25. Sáenz died before he could assume this post, and Manuel Gamio became the first director of the Instituto Interamericano Indigenista.

26. Aguirre Beltrán, "Introducción," 23.

Chapter 5

1. Clemente Cámara Ochoa, "Repúblicas independientes dentro de nuestro república," *El Universal,* 10 July 1944.

2. Cameron Townsend to José Pavia Crespo, 11 July 1944, doc. 03753, CTA.

3. Krauze, *Mexico,* 583. The best introduction to this period is found in Stephen Niblo's *Mexico in the 1940s,* although Niblo devotes scant attention to religious issues.

4. Read, *Latin American Church Growth,* 167. Although this chapter can only examine how the SIL responded to this situation, the question of how other Protestant groups in Mexico responded to the challenges of the 1940s and 1950s is clearly one of the key research questions for the study of Mexican Protantism.

5. The topic of state formation and popular resistance is dealt with extensively in Joseph and Nugent, *Everyday Forms of State Formation.*

6. Quoted in Negrete, *Relaciones,* 283.

7. "Propaganda Protestante en México," *La Prensa,* 20 February 1931; "El Protestantismo será combatido por los Católicos," *La Prensa,* 27 February 1931.

8. Báez-Camargo, "Missionary Task," 164.

9. Meyer, *Sinarquismo,* 31. The political heir of Sinarquismo, the Partido Demócrata Mexicano, existed until the mid-1990s.

10. "La campaña al protestantismo," *Novedades,* 17 November 1944; "El Señor Arzobispo de México organiza un comité de lucha," *El Popular,* 14 October 1944; "Múltiples obras de caridad para luchar contra el protestantismo," *El Universal,* 26 November 1944.

11. "La campaña católica no es de lucha, sino de paz," *Novedades,* 28 December 1944.

12. "Una sangrienta persecución contra los protestantes han desatado los sinarquistas en toda la República," *El Popular,* 6 May 1945. It is not clear that the persecutors were in fact sinarquistas. Protestants seem to have used the specter of sinarquismo to put a more political face on their enemies.

13. L. Scott, *Salt of the Earth,* 105–20.

14. "Acusan a Gobernación de dejar a los protestantes en completo desamparo," *El Popular,* 28 September 1948.

15. David Ruesga to Secretario de Gobernación, 9 March 1949, exp. 2/340(72)1, DGG.

16. "The religious associations called churches, whatever their creed, may never acquire, possess or administrate real estate or the improvements thereon. . . . Churches destined for public worship are the property of the Nation, represented by the Federal Government." *Constitución Política de los Estados Unidos Mexicanos,* Art. 27, Fracc. 2.

17. L. Scott, *Salt of the Earth,* 44–46. Ruesga includes a list of twenty churches of the Iglesia Cristiana Interdenominacional, five churches of the Iglesia Evangélica Independiente, and five other churches that had been waiting for official recognition for long periods, in one case since 1935. David Ruesga to Secretario de Gobernación, 9 March 1949, exp. 2/340(72)1, DGG.

18. David Ruesga to Secretario de Gobernación, 9 March 1949.

19. Ibid.; Estrada Martínez, *El problema.*

20. Elías Hernández to Secretario de Gobernación, 5 October 1945, exp. 2/340(72)1, DGG; Guillermo Macalpín to Secretario de Gobernación, 29 September 1945, exp. 2/340(72)1, DGG; Teresa Lara to Francisco Salcedo Casas, 2 February 1946, exp. 2/340(72)1, DGG; Antonio R. Farías et al. [officer of the Instituto Social Continental] to Manuel Avila Camacho, exp. 547.4/299, MAC.

21. Lydia Lino Sánchez et al. to Miguel Alemán, 6 May 1947, exp. 2/340(72)1, DGG.

22. Ibid.; Mary Cassaretto, "El movimiento protestante en México, 1940–1955," supplement to *Boletín del Secretariado Nacional de la Fe,* Guadalajara (January to April 1961), 46–59; Archivo General del Estado de Oaxaca, Dirrección Jurídica y de Gobierno (files referring to religious conflict are widely dispersed but usually are numbered between 140 and 149 after the first backslash, e.g., 4/149 "58"/1786 or 2/143.0 "60"/2298).

23. José Trueba, *El Sinarquista,* 20 March, 1 May 1941, cited in Meyer, *Sinarquismo,* 143–44.

24. Cameron Townsend and Elvira Townsend, prayer letter, 25 December 1938, doc. 02275, CTA.

25. Rowan Pearce et al. to Friends of Pioneer Mission Agency, Camp Wycliffe and the Wycliffe Bible Translators, 10 July 1942, PMA.

26. These figures are based on McKinlay, *Visits with Mexico's Indians,* 126–27; Elvira Townsend cites 109 workers for forty-five languages in 1943, but she is probably including indigenous languages from the United States, where the SIL had recently started working. Elvira Townsend to Moody Church, 10 November 1943, doc. 03465, CTA.

27. Cameron Townsend to Lázaro Cárdenas, 15 October 1942, doc. 03117, CTA; Cameron Townsend to Manuel Avila Camacho, 11 July 1944, exp. 705.2/659, MAC.

28. Francisco Trejo, Director, Dirección General de Población, Departa-

mento de Migración, to Gobernador del Estado de México, 26 June 1940, doc. 02690, CTA.

29. Elvira Townsend to fellow workers, 6 June 1941, doc. 02799, CTA.

30. "I would suggest that . . . Florence Hansen give Elvira's lectures on foreign courtesy. I consider these latter lectures very important and would hate very much to see them discontinued. Seeing so many new workers this time has emphasized the matter to me. Courtesy doesn't sound like linguistics but it sure does talk." Cameron Townsend to Ken Pike and Eugene Nida, 28 October 1942, doc. 03115, CTA.

31. E. Townsend, *Latin American Courtesy*.

32. Ibid., xi–xii.

33. Ibid., 11.

34. Ibid., 5, 6, 17, 21, 23, 24, 39, 44, 56, 58, 59.

35. Ibid., 61, 62.

36. Ibid., 61, 62.

37. For instance, one missionary to the Masai found that his experiences with them made him more critical of his own culture than of African culture: "The missionary facing an alien pagan culture, to be an efficient instrument of the Gospel, has to have the courage to cast off the idols of the tribe, the tribe he came from. There are many idols but two which, I believe, particularly mesmerize the Western church are individualism, on one hand, and the love of organization on the other." Vincent Donovan, *Christianity Rediscovered* (Maryknoll, N.Y.: Orbis, 1978), 12–13, cited in Sanneh, *Encountering the West,* 160. Similarly, after returning to Great Britain from India, retired missionary Leslie Newbigin devoted himself to criticism of the very foundations of Western culture: "And I could not have come to this critical stance in relation to my own culture without the experience of living in another, an Indian culture." Newbigin, *Foolishness to the Greeks,* 2.

38. Brainerd Legters, annual report, 1942, doc. 03269, CTA.

39. Dick Pittman to linguists, 18 February 1942, doc. 903353, CTA. The SIL was not alone as a missionary organization using science and technology as integral parts of its missionary strategy. As Edward Gitre points out in "The 1904–05 Welsh Revival," the Welsh Revival of 1904 relied on new technologies and spread quickly because of them.

40. Minutes of annual meeting of the Summer Institute of Linguistics, 5 September 1942, doc. 40250, CTA.

41. Cameron Townsend to Ken Pike, 24 February 1943, doc. 03505, CTA.

42. Townsend also needed to fight off internal critics who disliked his openness to Pentecostals and other non-fundamentalist Protestants. To him it was necessary to keep the SIL's ranks open to anyone who could sign the SIL's simple doctrinal statement, because it needed to be absolutely clear that the SIL was not propagating "some special system of theology, practice or discipline." Cameron Townsend to William Nyman, 23 February 1942, doc. 03269, CTA.

43. The figure of 381 publications includes approximately five written for

indigenous languages of the United States and Peru. Summer Institute of Linguistics, *Bibliography*, i.

44. L. L. Legters quoted in Steven, *Doorway to the World*, 17.

45. E. Pike, *Ken Pike*, 83. Pike had an incredibly fertile academic period from 1942 to 1951 during which, in addition to twenty articles, he produced the following books and monographs: *Pronunciation*, vol. 1 of *An Intensive Course in English for Latin American Students; Phonetics: A Critical Analysis of Phonetic Theory and a Technique for the Practical Description of Sounds; The Intonation of American English; Phonemics: A Technique for Reducing Languages to Writing; Tone Languages: A Technique for Determining the Number and Type of Pitch Contrasts in a Language, with Studies in Tonemic Substitution and Fusion;* and *Axioms and Procedures for Reconstruction in Comparative Linguistics: An Experimental Syllabus.*

46. E. Pike, *Ken Pike*, 130, 138, 171, 172.

47. The following SIL-Mexico linguists earned Ph.D.s between 1943 to 1959: Eugene Nida, UCLA, 1943; William Wonderly, University of Michigan, 1947; Dick Pittman, University of Pennsylvania, 1953; Robert Longacre, University of Pennsylvania, 1955; Ben Elson, Cornell, 1956; Howard McKaughan, Cornell, 1956; Sarah Gudschinsky, University of Pennsylvania, 1958; Viola Waterhouse, University of Michigan, 1958; Velma Pickett, University of Michigan, 1959. E. Pike, *Ken Pike*, 130.

48. Svelmoe, "A New Vision for Missions," 541.

49. UNESCO, *Empleo de las lenguas vernáculas en la enseñanza*, 75.

50. Aguirre Beltrán, "El Instituto Lingüístico de Verano," 446.

Chapter 6

1. Gregorio Reyes et al. to Gobernador Constitucional del Estado de Hidalgo, 26 August 1948, exp. 2/340(72)1, DGG; Francisco Salcedo Casas [head of Departamento de Gobierno] to Gobernador del Estado de Hidalgo, 9 September 1948, exp. 2/340(72)1, DGG; Francisco Salcedo Casas to Gregorio Reyes et al., 9 September 1948, exp. 2/340(72)1, DGG; David Ruesga and Agapito Ramos to Adolfo Ruiz Cortines [Secretario de Gobernación], exp. 2/340(72)1, DGG; F. Ocampo Noble [Secretario General de Gobierno del Estado de Hidalgo] to Presidente Municipal of Tepeji del Río, 18 October 1948, exp. 2/340(72)1, DGG; E. Martínez Adame [Director General, Secretaría de Comunicaciones y Obras Públicas] to Secretario de Gobernación, 20 October 1948, exp. 2/340(72)1, DGG; Francisco Salcedo Casas to David Ruesga and Agapito Ramos, 30 September 1948, exp. 2/340(72)1, DGG.

2. The timing of the Iglesia de Dios's request during the beginning months of Ruiz Cortines's term suggests that Protestants may have believed they had reason to hope for better treatment from the new president.

3. The bulk of this section on Tepeji del Río is based on "Informe que la Dirección General de Gobernación del Gobierno del Estado de Hidalgo se

permite rendir a la Secretaría de Gobernación, relativo a los actos realizados el 16 y 17 del presente mes en la población de Tepeji del Río de esta entidad federativa," by Gaudencio Morales, Director General de Gobernación del Gobierno del Estado de Hidalgo, 19 June 1953, exp. 2/340(72)1, DGG; other key documents include Revolucionario Veterano [signature illegible] to Presidente de la República, 17 October 1954, exp. 2/340(72)1, DGG; Próspero Macotela Craviota [Secretario General de Gobernación del Gobierno del Estado de Hidalgo] to Director General de Gobierno, 16 December 1952, exp. 2/340(72)1, DGG; Agapito Ramos [President of CNDE] to Angel Carvajal [Secretario de Gobernación], 17 June 1953, exp. 2/340(72)1, DGG; Alberto Violante Pérez [Brigadier General] to Estado Mayor Presidencial, 17 June 1953, exp. 2/340(72)1, DGG.

4. Revolucionario Veterano [signature illegible] to Presidente de la República, 17 October 1954, exp. 2/340(72)1, DGG.

5. Báez-Camargo, "Punish Mob for Attack on Chapel," 998, cited in L. Scott, *Salt of the Earth,* 46.

6. Taylor and Coggins, *Protestant Missions in Latin America,* cited in L. Scott, *Salt of the Earth,* 46.

7. Ruiz Cortines did not explain his religious policy (actually more of an implied threat than a defined policy), so it is difficult to know his motivations; however, it is possible that he believed the anti-Protestant violence had gone far enough and that the interests of the modernizing Mexican state were now best served by reining in Catholic activism. Genuine concern for the rights of Protestants is another possibility, as is the belief held by some indigenistas that Protestantism would modernize and Mexicanize the countryside. Ruiz Cortines's attitude toward Protestantism was actually more in tune with the Mexican state's approach during most of the twentieth century than the almost officially sanctioned violence of the Ávila Camacho and Alemán administrations.

8. Favre, *El indigenismo,* 8.

9. Alfonso Caso to Miguel Alemán, 24 December 1948, exp. 545.3/172, MAV.

10. Alfonso Caso to Miguel Alemán, 21 June 1949, exp. 522.1/12, MAV.

11. Caso, "El problema indígena de México," 152.

12. For many other examples of Mexican-U.S. cooperation during the 1940s and 1950s, see Stephen Niblo's *War, Diplomacy, and Development.*

13. Aguirre Beltrán, "El Instituto Lingüístico de Verano," 442–43.

14. Gonzalo Aguirre Beltrán to Alfonso Caso, 2 April 1951, exp. FD07/0005, INI.

15. Gonzalo Aguirre Beltrán to Alfonso Caso, 10 June 1951, exp. FD07/0005, INI; Gonzalo Aguirre Beltrán to Alfonso Caso, 10 August 1951, exp. FD07/0005, INI; Aguirre Beltrán, "El Instituto Lingüístico de Verano," 443; Romano Delgado, "Historia evaluativa," 3:41 (exp. FD07/0429, INI).

16. Romano Delgado, "Historia evaluativa," 3:42–44.

17. Aguirre Beltrán, "El Instituto Lingüístico de Verano," 446–47.

18. Gudschinsky, "Native Reaction"; Gudschinsky, "Toneme Representation in Mazatec Orthography."

19. Aguirre Beltrán, "El Instituto Lingüístico de Verano," 446–49.

20. Seven of the SIL "maestros rurales" in 1940 were Elizabeth Lathrop, Otis Leal, Florence Hansen, Victoria Pike, Jerdice Christiansen, Landis Christiansen. and Ken Pike. Francisco García to Brio. de Hacienda y Crédito Público, Dirrección General de Egresos, 8 March 1940, doc. 40270, CTA; Elvira Townsend to Charles Blatchley, 18 February 1941, doc. 02825, CTA.

21. Cameron Townsend to Secretario de Educación Pública, 24 December 1941, doc. 02697, CTA.

22. Emmanuel Palacios, Departamento de Asuntos Indígenas, to Cameron Townsend, 9 November 1946, "important documents, political" file, no number, CTA.

23. Aguirre Beltrán, "El Instituto Lingüístico de Verano," 442–43.

24. "Convenio celebrado entre la Secretaría de Educación Pública de México, a través de la Dirección General de Asuntos Indígenas, y el Sr. Guillermo Townsend, Director General del Summer Institute of Linguistics, Inc, de la Universidad del Edo. de Oklahoma de los Estados Unidos de América," 15 August 1951, in Colegio de Etnólogos y Antropólogos Sociales, *Dominación ideológica y ciencia social,* 41–48.

25. Secretaría de Educación Pública, "La obra indigenista del Presidente Alemán," n.d., exp. 940/12973, MAV.

26. Townsend quoted in Hefley and Hefley, *Uncle Cam,* 76.

27. The SIL itself did not necessarily share this view about the superiority of Western culture. The issue here is that Gamio perceived the SIL as the bearer of Western culture and thus as a positive influence in indigenous communities.

28. Gamio, "Consideraciones sobre el problema indígena en América," 136 (first published in *América Indígena* [Mexico City] in April 1942).

29. Manuel Gamio, "Consideraciones sobre el Instituto Indigenista Nacional" [*sic*], 3 January 1947, exp. 62, caja 2, MG.

30. Gamio, "La investigación de los grupos indígenas mexicanos," 119, 122 (first published in *Hacia un nuevo México* [Mexico City] in 1935).

31. Gamio, "Consideraciones sobre el problema indígena en América," 125.

32. Manuel Gamio, "Moral Concepts and the Religious Problem in Mexico," n.d., caja 1, MG. This address in English appears to be an adaptation of an article that Gamio wrote for *La Nueva Democracia* in April 1920 ("El problema religioso en México"). The earlier version is discussed at length in Ruíz Guerra, "Panamericanismo y protestantismo."

33. Gamio, "Nuestra estructura social," 152 (first published in *Hacia un nuevo México*).

34. Manuel Gamio to Cameron Townsend, 23 April 1952, exp. 89, caja 2, MG; Manuel Gamio to Cameron Townsend, 13 May 1952, exp. 92, caja 2, MG; Manuel Gamio to Ethel Wallis, 23 August 1952, exp. 6, caja 3, MG; Manuel Gamio to Cameron Townsend, 12 January 1955, exp. 13, caja 3, MG.

35. Manuel Gamio to Manuel Gual Vidal, 28 August 1952, exp. 7, caja 3, MG; Manuel Gamio to Javier Desentis, 12 March 1952, exp. 82, caja 2, MG; Manuel Gamio to Quintin Rueda Villagrán, 1 April 1952, exp. 85, caja 2, MG; Summer Institute of Linguistics, "Bibliography of Linguistic, Ethnographic and Literacy Materials by Members of the Summer Institute of Linguistics," September 1951, exp. 704/571, ARC.

36. Manuel Gamio to Jaime Torres Bodet, 3 January 1956, exp. 22, caja 3, MG; Raquel M. de Hoyle to Ethel Wallis, 1 March 1952, exp. 81, caja 2, MG; Manuel Gamio to Ken Pike, 22 July 1952, exp. 2, caja 3, MG; Manuel Gamio to Ethel Wallis, 23 August 1952, exp. 6, caja 3, MG; Manuel Gamio, untitled document, exp. 8, caja 7, MG.

37. Manuel Gamio, "El Instituto Lingüístico de Verano y la redención de los indios monolíngues," in Gamio and Noriega, *A William Cameron Townsend*, 14.

38. Another of Gamio's plans to raise the cultural level of indigenous populations was to bring home Mexicans who had attained an "elevated" lifestyle by living in the United States and to use them as examples for their compatriots. Wilberto Cantón, "Más que a leer, precisa enseñar a que vivan mejor," *Excélsior*, 17 August 1945.

39. Francisco Arellano Belloc, "Townsend, un norteamericano excepcional," *Novedades*, 25 March 1964.

40. Colby and Dennett, *Thy Will Be Done*, 102.

41. One American reviewer called the book "more than slightly prejudiced in favor of Gen. Cardenas," finding it "rather a study of character than an unbiased survey of events" (W. K. Kelsey, "The Commentator," *Detroit News*, 18 February 1952). Mexico's *Tiempo*, however, gave it a glowing review (14 March 1952), as did Pedro Gringoire in *Excélsior* ("Una biografia del Gral. Cárdenas," 7 April 1952), praising it for "doing simple justice to its subject" without "the least hint of fawning." Townsend himself ascribed his writing of the book to divine providence: "Why did I work for almost a year and a quarter writing a biography of Cárdenas? Because God knew it was needed in the Philippines," where President Magsaysay extended an invitation to the SIL after reading the book. C. Townsend, "You're Back Again, Uncle Cam," 34.

42. C. Townsend, *Lázaro Cárdenas*, vi, 372.

43. Ibid., 371–72.

44. Cameron Townsend to Raul Noriega, Oficial Mayor, Secretaría de Hacienda, 13 July 1953, exp. 130/127, ARC. It is not clear whether Townsend received this money.

45. "Desconfianza contra EEUU," *El Universal*, 27 November 1957; "El alza ayuda al comunismo continental," *El Nacional*, 27 November 1957; "Ayudaría al comunismo el alza de Aranceles," *Excélsior*, 27 November 1957; "Mexicanos contra Aranceles," *Tiempo*, 2 December 1957.

46. Cameron Townsend to John F. Kennedy, 23 March, 25 April, 29 April 1961, doc. 45257, CTA; Cameron Townsend, "Oportunas advertencias al President Kennedy," *Magisterio* (Mexico City), May 1961, doc. 45257, CTA; "Tribuna nacional," *Novedades*, 6 May 1961, doc. 45256, CTA.

47. "SIL 1999 Annual Report," http://www.sil.org/sil/annualreport/English.pdf.

48. In perhaps his most damning revelations, Colby points to a $11,000 donation for the SIL's pavilion at the 1964–65 World's Fair made by the Pew family of Sun Oil Company, which later drilled for oil in regions where the SIL had worked, and a $200,000 gift from Nelson Bunker Hunt, another oil man who could be construed to have designs on oil in lands where the SIL worked. In 1967, Colby shows, the SIL received a total of $450,000 from large institutions, including the Ford Foundation, the Crowell Trust, the Glenmeade Trust, the Lilly Foundation, and the U.S. government. In 1969 the Woodward Foundation, "founded and run by the brother of Rockefeller aide Harper Woodward," gave the SIL $25,000. Colby and Dennett, *Thy Will Be Done*, 487, 567–70, 678.

49. The list of "major donors to the SIL/WBT" that Colby identifies includes the following: Pew family (Sun Oil), Pitcairn family (Pittsburgh Plate Glass), Clark Breeding (Aztec Oil), Nelson Bunker Hunt (Placid Oil), James Ezell, Le Tourneau family, Weldon Thomas, Frank Sherrill (S & W Cafeterias), Lawrence Routh, Belk family, G. S. Jones, Woodward Foundation, Trammel Crow, Samuel Milbank (Corn Products Corp.), Cerro de Pasco Corp., Standard Oil of New Jersey, Albert Johnson, David Weyerhauser, Aarón Sáenz, Amos Baker, Henry Crowell (Quaker Oats), Kejn Foundation, Maxey Jarman (Genesco), Robert Welch, Earl Miller, Irvine Foundation, and Herbert Rankin. Colby and Dennett, *Thy Will Be Done*, 488. The largest gift I have identified is "one million dollars in outdated communications equipment" from Pacific Telephone and Telegraph, mentioned in L. Hart, "Story of the Wycliffe Translators," 22.

50. L. Hart, "Story of the Wycliffe Translators," 22.

51. Hefley and Hefley, *Uncle Cam*, 160, 191–95.

52. Colby and Dennett, *Thy Will Be Done*, 571, 779.

53. Hamilton, "We're in the Money," 41.

54. Ibid.

55. Svelmoe, "A New Vision for Missions," 636.

56. Stoll, *Fishers of Men*, 86.

Chapter 7

1. Joseph, "Close Encounters," 15.

2. Siverts, *Oxchuc*, 205.

3. Esponda Jimeno, *La organización social de los tzeltales*, 88.

4. Marianna Slocum to Elvira Townsend and Cameron Townsend, 10 December 1941, doc. 02844, CTA; Slocum and Watkins, *The Good Seed*, 1–34.

5. Marianna Slocum, report, October 1941 to June 1942, doc. 903319, CTA.

6. Slocum and Watkins, *The Good Seed*, 35–59.

7. Marianna Slocum, quoted in "Steam from the Kettle" (SIL Mexico

newsletter), 25 October 1946, 40239, CTA; Slocum and Watkins, *The Good Seed*, 60–93.

8. Slocum and Watkins, *The Good Seed*, 93–139.

9. "Cuidado católico, mucho cuidado!" Acción Católica Mexicana, c. 1950, doc. 45167, CTA. The SIL received other negative publicity at this time. See "Falsos hombres de ciencia que en realidad son catequistas," *El Universal*, 10 March 1951; "Buscan proselitos entre nuestros indígenas," *Excélsior*, 12 October 1951.

10. Anselmo Hernández to Miguel Alemán, 2 January 1951, exp. 254/14437, MAV.

11. Ethel Wallis, "History," c. 1950, doc. 40174, CTA.

12. Alejandro Hernández Bermudez [Presidential Chief of Staff] to Angel Carvajal [Secretario de Gobernación], 12 May 1953, exp. 2/340(72)1, DGG.

13. Fernando Suárez del Solar, Director General de Gobierno, to Governor of Chiapas, 20 May 1953, exp. 2/340(72)1, DGG; Eduardo Poumian Selvas, Procurador General de Justicia del Estado de Chiapas, to Oficial Mayor de Gobierno, 29 June 1953, 2/340(72)1, DGG. "Morrinson" was Mary Morison, a nurse who helped Slocum for a short time.

14. Cameron Townsend to Jerry Cobb, 20 July 1962, doc. 40311, CTA; "News Notes from among the Tzeltals," fall 1956, doc. 40347, CTA; Slocum and Watkins, *The Good Seed*, 200–206.

15. "Perspectiva," *Tiempo*, 9 December 1957.

16. Slocum and Watkins, *The Good Seed*, 106, 112–13, 256. For a more negative assessment of how the SIL worked in Chiapas, see Stoll, *Is Latin America Turning Protestant?* 86–87.

17. Siverts, *Oxchuc*, 175–84. The religious situation became even more strained and complex in the 1960s when Bishop Samuel Ruiz began working with Marist monks and nuns in the Ocosingo, Bachajón, and Comitán areas, eventually training more than six hundred catechists who adopted some of the values of liberation theology. Stephen, *Zapata Lives!* 111.

18. Siverts, *Oxchuc*, 175.

19. Sebastián Ichín López, quoted in Angel Baltazar Caballero, "Historia evaluativa," 4:15 (exp. FD07/0429, INI).

20. Hernández Castillo identifies a similar dynamic among Mam Presbyterians and Jehovah's Witnesses in Chiapas in *Histories and Stories from Chiapas*, 47.

21. Raat and Janecek, *Mexico's Sierra Tarahumara*, 56.

22. Bennett and Zingg, *Los tarahumaras*, 487–96; González Rodríguez, *Tarahumara*, 108–15; Raat and Janacek, *Mexico's Sierra Tarahumara*, 54.

23. Cameron Townsend, "Camp Wycliffe's Activities during the Past Year," September 1936, doc. 02024, CTA; Eugene Nida to "folks," 15 October 1936, doc. 02065, CTA; Eugene Nida to Cameron Townsend, 22 October 1936, doc. 02019, CTA; Eugene Nida to Cameron Townsend, 2 December 1936, doc. 02000, CTA; Steven, *Doorway to the World*, 61, 67–71, 76–83, 85, 87–88, 91–96, 117.

24. Cameron Townsend to Lázaro Cárdenas, 5 September 1940, exp. 710.1/1598, LC.

25. Hilton, *They Were Considered Faithful*, 1–59, 103–4.
26. Ibid., 59–66.
27. Ibid., 67–68.
28. Ibid., 66–68.
29. Ibid., 67–104. In 1990 Ramón López wrote the Hiltons that the church he was leading included sixty-five adult Tarahumaras. It is not clear whether the Hiltons' presence had been counterproductive or whether the Tarahumaras had become more receptive to Protestantism for some other reason (ibid., 100).
30. I do not mean to imply here that they lost their indigenous identities. To the contrary, they usually maintained strong ethnic identities, often enforced by vernacular literacy. The change was toward a dual, Mexican/indigenous identity.
31. Purnell, *Popular Movements and State Formation*, 70–71.
32. "Believers in Tribes in Mexico," January 1962, doc. 40314, CTA. Brainerd and Elva Legters, translators of Yucatec Maya, had been some of the original SIL translators but had resigned to become independent missionaries. Statistics for three groups were not available.
33. In naming her book on the Tzeltals *The Good Seed*, a reference to the Tzeltal name for the Bible, which evokes the parable of the sower and the seed (Mark 4:1–20), and in which seed sown on good soil multiplies a hundredfold, Slocum seeks to give the credit for the Tzeltal revival to God rather than to herself. The title *They Were Considered Faithful*, chosen by Ken and Martha Hilton's daughter Roseanne for the story of her parents' work, comes from Nehemiah 13:13, where the faithful discharge of divinely appointed duties does not lead to obvious religious successes.

Chapter 8

1. This chapter is based on interviews using a bilingual (Otomi/Spanish) translator done in May, June, July, and September 1999 in the following parts of Mexico: San Antonio el Grande, Hidalgo; San Gregorio, Hidalgo; Tulancingo, Hidalgo; and Oaxaca de Juárez, Oaxaca.
2. Felipe Ventura Rodríguez, interview, June 1999.
3. In 1943 Huehuetla built a gas-powered coffee grinder, thereby encouraging a general intensification of coffee growing in the whole municipio by 1950. Prado Gutiérrez, *Monografía del Estado de Hidalgo*.
4. Fidencio Montes Romero, interview, June 1999.
5. Pérez Francisco, *Ra dathu bin ja (El hambre)*.
6. Hidalgo's little-studied Sierra Oriente (also known as the Sierra de Tenango or Sierra de Puebla) is located at the southernmost end of the area known as the Huasteca in the state of Hidalgo. Dow divides the Otomis of the Sierra Oriente into three subregions: the Sierra Alta, Tutotepec, and the Sierra Baja, of which San Antonio el Grande is probably the most important community. Dow, *Santos y Supervivencias*, 65.
7. In 1963 the more accessible Tenango de Doria was still a rather feared and unknown area to the inhabitants of the state capital. "Misteriosa

desaparición de una colega," *El Observador,* 7 September 1963. In 1993 San Antonio had 2,171 of the municipio's 23,000 inhabitants. Prado Gutiérrez, *Monografía del Estado de Hidalgo,* 16.

8. De la Rosa and Campos Cabrera, "Presbiterianismo," 29.

9. Guerrero Guerrero, *Otomíes,* 32, 39.

10. Dow, *Santos y Supervivencias,* 143–57.

11. Guerrero Guerrero, *Otomíes,* 59.

12. De la Rosa and Campos Cabrera, "Presbiterianismo," 80–85, 95.

13. Tepehua is a very small language group unrelated to Otomi. Despite this fact, present-day Tepehuas and Otomis in the Sierra Oriente share many cultural practices because of their interactions over generations. The more numerous and well-known Otomis of Hidalgo's Mezquital Valley speak a variant of Otomi that is incomprehensible to speakers of Eastern Otomi.

14. Katherine Voigtlander, interview, June 26, 1999.

15. Voigtlander, "Sketch of the Lord's Work," 2.

16. Fidencio Montes Romero, interview, June 1999.

17. In *Protestantism in Guatemala,* Virginia Garrard-Barnett notes that indigenous areas of Guatemala affected by violence in the 1980s often saw high rates of Protestant growth because, among other reasons, Protestants received preferential treatment from the state and small Protestant churches offered a sense of community in the midst of chaos.

18. Joaquín Cayetano Ponce, interview, June 1999; Ernesto Pérez Francisco, interview, June 1999.

19. Joyce Jenkins was diagnosed with cancer in 1953 and died in 1958. At about this time, SIL Mexico branch director Ben Elson decided that Voigtlander would go to another town and that Griste would stay in San Gregorio. Griste, in her mid-seventies, soon retired, but not before producing the preliminary translation of the Gospel of John that Voigtlander used in her early years in San Antonio.

20. Juan Santiago, interview, June 1999.

21. Fidencio Rosas Caballero, interview, June 1999.

22. Katherine Voigtlander, interview, 26 June 1999.

23. Macario Santiago Altamirano, interview, June 1999.

24. Fidencio Rosas, interview, June 1999. Many evangelical Protestants believe that women should not serve as pastors, although this prohibition is often bent or broken on the mission field. Rosas was one of two main Otomi translation associates for the translation of the New Testament.

25. Katherine Voigtlander, interview, 26 June 1999.

26. Voigtlander and Echegoyen also depended on community acceptance and feedback in their linguistic work of developing a readable orthography (alphabet), the necessary prerequisite to translation: "Many of the changes were incorporated bit by bit in the published materials, according to the reactions of Otomi readers." Although they had their own ideas about how best to render certain sounds, in the end they had to defer to the indigenous experts, as in a case where Echegoyen and Voigtlander made a change in the orthography that "better reflects the language as the Otomis themselves percieve it." Echegoyen, "Factores," 44, 51.

27. In addition to their SIL linguistic training, Voigtlander had graduated from the Pennsylvania Academy of Fine Arts and the University of Pennsylvania and Echegoyen from the Bible Institute of Los Angeles. Even after fourteen years of study of Otomi, in the midst of writing a descriptive grammar, Echegoyen had no illusions about her knowledge of the language, distinguishing her work of mere description from the higher knowledge held by a native speaker: "If it is proper to establish rules of 'correct' speech, that job belongs to the native speakers of that language." Echegoyen, *Luces contemporáneas del Otomí*, i.

28. Katherine Voigtlander, interview, 26 June 1999.

29. Agustín Arroyo Tolentino, interview, July 1999.

30. Katherine Voigtlander, interview, 26 June 1999.

31. For the African case see Sanneh, *Encountering the West*.

32. Felipe Ventura Rodríguez, interview, June 1999.

33. Francisco San Juan Tolentino, interview, May 1999. The Otomis believed that linguists' familiarity with Pachuca and Mexico City would help San Antonio in its dealings with government bureaucracies. Voigtlander denies that such a meeting ever took place: "I can't imagine my acting like this." Katherine Voigtlander, personal communication, December 2003. Perhaps one of the Otomi Protestants made a similar statement, based on what he had learned from studying the New Testament with Voigtlander.

34. Marcelino Lorenzo Mejía, interview, June 1999. Lorenzo was one of the two main Otomi translation associates in the New Testament translation project. Although many of the early cinder block houses did belong to Protestants, the first two "good" houses were built by Salvador Lazcano and Francisco San Vicente, neither one a Protestant. Antonio Santiago Altamirano, interview, June 1999.

35. Joaquín Cayetano Ponce, interview, July 1999. Two of those who sold their lands were Francisco San Juan Tolentino and Macario García. Macario Santiago Altamirano, interview, June 1999.

36. Antonio Santiago Altamirano, interview, June 1999. One member of the community believes that mayordomías had stopped being mandatory in 1958, before the arrival of the missionaries. Macario Santiago Altamirano, interview, June 1999.

37. Felipe Naranjo Santiago, interview, June 1999.

38. Fidencio Montes Romero, interview, June 1999. Later, Panfilo Mendozo admitted to Domingo Santiago that he had wanted to do violence to some of the Protestants and to Juan Santiago and that he did not carry out plans to bomb the Protestants because he had a vision of a vast army protecting them. Juan Santiago, interview, June 1999.

39. Modesta Santiago Altamirano, interview, May–June 1999; Kastula Esteban, interview, July 1999.

40. Joaquín Miranda San Vicente, interview, June 1999.

41. In Tepeji del Río, Hidalgo, for instance, in 1948 Catholics had burned an evangelical church and managed to prevent Protestants from working in a local factory. Exp. 2/340(72)1, DGG.

42. Neither the missionaries nor their Protestant converts in San Antonio

deny the existence of the beings worshipped by the bädis, as is demonstrated by this quote from Voigtlander about a powerful shaman, the grandfather of Fidencio Rosas: "This man did not use ventriloquism or any kind of pretense when the spirits were talking with him in his house." Katherine Voigtlander, interview, June 1999.

43. Artemisa Echegoyen, interview, 17 September 1999.

44. Ibid.

45. De la Rosa and Campos Cabrera, "Presbiterianismo," 32; Fidel Velasco Mejía, interview, July 1999.

46. Artemisa Echegoyen, interview, 17 September 1999.

47. Ibid. Pachuca is the capital of the state of Hidalgo.

48. De la Rosa and Campos Cabrera, "Presbiterianismo," 126.

49. In a similar case in the municipio of Tenango de Doria, Dow found that the division of the pueblo of San Nicolás into Protestant and Catholic factions had been preceded by a previous division along political lines. Dow, *Santos y Supervivencias*, 87.

50. De la Rosa and Campos Cabrera, "Presbiterianismo," 77.

51. De la Rosa and Campos Cabrera, "Presbiterianismo," 145.

52. The cultural dynamic in San Antonio is very similar to what Bonnie Sue Lewis describes in *Creating Christian Indians*, where she posits that Nez Perce and Dakota conversion to Christianity did not signal a rejection of indigenous culture.

53. Although Gould has argued that "it is erroneous to equate language with identity and that elimination of the former does not extinguish the latter" (*To Die in This Way*, 7), it seems clear from his work that when Nicaragua's indigenous peoples lost their vernacular languages they also lost one of the major tools they could have used to resist acculturation. Perhaps it would be more accurate to say that, although we cannot equate language and identity, the loss of the former often signals the beginning of the process of adopting a mestizo identity.

54. It seems unfair for secular academics to insist on continued adherence to traditional religion as a requirement of indigenous peoples' ethnic identity while simultaneously asserting their own independence from the traditional religion of the West. A more helpful (and more accurate) formulation would be to admit that Christianity and many other religions are compatible with a multiplicity of cultures. For instance, the contemporary shift of Christianity's center, both numerically and in terms of intensity of belief, from Europe to Africa has not made Africa less African; rather, it has demonstrated the compatibility of Christianity with a wide variety of African cultures. The obverse of the African case can be seen in the West, where de-Christianization has by no means led to de-Westernization. See Sanneh, *Translating the Message*.

55. Although Voigtlander and Echegoyen rarely made the journey to San Antonio during the 1990s—both were in their late seventies by the end of the decade—they still maintained a strong influence on the village, largely through their continued patronage of written Otomi. Although the Mexican

state officially supported bilingual education and had instituted it in San Antonio, the fact was that of twenty teachers in the village in 1999, five did not speak Otomi at all and only three could read and write Otomi. Even these three do not use or teach the written language in the classroom. The version of bilingual education practiced in San Antonio consisted of teachers using Otomi as a means of better teaching Spanish and of explaining what students could not understand in their Spanish-language textbooks. Most teachers, products of an educational system that presented Spanish as the key to success and the mestizo culture as superior to indigenous cultures, simply had no desire to learn to read and write in Otomi. Their goal and their functional role, regardless of what the SEP officially espoused, was to Mexicanize their students, not to affirm the validity of Otomi language and culture. To be fair to the local teachers, it also must be pointed out that the SEP had provided them with written materials only in Mezquital Otomi, a variant of Otomi that is as different from Eastern Otomi as Spanish is from French. Hence, even if they had wanted to teach written Otomi, they lacked the appropriate materials. Still, in the late 1990s students in San Antonio *were* learning to read and write Otomi. Voigtlander and Echegoyen, despairing of any hope that the youth of San Antonio would learn written Otomi in the school system, and unable to teach it themselves, contracted with two young Protestants to teach it and secured permission from the local primary school director for this program. For educational officials the linguists' offer provided a way of better fulfilling their mandate for bilingual education; for Voigtlander and Echegoyen this attempt at producing widespread literacy in Eastern Otomi appeared to be the best way of producing a potential pool of readers for the Otomi New Testament.

Chapter 9

1. Frank Robbins to Ernesto Enríquez Jr., Subsecretario of the SEP, 26 January 1962, doc. 40315, CTA.
2. Invitation from SEP, INI, III, and SIL, April 1964, doc. 40305, CTA; "Indigenismo: Nada menos que cien lenguas," *Tiempo,* 27 April 1964; Mario Martini, "Extraordinaria obra humana y científica del Instituto Lingüístico de Verano," *Novedades,* 3 May 1964; Summer Institute of Linguistics, "Día Americano del Indio, 1964–1965" (booklet), 1966, doc. 40304, CTA.
3. Alejandro Ortiz Reza, "La obra indigenista de México, un ejemplo para todo el continente," *Excélsior,* 22 August 1962; "Se aprovechará nuestra experiencia indigenista," *El Universal,* 24 January 1964.
4. Antonio Garza, "Defensa de 30 millones de indígenas," *Novedades,* 17 April 1968.
5. Ben Elson, "Director's Report, Mexico Conference," 1965, doc. 940304, CTA.
6. Benito Coquet to Alfonso Caso, 3 December 1957, exp. 418.2/623, ARC; Cameron Townsend to Adolfo Ruiz Cortines, 16 October 1956, "Heads of State" file, CTA; *Diario Oficial,* 28 July 1960, 3; Cameron Townsend to

Adolfo López Mateos, 26 January 1960, "Heads of State" file, CTA; "Mexico City Headquarters Project," 1961, doc. 40320, CTA; "Posibilidad de construir un gran centro indigenista," *Novedades,* 16 June 1961; Aaron Sáenz to Jaime Torres Bodet, 13 September 1962, doc. 40307, CTA; "Aaron Sáenz donó medio millón para la construcción de la Casa de las 100 Lenguas," *Excélsior,* 30 September 1962, doc. 45244, CTA. Since teaching Spanish and increasing Spanish literacy were perceived as such high priorities by many officials, the SIL emphasized the role of vernacular literacy in pointing indigenous people toward the learning of Spanish and produced some materials designed to teach Spanish to those who could read indigenous languages, even though the teaching of Spanish could work at cross-purposes to their vernacular project. John Beekman, translator of the Chol New Testament, for instance, wrote a booklet called *Spanish Lessons for the Chols,* which attempted to use vernacular literacy "as a psychological and practical bridge to the learning of Spanish," and Artemisa Echogoyen wrote *Hablemos español* for Otomi speakers.

7. The student movement of 1968, which had included demonstrations by as many as three hundred thousand people, came to a bloody conclusion when soldiers and police opened fire on a gathering of ten thousand students at the Plaza de las Tres Culturas (Tlatelolco) and killed two to three hundred of them. Thousands more were injured or arrested. More than any other single event, the Tlatelolco massacre pushed intellectuals out of the PRI and into critical postures toward the regime, some going so far as to join guerrilla movements.

8. González Casanova, "Sociedad plural," 27; González Casanova, *La democracia en México.*

9. Rodolfo Stavenhagen, "Essai comparatif sur les clases sociales et la stratification dans quelques pays sousdeveloppés" (Ph.D., Paris, 1964), cited in Aguirre Beltrán, *Lenguas vernáculas,* 369; Stavenhagen, "Clases, colonialismo y aculturación."

10. Part of the tension between generations involved older Marxist indigenistas indicting their younger neo-Marxian colleagues for "heterodox" interpretations of Marxism, while the younger generation chafed at the rigidity of their elders' "dogmatic" adherence to orthodox Marxism. Gonzalo Aguirre Beltrán, for instance, advocated Mexicanization because he believed it would hasten the creation of a class society. He could not understand why younger anthropologists would impede this necessary and ultimately beneficial process, and he had little sympathy for the "utopian indigenismo" that they advocated. Aguirre Beltrán, *Lenguas vernáculas,* 368–72.

11. Hefley and Hefley, *Uncle Cam,* 197–99; Wallis, *The Dayuma Story;* Wallis and Bennett, *Two Thousand Tongues to Go.*

12. Hefley and Hefley, *Uncle Cam,* 238.

13. Cowan, *The Word That Kindles,* 137–39.

14. Ben Elson, "Permission Is Not Enough," in Pittman et al., *The Wycliffe Sapphire,* 101–4.

15. Richard Pittman, "The Patronato Pattern," in Pittman et al., *The Wycliffe Sapphire,* 144.

16. Hefley and Hefley, *Uncle Cam,* 200–206.

17. Ibid., 270; Cowan, *The Word That Kindles,* 84, 143.

18. Aguirre Beltrán, *Lenguas vernáculas,* 369. For an insightful discussion of anthropology and nationalism in Mexico, see Lomnitz's essay "Bordering on Anthropology: Dialectics of a National Tradition" in his *Deep Mexico, Silent Mexico,* 228–62.

19. Cazés, "Comments," 408, 409.

20. *América Indígena* 29, no. 3 (1969): 787–863.

21. Berreman, "Is Anthropology Alive?" 391.

22. Gunder Frank, "Comments," 412, 414. In response to Frank's attacks on her article "New Proposals for Anthropologists," Gough clarified, "I think, with Frank, that it is my duty to aid revolution as best I can." Gough, "Comment," 429.

23. Rudolf van Zantwijk to Alfonso Caso, 2 July 1969, and Alfonso Caso to Rudolf van Zantwijk, 11 July 1969, caja 6, leg. 67, Archivo Alfonso Caso, INAH.

24. Jose M. Massip, "Un idilio . . . y el escándolo," *Excélsior,* 28 February 1967; Steven Roberts, "Students Opposing U.S.-Aided Regimes Got C.I.A. Subsidies," *New York Times,* 21 February 1967; E. W. Kenworthy, "Hobby Foundation of Houston Affirms C.I.A. Tie," *New York Times,* 21 February 1967; "Repercussions of the C.I.A.," *New York Times,* 26 February 1967.

25. "La C.I.A. en Iberoamérica," *Excélsior,* 23 April 1967 (originally printed in *Marcha* [Montevideo]).

26. "La CIA y sus sucesoras financieras," *El Día,* 10 June 1968.

27. Alain Buler, "La CIA: ¿Gobierno oculto o gran red de espionaje?" *Excélsior,* 20 December 1970 (originally printed in *Realités* [Paris]).

28. José Valderrama, "Homenaje del Instituto Linguistico a la memoria de Dn. Ramón Beteta," *Novedades,* 22 June 1966.

29. Yañez spoke at the SIL's international conference: "Comunicación y Comprensión" *Tiempo,* 29 May 1967; SEP, INI, III, and SIL, invitation to Day of Indian celebration, April 1969, doc. 40287, CTA.

30. "Report to Corporation Conference 1971, Mexico Branch," 1971, doc. 40381, CTA.

31. Cameron Townsend to Luis Echeverría, 19 November 1971, "Heads of State" file, CTA; "Excerpts from Sunday evening reports," July 1972, doc. 40380, CTA.

32. Don Burgess, "Report on the Tercer Seminario de Educacion Indigena," July 1972, doc. 40379, CTA.

33. "Report to Corporation Conference 1971, Mexico Branch," 1971, doc. 40381, CTA. In 1971, fifteen New Testaments had been published; translators were currently working on ninety-five languages, and the task was complete in only two.

34. "México ha logrado estimular el desarrollo de comunidades indias y les ha restituido tierras," *Excélsior,* 9 August 1972.

35. Organization of American States, certificate of recognition, 18 September 1972, in Ochoa Zazueta, "El Instituto Lingüístico de Verano, A.C.";

Emilio Rabas, Secretario de Relaciones Exteriores, to Secretario General del Séptimo Congreso Indigenista Interamericano, 29 July 1972, doc. 40378, CTA.

36. "Dura crítica a la política indigenista de México," *El Universal*, 11 August 1972.

Chapter 10

1. Jaulin, "Introducción," 8–10.
2. Ibid., 12.
3. Keith, "Los indios de América del Norte"; and Meyer, "El problema indio."
4. Aguirre Beltrán, *Lenguas vernáculas*, 370.
5. Warman, "Todos santos y todos difuntos," 10, 36, 37.
6. Valencia, "La formación de nuevos antropólogos," 149; Olivera "Algunos problemas," 98, 108, 115.
7. Bonfil Batalla, "Del indigenismo," 65.
8. Sjollema, preface, 11.
9. For Grünberg's work see his "Urgent Research in North-West Mato Grosso" and his "Beiträge zur Ethnographie der Kayabí Zentralbrasiliens."
10. The participants in the symposium were Grünberg, Pedro Manuel Agostinho da Silva (Brazil), Bernard Arcand (Denmark), Nelly Arvelo de Jiménez (Venezuela), Miguel Bartolomé (Argentina/Mexico), Guillermo Bonfil Batalla (Mexico), Víctor Daniel Bonilla (Colombia), Gonzalo Castillo (Colombia), Miguel Chase (Paraguay), Carlos de Araujo (Brazil), Esteban Mosonyi (Venezuela), Scott Robinson (United States/Mexico), Silvio Coelho (Brazil), Stefano Varese (Peru/Mexico), and Darcy Ribeiro (Brazil); Dostal, *Situation of the Indian*, 12.
11. Bonilla, "Destruction of the Colombian Indian Groups," 61, 71.
12. Robinson, "Some Aspects," 112, 113.
13. Varese, "Inter-ethnic Relations," 136–38.
14. Bonfil Batalla, "The Indian and the Colonial Situation."
15. Ibid., 26, 28.
16. Bartolomé et al., "Declaration of Barbados"; Davis, "Guillermo Bonfil Batalla," 411.
17. Bartolomé et al., "Declaration of Barbados," 376, 378.
18. Ibid., 377, 380. There is a certain amount of irony inherent in these European and mestizo anthropologists' faith in themselves and their discipline, for elsewhere in the declaration they assert that "Indians must organize and lead their own liberation movement otherwise it ceases to be liberating. When non-Indians pretend to represent Indians, even on occasion assuming leadership of the latter's groups, a new colonial situation is established. This is yet another expropriation of the Indian populations' inalienable right to determine their future" (381).

19. Ibid., 378, 379; David Belnap, "Condena internacional de las misiones," *Novedades*, 27 August 1971.

20. Mondragón, "Protestantismo, Panamericanismo, e identidad nacional," 327–31.

21. Martin, *Tongues of Fire*, 262; Bastian, "Protestantismos latinoamericanos."

22. Ochoa Zazueta, "El Instituto Lingüístico de Verano, A.C.," 7. The name of the report was "El protestantismo: Factores para su estudio," but it is unclear whether it was ever published.

23. L. Hart, "Story of the Wycliffe Translators."

24. NACLA Church Research Project, "Introduction" and "The Benevolent Empire"; Edwards, "Protestant Ethic and Imperial Mission."

25. Important denunciations citing *NACLA's Latin America and Empire Report* 7, no. 10, include the following: Cano et al., *Los nuevos conquistadores;* Palomino, *El Instituto Lingüístico de Verano;* and Colegio de Etnólogos y Antropólogos Sociales, *Dominación ideológica y ciencia social* [hereafter CEAS, *Dominación ideológica*].

26. L. Hart, "Story of the Wycliffe Translators," 24, 30, 21.

27. *Translation,* October–December 1972, 2, cited in L. Hart, "Story of the Wycliffe Translators," 21. The "God uses military troops" quotation is repeated by Manuel Buendía ("Dios golpista," *Excélsior,* 20 April 1983) and Andrés Fábregas ("El Instituto Lingüístico de Verano," 154), among others.

28. For instance, Isaiah 10:5, "Woe to the Assyrian, the rod of my anger, in whose hand is the club of my wrath" (King James Version). God uses the Assyrians as an instrument of judgment on Israel, then judges the Assyrians themselves for their actions and their attitudes toward Israel.

29. In the same issue of *NACLA's Latin America and Empire Report*, Douglas Hostetter makes the point that, although "politically very naïve in their relations with other Americans," the SIL linguists whom he knew in Vietnam "lived a simple life," "made a real attempt to understand the culture as well as the language and the history of the people," and, unlike missionaries from other organizations, avoided contact with known CIA collaborators. Hostetter, "An Insider's Story," 8.

30. Fernando Cantu, "Jesucristo es utilizado entre los indios para hacerles aceptar la explotación," *Excélsior,* 3 January 1974; Pedro Gringoire, "Qué hace la CIA en México," *Excélsior,* 27 July 1974; Rafael Rodríguez Castañeda, "Usa intercambios de jóvenes para filtrarlos," *Excélsior,* 15 September 1974; "A lo largo del año y del espacio, la CIA presente," *El Nacional,* 30 December 1974; Vicente Leñero, "Indígenas y minorías, olvidados," *Excélsior,* 23 August 1975.

31. "Un instituto lingüístico de EU acusado de Saqueos en Colombia," *Excélsior,* 16 July 1975; Gregorio Selser, "Estirilización, contrabando, exploración de recursos," *Excélsior,* 9 November 1975.

32. Allegro Marzialle, "Concierto político: Penetran agentes de E.U.," *El Día,* 14 September 1975.

33. "Declaración al primer congreso de pueblos indígenas," *El Día*, 5 October 1975.

34. "Denuncia de Pátzcuaro," in Ochoa Zazueta, "El Instituto," 78–81; "La CIA en casa," *El Día*, 13 October 1975.

35. "Cien idiomas aborígenes estudia el Instituto Lingüísto de Verano," *El Nacional*, 14 February 1971; Salomón Nahmad to Frank Robbins [Director of SIL], April 1971, SNS; Salomón Nahmad to John Alsop [Director of SIL], 18 October 1972, SNS; Stoll, *Fishers of Men*, 226.

36. Salomón Nahmad, interview, November 1999.

37. Alejandro Sorondo, "La última carta de Lázaro Cárdenas fue una dirigida a Salvador Allende," *Excélsior*, 28 June 1976; Antonio Magaña-Esquivel, "El nacionalismo de Lázaro Cárdenas," *Novedades*, 10 July 1976.

38. "La senora Viuda de Cárdenas tomó posesión de un importante cargo," *El Nacional*, 30 June 1976.

39. "Plática por el Sr. Ing, Cuauhtémoc Cárdenas al Instituto Lingüístico," September 1976, doc. 40361, CTA; Dick Pittman to Cameron Townsend, 26 September 1976, doc. 40360, CTA.

40. Grupo de Barbados, "Antecedentes," 13; Pérez and Robinson, *La misión detrás de la misión*, 17.

41. Grupo de Barbados, *Indianidad*, 397; Nemesio J. Rodríguez later edited *Apuntes para la interpretación de una transnacional misionera: El caso del ILV* (1981); that same year, Aaby and Hvalkof edited *Is God an American?*

42. Grupo de Barbados, "La política colonialista del ILV," 399.

43. Ibid.

44. Grupo de Barbados, "Declaración de Barbados II," 391.

45. Grupo de Barbados, "La política colonialista del ILV," 397.

46. In 1968, for instance, the SIL was working on thirteen variants of Mixtec and nine variants of Zapotec (Hefley, *Peril by Choice*, opening map). It takes great faith in the subversive nature of the SIL's mission to assume that twelve of the Mixtec translation teams and eight of the Zapotec teams were superfluous. The fact is that, after centuries of idiosyncratic development in isolated communities, there are no such languages as "Mixtec" and "Zapotec," only families of languages as diverse as the Romance languages in Europe. The SIL, in fact, would have loved to do one translation for all the various Zapotec communities in order to save itself time and effort, but this would have been about as effective as using Portuguese textbooks in Italy or publishing French newspapers in Madrid.

47. Bonfil Batalla, "Sobre la liberación del indio," 95.

48. Margarita Nolasco, "Educación indígena: Las cartillas bilingües," *El Sol de México*, 26 September 1977; Víctor de la Cruz, "En el simposio de Barbados II," *El Nacional*, 15 October 1977; Margarita Nolasco, "Ayuda social y penetración imperial," *El Sol de México*, 10 December 1977.

49. "P.R. Coordinator's Report," October 1977, doc. 40368, CTA.

50. Ibid.

51. Cameron Townsend to Gerald Ford, 13 May 1976, and Cameron

Townsend to Jimmy Carter, 9 November 1976, 11 August 1977, 4 November 1977, "Heads of State" file, CTA.

52. Millán, "Al recibir," 85.

53. The CEAS, founded in 1977 for the "vigilance" of its field so that "the practice of anthropology would not become another weapon of exploitation and domination" (CEAS, *Dominación ideológica*, 1), was attempting to become "the most important organization" in Mexico for ethnologists and social anthropologists by initiating a "national debate" about applied anthropology that would focus, at least initially, on the SIL. Colegio de Etnólogos y Antropólogos Sociales, "Carta circular," 26 March 1979, SNS.

54. Nahmad Sitton, "La educación bilingüe y bicultural," 16.

55. "Espias de EU, supuestos investigadores, operan sin control en México: Nahmad," *Excélsior*, 7 May 1978.

56. Fernando Meráz, "Boicot contra el gobierno, dice el INI," *Uno Más Uno*, 27 July 1978. This is an odd charge, given the SIL's willingness to work closely with a variety of government agencies.

57. "Capacitan a jóvenes indígenas en técnicas lingüísticas y etnológicas," *El Nacional*, 23 January 1978.

58. Bonfil Batalla, "Programa de formación," 61, 64, 76, 77. An interesting aspect of Nahmad's new indigenismo and Bonfil Batalla's ethnolinguistic degree program was that both were perceived by many other Mexican anthropologists as just more of the same, old state-sponsored paternalism. Marcela Lagarde and Daniel Cazés, for instance, referred to the new school of ethnolinguistics as "The National School for Enlightened Caciques and Professional Indians." Lagarde and Cazés, "Política del lenguaje y lingüística aplicada," 168. But most could agree that the SIL had to go.

59. Salomón Nahmad Sitton to Secretaría de Educación, 26 January 1979, SNS.

60. Andrés Fábregas Puig [Presidente del Consejo Directivo, Colegio de Etnólogos y Antropólogos Sociales] to Fernando Solana, 8 March 1979, SNS. An article in *Excélsior* ("Discusión en el Colegio de Etnólogos," 13 May 1978) mentions the participation of Bonfil Batalla, Stavenhagen, and Ovalle in one of the early meetings of the CEAS.

61. "Cronología de noticias acerca del ILV en México, 1975–1979," in CEAS, *Dominación ideológica*, 110–16. Stavenhagen responded in 2001, "I think I meant that its own serious linguistic work on indigenous languages had done little to train Mexican linguists and further the development of linguistic science in Mexico." Rodolfo Stavenhagen, personal communication, 11 May 2001.

62. Salomón Nahmad Sitton, Ignacio Ovalle Fernández, Guillermo Bonfil Batalla, and Rodolfo Stavenhagen to Fernando Solana, "Memorandum Confidential," 19 June 1979, SNS.

63. Ibid.

64. Ibid. Zilg later adopted the name "Gerald Colby." For the controversy generated by Zilg and Dennett's book, *Thy Will Be Done* (1995), see *Anthro-*

pology Newsletter for Marc Edelman's interview with Zilg and Dennett ("Nelson Rockefeller and Latin America") and Kenneth Pike and Thomas Headland's response ("SIL and Genocide: Well-Oiled Connection?"). The statement about the Cárdenas family was untrue (whether intentionally or unintentionally is hard to tell), for shortly thereafter, in September 1980, Cuauhtémoc Cárdenas invited members of the SIL to attend his inauguration as governor of Michoacán. Cuauhtémoc Cárdenas, 15 September 1980, doc. 40358, CTA.

65. "Declaración de Temoaya," *El Día*, 30 July 1979.

66. Daniel Cazés, "Mas sobre el ILV," *Uno Más Uno*, 22 August 1979.

67. CEAS, *Dominación ideológica*, 37–38.

68. "La SEP da por terminado el convenio," in Alisedo et al., *El Instituto Lingüístico de Verano*, 75.

69. Earl Adams, "The End of an Era: Closing up Jungle Camp," 11 April 1980, doc. 40428, CTA.

70. John Alsop, personal communication, 11 December 2003; C. Townsend, "Two Presidents . . . and the Chamulas," 143.

71. Ben Elson, "Mexican Branch Report to the Biennial Conference 1961," doc. 940351, CTA.

72. *Acta final del VIII Congreso Indigenista Interamericano* (Mexico City: III, 1980), 97; Stoll, "¿Con qué derecho adoctrinan ustedes a nuestros indígenas?" 10–11; Stoll, *Fishers of Men*, 230–31.

73. King, *Roots of Identity*, 115; Bravo Ahuja, *Los materials didácticos*, 147.

74. L. Hart, "Story of the Wycliffe Translators," 22; Stoll, *Fishers of Men*, 85; Pérez and Robinson, *La misión detrás de la misión*, 23.

75. Stoll, *Fishers of Men*, 83–86.

76. As William Svelmoe points out in "The General and the Gringo" (304n), the fervor of the campaign against Townsend was directed at "precisely the wrong man," for it is difficult to imagine an American more willing to cast off his American-ness and to adopt the perspective of Latin America than Townsend.

77. C. Townsend, "Two Presidents . . . and the Chamulas," 144; Cameron Townsend to José López Portillo, 16 January 1981, "Heads of State" file, CTA.

Conclusion

1. Catholic universities would be another example of institutions combining religion, politics, and science.

2. Roseberry, "Hegemony and the Language of Contention"; Purnell, *Popular Movements and State Formation*.

3. Steven, *They Dared to Be Different*, 115, 129, 141, 189.

4. Estrada Martínez, *El problema*, 41.

5. In 1985 the Chamulan colonia of Betania had 1,028 inhabitants. Of its 177 families, 8 were Jehovah's Witnesses, 2 or 3 were Catholic, and the rest were Presbyterian. Although there were civil authorities, in practice the pastor of the largest of its two Presbyterian churches was the real leader of the community. Other than two North American missionaries, the commu-

nity has not allowed non-Chamulas to settle in its territory. Robledo Hernández, *Disidencia y religión*, 87–93.

6. Estrada Martínez, *El problema*, 15–27.

7. *Ladino* is the term used in Chiapas for mestizos and acculturated (hispanicized) Indians.

8. Estrada Martínez, *El problema*, 33.

9. Rus, "The 'Comunidad Revolucionaria Institucional' "; for more on the importance of *posh* to Chamulan culture, see Pozas, *Juan the Chamula*.

10. Fernando Meraz, "Boicot contra el gobierno, dice el INI," *Uno Más Uno*, 27 July 1978.

11. Ramón Llarena y del Rosario, "San Juan Chamula: ¿Qué hay detrás?" *El Universal*, 19 October 1978.

12. CEAS, *Dominación ideológica*, 16–17; Enrique Maza echoes almost exactly the CEAS criticisms of the SIL's role among the Chamulas in "El ILV: Antimexicano, pero 'al servicio del estado,' " in Alisedo et al., *El Instituto Lingüístico de Verano*, 27–38.

13. Enrique Maza, "El Colegio de Etnólogos y Antropólogos demanda la expulsión del ILV" (interview with Andrés Fábregas), in Alisedo et al., *El Instituto Lingüístico de Verano*, 56.

14. Rus and Wasserstrom, "Evangelization and Political Control," 170; Rus, "The 'Comunidad Revolucionaria Institucional,' " 299–300.

15. Benjamin, "A Time of Reconquest"; Stephen, *Zapata Lives!* 91–215.

16. The SIL worked on exactly the languages that Benjamin cites in his article: San Andrés Larraínzar Tzotzil, San Juan Chamula Tzotzil, Chenalhó Tzotzil, Huixtec Tzotzil, Oxchuc Tzeltal, Bachajón Tzeltal, Chol, and Tila Chol. Hefley, *Peril by Choice*, frontispiece.

17. Benjamin, "A Time of Reconquest," 429, 436.

18. Stephen, *Zapata Lives!* 112.

19. Benjamin, "A Time of Reconquest," 427.

20. Rus's 1994 article argues in a similar vein that Protestantism served as a site of resistance to the corrupt Chamulan civil-religious hierarchy, a much more positive view of Protestantism than his view in 1981, but does not go so far as to give credit to the SIL for providing an ideological alternative for San Juan Chamula. Rus, "The 'Comunidad Revolucionaria Institucional,' " 300; Rus and Wasserstrom, "Evangelization and Political Control," 170.

21. The shrewdness of defining economic, political, religious, and even agricultural dissidence as "heresy" is demonstrated by the PRI's continuing ability to legitimize its support of caciques as support for "traditional religion." The enduring desire among political progressives for the preservation of indigenous cultures meant that many on the left were reluctant to speak out for fear of appearing insensitive to Chamulan "tradition." See Rus, "The 'Comunidad Revolucionaria Institucional,' " 300.

22. Chamulas were not unfamiliar with wage labor, but the kind of seasonal work that men traditionally did on large plantations was far different from urban forms of domestic and commercial labor. Many Chamulas tried

to continue their agricultural lifestyles in the environs of San Cristóbal de Las Casas, but the scarcity, expense, and poor quality of cultivable land made this quite difficult. Some Chamulan Protestants, like other dissidents, also formed new communities in the Lacandón jungle, but the vast majority of Protestant expulsados moved to the environs of San Cristóbal de Las Casas.

23. In the rare cases where a written language already exists, the New Testament still serves as a major addition to the existing literature. Isthmus Zapotec, for instance, had an emerging written literature when Velma Pickett and other SIL linguists began their work in that language in the early 1940s, but their presence spurred Zapotec intellectuals to participate in a "round table" with the SIL linguists to unify the various alphabets that were being used. Velma Pickett, interview, January 1998.

24. Nahmad, "Oaxaca y el CIESAS," 23.

25. Bonfil Batalla, *Utopía y revolución*.

26. Bonfil Batalla quoted in Davis, "Guillermo Bonfil Batalla," 414.

27. Bonfil Batalla, *México Profundo*, 148; Bartolomé et al., "Declaration of Barbados," 378–79.

28. Bonfil Batalla, *México Profundo*, 149. Sociologist Jean-Pierre Bastian proposes a similar view of religious change, pointing out that the Indian is not a passive receptor of external religions but "a social actor who chooses from outside beliefs, practices, and offerings as part of strategies that correspond as much to global realities as to affairs within his own ethnic group." Bastian, *La mutación religiosa*, 101–3.

29. Solomón Nahmad, interview, November 1999.

30. Bastian, *La mutación religiosa*, 121.

Bibliography

Archives and Libraries

Archivo General de la Nación, Mexico City
    Ramo Miguel Alemán Velasco
    Ramo Manuel Avila Camacho
    Ramo Lázaro Cárdenas del Rio
    Archivo Particular Lázaro Cárdenas, Microfilm
    Dirección General de Gobierno
    Ramo Adolfo López Mateos
    Ramo Adolfo Ruiz Cortines
Archivo General del Estado de Hidalgo, Pachuca
Archivo General del Estado de Oaxaca, Oaxaca
    Dirección Jurídica y de Gobierno
Biblioteca Miguel Lerdo de Tejada, Mexico City
    Archivo Económico
Franklin D. Roosevelt Presidential Library, Hyde Park, New York
    Josephus Daniels Collection
    Microfilm Collection: Josephus Daniels
    President's Secretary's File
    Sumner Welles Collection
Hemeroteca Pública de Oaxaca Nestor Sánchez H., Oaxaca
Instituto Dr. José María Luis Mora, Biblioteca, Mexico City
Instituto Nacional de Antropología e Historia, Archivo Histórico, Mexico City
    Archivo Alfonso Caso
    Archivo Manuel Gamio
Instituto Nacional Indigenista, Archivo Histórico, Mexico City
Instituto Nacional Indigenista, Biblioteca Pública, Oaxaca

Jungle Aviation and Radio Service Headquarters, Waxhaw, North Carolina
    Cameron Townsend Archive
Library of Congress, Washington, D.C.
National Archives, College Park, Maryland
    State Department Central Files, Record Group 59
Personal Archive of Salomón Nahmad Sitton (to be donated to the Centro
    de Investigacione y Estudios Superiores en Antropología Social), Oaxaca
Secretaría de Relaciones Exteriores, Archivo Histórico, Mexico City
Yale University, Divinity School Library
    Records of the Pioneer Mission Agency
Yale University, Sterling Library

Interviews

Daniel Agee, December 1997, Oaxaca
Agustín Arroyo Tolentino, July 1999, San Antonio el Grande, Hidalgo
Francisco Bacilio Eusebio, June 1999, San Antonio el Grande, Hidalgo
Zenón Bacilio Eusebio, June 1999, San Antonio el Grande, Hidalgo
Fidencio Bacilio Santiago, June 1999, San Antonio el Grande, Hidalgo
Doris Bartholomew, January 1998, Catalina, Arizona
María Bernardino Tolentino, May 1999, San Antonio el Grande, Hidalgo
Venancio Calletano, June 1999, San Antonio el Grande, Hidalgo
Joaquín Cayetano Ponce, June 1999, San Antonio el Grande, Hidalgo
Marian Cowan, January 1998, Catalina, Arizona
Artemisa Echegoyen, July 1997, August and September 1999, Oaxaca
Ben Elson, January 1998, Catalina, Arizona
Benigno Encarnación Ventura, June 1999, San Antonio el Grande, Hidalgo
Kastula Esteban, July 1999, San Antonio el Grande, Hidalgo
Tomás Flores Tolentino, July 1997 and June 1999, San Antonio el Grande,
    Hidalgo
Modesta García, May 1999, San Antonio el Grande, Hidalgo
Armando González Naranjo, June 1999, San Antonio el Grande, Hidalgo
María Gregorio, June 1999, San Antonio el Grande, Hidalgo
Barbara Hollenbach, 4 July 1997, Tlaxiaco, Oaxaca
Bruce Hollenbach, 4 July 1997, Tlaxiaco, Oaxaca
Pedro Lewin, 12 July 1997, Oaxaca
John Lind, January 1998, Willcox, Arizona
Royce Lind, January 1998, Willcox, Arizona
Francisco Lorenzo Bacilio, May 1999, San Antonio el Grande, Hidalgo
Marcelino Lorenzo Mejía, June 1999, San Antonio el Grande, Hidalgo
Eulogio Lorenzo Santiago, June 1999, San Antonio el Grande, Hidalgo
Ulises Lorenzo, June 1999, San Antonio el Grande, Hidalgo
Steve Marlett, January 1998, Catalina, Arizona
Francisco Mejía Licona, June 1999, San Antonio el Grande, Hidalgo
Macario Mejía Licona, June 1999, San Antonio el Grande, Hidalgo
Margarita Miranda Altamirano, May 1999, San Antonio el Grande, Hidalgo

Fidencio Miranda García, June 1999, San Antonio el Grande, Hidalgo
Pablo Miranda Mendoza, June 1999, San Antonio el Grande, Hidalgo
Javier Miranda San Vicente, May 1999, San Antonio el Grande, Hidalgo
Joaquín Miranda San Vicente, June 1999, San Antonio el Grande, Hidalgo
Fidencio Montes Romero, June 1999, San Antonio el Grande, Hidalgo
Salomón Nahmad Sitton, November 1999, Oaxaca
Felipe Naranjo Santiago, June 1999, San Antonio el Grande, Hidalgo
Francisco Naranjo Santiago, May 1999, San Antonio el Grande, Hidalgo
Juvencio Naranjo Santiago, May 1999, San Antonio el Grande, Hidalgo
Epifanio Neria José, May 1999, San Antonio el Grande, Hidalgo
Verónica Paulino Encarnación, June 1999, San Antonio el Grande, Hidalgo
Margarita Pérez, June 1999, San Antonio el Grande, Hidalgo
Ernesto Pérez Francisco, June 1999, San Antonio el Grande, Hidalgo
Lázaro Pérez Naranjo, June 1999, San Antonio el Grande, Hidalgo
Velma Pickett, January 1998, Catalina, Arizona
Francisco Romero Altamirano, May 1999, San Antonio el Grande, Hidalgo
Fidencio Rosas Caballero, June 1999, San Antonio el Grande, Hidalgo
Francisco San Juan Tolentino, May 1999, San Antonio el Grande, Hidalgo
Juan Santiago, June 1999, San Antonio el Grande, Hidalgo
Antonio Santiago Altamirano, June 1999, San Antonio el Grande, Hidalgo
Macario Santiago Altamirano, June 1999, San Antonio el Grande, Hidalgo
Modesta Santiago Altamirano, May 1999, San Antonio el Grande, Hidalgo
Victor Santiago Hernández, June 1999, San Antonio el Grande, Hidalgo
Glenn Stairs, November 1999, Oaxaca
Lucero Topete, 3 July 1997, Oaxaca
David Tuggy, January 1998, Catalina, Arizona
Fidel Velasco Mejía, July 1999, San Antonio el Grande, Hidalgo
Felipe Ventura Rodríguez, June 1999, San Antonio el Grande, Hidalgo
Francisco Ventura Rodríguez, May 1999, San Antonio el Grande, Hidalgo
Katherine Voigtlander, July 1997 and June 1999, Tulancingo, Hidalgo
Milton Warkentin, January 1998, Catalina, Arizona
Tom Willett, 10 July 1997, Puebla

Newspapers

Baltimore Catholic Review
Carteles del Sur (Oaxaca)
Chicago Daily Tribune
Dallas Times-Herald
El Día (Mexico City)
Excélsior (Mexico City)
Gazette (Montreal)
Gráfico (Mexico City)
El Independiente (Pachuca)
La Jornada (Mexico City)
Light (San Antonio, Texas)

La Nación (Buenos Aires)
El Nacional (Mexico City)
New York Herald Tribune
New York Post
New York Times
New York World Telegram
Noticias (Oaxaca)
Novedades (Mexico City)
El Observador (Pachuca)
El Popular (Mexico City)
La Prensa (Mexico City)
La Prensa (San Antonio, Texas)
Renovación (Pachuca)
El Sol de México
El Universal
Uno Más Uno
Washington Post

Books and Articles

Adams, Richard N. "Strategies of Ethnic Survival in Central America." In *Nation-States and Indians in Latin America,* ed. Greg Urban and Joel Sherzer, 181–206. Austin: University of Texas Press, 1991.

Agence Latino-Americaine d'Information. "El Instituto Lingüístico de Verano, instrumento del imperialismo." *Nueva Antropología* 3, no. 9 (1978): 118–33.

Aguirre Beltrán, Gonzalo. *Crítica antropológica: Hombres e ideas.* Mexico City: Fondo de Cultura Económica, 1990.

———. "El Instituto Lingüístico de Verano." *América Indígena* 41, no. 3 (1981): 435–61.

———. "Introducción." In Vicente Lombardo Toledano, *El problema del indio,* 7–8. Mexico City: SEP Setentas, 1973.

———. *Lenguas vernáculas: Su uso y desuso en la enseñanza: La experiencia de México.* Mexico City: Fondo de Cultura Económica, 1993.

———. *Teoría y práctica de la educación indígena.* Mexico City: SEP Setentas, 1973.

Alisedo, Pedro, et al. *El Instituto Lingüístico de Verano.* Mexico City: Proceso, 1981.

Anderson, Justice C. Review of *Thy Will Be Done,* by Gerald Colby and Charlotte Dennett. *International Review of Missionary Research* 20, no. 3 (1996): 129.

Anhalt, Diana. *A Gathering of Fugitives: American Political Expatriates in Mexico, 1948–1965.* Santa Maria, Calif.: Archer, 2001.

Báez-Camargo, Gonzalo. *Is There Religious Persecution in Mexico?* New York: N.p., 1926.

———. "The Missionary Task of the Church in Mexico and Central America." *International Review of Missions* 36 (1947): 163–74.

———. "Protestantism in Latin America: Mexico." *Religion in Life* 27, no. 1 (1957–58): 45–53.

———. "Punish Mob for Attack on Chapel." *Christian Century*, 2 September 1953, 998.

Bailey, David. "The Church since 1940." In *Twentieth-Century Mexico*, ed. W. Dirk Raat and William Beezley, 236–42. Lincoln: University of Nebraska Press, 1986.

Baldwin, Deborah. *Protestants and the Mexican Revolution: Missionaries, Ministers, and Social Change*. Urbana: University of Illinois Press, 1990.

Barrios Ruiz, Walda, and Leticia Pons Bonals. *Sexualidad y religión en los Altos de Chiapas*. Tuxtla Gutiérrez: Universidad Autónoma de Chiapas, 1995.

Bartolomé, Miguel, et al. "Declaration of Barbados: For the Liberation of the Indians." In *The Situation of the Indian in South America: Contributions to the Study of Inter-ethnic Conflict in the non-Andean Regions of South America*, ed. Walter Dostal, 376–81. Geneva: World Council of Churches, 1972.

Bastian, Jean-Pierre. *Los disidentes: Sociedades protestantes y revolución en México, 1872–1911*. Mexico City: Fondo de Cultura Económica, 1989.

———. *La mutación religiosa de América Latina: Para una sociología del cambio social en la modernidad periférica*. Mexico City: Fondo de Cultura Económica, 1997.

———. "Protestantismos latinoamericanos entre la resistencia y la sumisión, 1961–1983." *Cristianismo y Sociedad* 82 (1984): 49–68.

———. "Protestantismos minoritarios y protestarios en México." *Taller de Teología* 10 (1982): 5–11.

———. *Protestantismo y sociedad en México*. Mexico City: Casa Unida de Publicaciones, 1983.

Bays, Daniel, and Grant Wacker. "Introduction: The Many Faces of the Missionary Enterprise at Home." In *The Foreign Missionary Enterprise at Home: Explorations in North American Cultural History*, ed. Bays and Wacker, 1–12. Tuscaloosa: University of Alabama Press, 2003.

———, eds. *The Foreign Missionary Enterprise at Home: Explorations in North American Cultural History*. Tuscaloosa: University of Alabama Press, 2003.

Becker, Marjorie. *Setting the Virgin on Fire: Lázaro Cárdenas, Michoacán Peasants and the Redemption of the Mexican Revolution*. Berkeley: University of California Press, 1995.

———. "Torching La Purísima, Dancing at the Altar: The Construction of Revolutionary Hegemony in Michoacán, 1934–1940." In *Everyday Forms of State Formation: Revolution and the Negotiation of Rule in Modern Mexico*, ed. Gilbert Joseph and Daniel Nugent, 247–64. Durham, N.C.: Duke University Press, 1994.

Beekman, John. *Spanish Lessons for the Chols*. Mexico City: Summer Institute of Linguistics, 1953.

Benjamin, Thomas. "A Time of Reconquest: History, the Maya Revival and the Zapatista Rebellion in Chiapas." *American Historical Review* 105, no. 2 (2000): 417–50.

Bennett, Wendell, and Robert Zingg. *Los tarahumaras: Una tribu india del norte de México.* Mexico City: Instituto Nacional Indigenista, 1986.

Berreman, Gerald. "Is Anthropology Alive? Social Responsibility in Social Anthropology." *Current Anthropology* 9, no. 5 (1968): 391–96.

Bethell, Leslie, ed. *Mexico since Independence.* New York: Cambridge University Press, 1991.

Blancarte, Roberto. "Aspectos internacionales del conflicto religioso mexicano en la década de los treinta." In *Cultura e identidad nacional,* ed. Blancarte, 233–60. Mexico City: Fondo de Cultura Económica, 1994.

———, ed. *Cultura e identidad nacional.* Mexico City: Fondo de Cultura Económica, 1994.

Bonfil Batalla, Guillermo. "Del indigenismo de la Revolución a la antropológica crítica." In Arturo Warman et al., *De eso que llaman antropología mexicana,* 30–65. Mexico City: Nuestro Tiempo, 1970.

———. "The Indian and the Colonial Situation: The Context of Indigenist Policy in Latin America." In *The Situation of the Indian in South America: Contributions to the Study of Inter-ethnic Conflict in the non-Andean Regions of South America,* ed. Walter Dostal, 21–28. Geneva: World Council of Churches, 1972.

———. *México Profundo: Reclaiming a Civilization.* Trans. Philip A. Dennis. Austin: University of Texas Press, 1996.

———. "Las nuevas organizaciones indígenas." In *Indianidad y descolonización en América Latina: Documentos de la segunda reunión de Barbados,* 23–40. Mexico City: Nueva Imagen, 1979.

———. "Programa de formación profesional de etnolingüístas." In Mercedes Olivera et al., *Indigenismo y lingüística: Documentos del foro "La política del lenguaje en México,"* 61–82. Mexico City: Universidad Nacional Autónoma de México, 1980.

———. "Sobre la liberación del indio." *Nueva Antropología* 2, no. 8 (1978): 95–100.

———. *Utopía y revolución: El pensamiento político contemporáneo de los Indios de América Latina.* Mexico City: Nueva Imagen, 1981.

Bonilla, Víctor Daniel. "The Destruction of the Colombian Indian Groups." In *The Situation of the Indian in South America: Contributions to the Study of Inter-ethnic Conflict in the Non-Andean Regions of South America,* ed. Walter Dostal, 56–75. Geneva: World Council of Churches, 1972.

Borman, Randall. "Survival in a Hostile World: Culture Change and Missionary Influence among the Cofan People of Ecuador, 1954–1994." *Missiology: An International Review* 24, no. 2 (1996): 185–200.

Bravo Ahuja, Gloria. *Los materials didácticos para la enseñanza del español a los indígenas mexicanos.* Mexico City: Colegio de México, 1977.

Breton, Alain. *Bachajón: Organización socioterritorial de una comunidad tzeltal.* Mexico City: Instituto Nacional Indigenista, 1984.

Britton, John. *Educación y radicalismo en México.* Vol. 2. *Los años de Cárdenas.* Mexico City: SEP Setentas, 1976.

————. *Revolution and Ideology: Images of the Mexican Revolution in the United States*. Lexington: University Press of Kentucky, 1995.

Buendía, Manuel. *La CIA en México*. Mexico City: Ediciones Océano, 1983.

Calderón, Lisandro. *La educación moral en la escuela socialista*. Mexico City: DAPP, 1938.

Calles, Plutarco Elías. *México before the World: Public Documents and Addresses of Plutarco Elías Calles*. New York: Academy Press, 1927.

Cano, Ginette, et al. *Los nuevos conquistadores: El Instituto Lingüístico de Verano en América Latina*. Quito: CEDIS, 1981.

Cárdenas, Lázaro. "Discurso en apoyo de la educación socialista." In *La educación socialista, 1934–1945,* ed. Gilberto Guevara Niebla, 85–88. Mexico City: SEP, 1985.

————. *Obras*. Vol. 1. *Apuntes, 1913–1940*. Mexico City: Universidad Nacional Autónoma de México, 1972.

Carpenter, Joel. *Revive Us Again: The Reawakening of American Fundamentalism*. New York: Oxford University Press, 1997.

Caso, Alfonso. "Los fines de la acción indigenista en México." In Caso, *La comunidad indígena*, 137–45. Mexico City: SEP, 1980.

————. "Los ideales de la acción indigenista." In Caso, *La comunidad indígena*, 154–61. 1962. Mexico City: SEP, 1980.

————. "Lo que no es el indigenismo." In Caso, *La comunidad indígena*, 162–78. Mexico City: SEP, 1980.

————. "El problema indígena de México." In Caso, *La comunidad indígena*, 146–53. Mexico City: SEP, 1980.

Cassaretto, Mary. "El movimiento protestante en México, 1940–1955." Supplement to *Boletín del Secretariado Nacional de la Fe,* Guadalajara (January–April 1961).

Castellanos, Alicia. *Notas sobre la identidad étnica en la región tzotzil tzeltal de Los Altos de Chiapas*. Mexico City: Universidad Autónoma Metropolitana, 1988.

Cazés, Daniel. "Comments." In "Social Responsibilities Forum." *Current Anthropology* 9, no. 5 (1968): 408–9.

Clark, Larry. *Not Silenced by Darkness*. Langley, B. C.: Credo, 1992.

Colby, Gerald, and Charlotte Dennett. *Thy Will Be Done: The Conquest of the Amazon: Nelson Rockefeller and Evangelism in the Age of Oil*. New York: Harper Collins, 1995.

Colegio de Etnólogos y Antropólogos Sociales, A.C. *Dominación ideológica y ciencia social: El I.L.V. en México*. Mexico City: Nueva Lectura, 1979.

Comas, Juan. "La lengua vernácula y el bilingüismo en la educación." *América Indígena* 16, no. 2 (1956): 93–109.

Cowan, George W. *The Word That Kindles*. Chappaqua, N.Y.: Christian Herald Books, 1979.

Cronon, David. "American Catholics and Mexican Anticlericalism, 1933–1936." *Mississippi Valley Historical Review* 45, no. 2 (1958): 201–30.

————. *Josephus Daniels in Mexico*. Madison: University of Wisconsin Press, 1960.

Dame, Lawrence. *Maya Mission*. Garden City: Doubleday, 1968.

Daniels, Josephus. *Shirt-Sleeve Diplomat*. Chapel Hill: University of North Carolina Press, 1942.

Davis, Shelton. "Guillermo Bonfil Batalla y el movimiento indio latinoamericano." *América Indígena* 51, nos. 2–3 (1991): 411–16.

Dayton, Donald, and Robert Johnston, eds. *The Variety of American Evangelicalism*. Downers Grove, Ill.: InterVarsity Press, 1991.

Delpar, Helen. *The Enormous Vogue of Things Mexican: Cultural Relations between the United States and Mexico, 1920–1935*. Tuscaloosa: University of Alabama Press, 1992.

Dostal, Walter, ed. *The Situation of the Indian in South America: Contributions to the Study of Inter-ethnic Conflict in the Non-Andean Regions of South America*. Geneva: World Council of Churches, 1972. Originally published as *La situación del indígena en América del Sur: Aportes al estudio de la fricción interétnica en los indios no-andinos*. Montevideo: Tierra Nueva, 1972.

Dow, James. *Santos y Supervivencias: Funciones de la religión en una comunidad otomí, México*. Mexico City: Instituto Nacional Indigenista, 1974.

———. *The Shaman's Touch: Otomi Indian Symbolic Healing*. Salt Lake City: University of Utah Press, 1986.

Dumont, Jean-Paul. "El occidente y los bárbaros." *Anuario Indigenista* 30 (1970): 7–11.

Durán Solís, Leonel, ed. *Religión y sociedad en el sureste de México*. 7 vols. Mexico City: Cuadernos de la Casa Chata, 1987–89.

Dye, T. Wayne. *Bible Translation Strategy: An Analysis of Its Spiritual Impact*. Dallas: Wycliffe Bible Translators, 1985 (1980).

Echegoyen, Artemisa. "Factores en el desarollo de una ortografía para el otomí de la Sierra." In *Escritura y alfabetización*, ed. Luis Fernando Lara and Felipe Garrido, 39–59. Mexico City: Ediciones del Hermitaño, 1986.

———. *Hablemos español*. Mexico City: Summer Institute of Linguistics, 1964.

———. *Luces contemporáneas del Otomí: Gramática del Otomí de la Sierra*. Mexico City: Instituto Lingüístico de Verano, 1979.

Edelman, Marc. "Nelson Rockefeller and Latin America." *Anthropology Newsletter,* January 1997, 36–37.

Edwards, Rick. "Protestant Ethic and Imperial Mission: The Latin American Case." *NACLA's Latin America and Empire Report* 6, no. 2 (1972): 2–13.

Eley, Geoff, and Ronald Grigor Suny. "Introduction: From the Moment of Social History to the Work of Cultural Representation." In *Becoming National: A Reader,* ed. Eley and Suny, 3–38. New York: Oxford University Press, 1996.

———, eds. *Becoming National: A Reader*. New York: Oxford University Press, 1996.

Elson, Benjamin, ed. *Language in Global Perspective: Papers in Honor of the Fiftieth Anniversary of the Summer Institute of Linguistics*. Dallas: Summer Institute of Linguistics, 1986.

Espejel López, Laura, and Rubén Ruíz Guerra, eds. *El protestantismo en México*

(1850–1940): La Iglesia Metodista Episcopal. Mexico City: Instituto Nacional de Antropología e Historia, 1995.

Esponda Jimeno, Víctor Manuel. *La organización social de los tzeltales*. Tuxtla Gutiérrez: Instituto Chiapaneco de Cultura, 1994.

Estrada Martínez, Rosa Isabel. *El problema de las expulsiones en las comunidades indígenas de los Altos de Chiapas y los derechos humanos*. Mexico City: Comisión Nacional de Derechos Humanos, 1995.

Fábregas, Andrés. "El estudio antropológico de la religión." In *Religión y sociedad en el sureste de México*, ed. Leonel Durán Solís, 2:1–26. Mexico City: Cuadernos de la Casa Chata, 1987–89.

———. "El Instituto Lingüístico de Verano y la penetración ideológica." In Mercedes Olivera et al., *Indigenismo y lingüística: Documentos del foro "La política del lenguaje en México,"* 153–58. Mexico City: Universidad Nacional Autónoma de México, 1980.

Favre, Henri. *El indigenismo*. Trans. Glenn Amado Gallardo Jordán. Mexico City: Fondo de Cultura Económica, 1998.

Fein, Seth. "Everyday Forms of Transnational Collaboration: U.S. Film Propaganda in Cold War Mexico." In *Close Encounters of Empire: Writing the Cultural History of U.S.–Latin American Relations*, ed. Gilbert Joseph, Catherine LeGrand, and Ricardo Salvatore, 400–450. Durham, N.C.: Duke University Press, 1998.

Frank, Andre Gunder. "Comments." *Current Anthropology* 9, no. 5 (1968): 412–14.

Friedlander, Judith. *Being Indian in Hueyapan: A Study of Forced Identity in Contemporary Mexico*. New York: St. Martin's, 1975.

Friedrich, Paul. *The Princes of Naranja*. Austin: University of Texas Press, 1986.

Gamio, Manuel. *Antología*. Mexico City: Universidad Nacional Autónoma de México, 1985.

———. *Arqueología e indigenismo*. Mexico City: SEP Setentas, 1972.

———. "Consideraciones sobre el problema indígena en América." In Gamio, *Arqueología e indigenismo*, 123–36. 1942. Mexico City: SEP Setentas, 1972.

———. "La investigación de los grupos indígenas mexicanos." In Manuel Gamio, *Arqueología e indigenismo*, 105–22. 1935. Mexico City: SEP Setentas, 1972.

———. "Nuestra estructura social, el nacionalismo y la educación." In Gamio, *Arqueología e indigenismo*, 152–75. 1935. Mexico City: SEP Setentas, 1972.

———. "El problema religioso en México." *La Nueva Democracia* 1, no. 4 (1920): 11–12.

Gamio, Manuel, and Raúl Noriega, eds. *A William Cameron Townsend en el vigésimoquinto aniversario del Instituto Lingüístico de Verano*. Cuernavaca: Summer Institute of Linguistics, 1961.

García Ugarte, Marta Eugenia. *La nueva relación iglesia-estado: Un análisis de la problemática actual*. Mexico City: Nueva Imagen, 1993.

Garma Navarro, Carlos. "Liderazgo protestante en una lucha campesina en México." *América Indígena* 44, no. 1 (1984): 127–41.

———. *Protestantismo en una comunidad totonaca de Puebla*. Mexico City: Instituto Nacional Indigenista, 1983.

Garrard-Burnett, Virginia. *Protestantism in Guatemala: Living in the New Jerusalem*. Austin: University of Texas Press, 1998.

Giménez Montiel, Gilberto. "La Iglesia Católica y las sectas en reciprocidad de perspectivas." In *Religión y sociedad en el sureste de México*, ed. Leonel Durán Solís, 7:1–22. Mexico City: Ediciones de la Casa Chata, 1987–89.

Gitre, Edward. "The 1904–1905 Welsh Revival: Modernization, Technologies, and Techniques of Self." *Church History: Studies in Christianity and Culture* 73, no. 4 (2004): 792–827.

González Casanova, Pablo. *La democracia en México*. Mexico City: Era, 1965.

———. "Sociedad plural, colonialismo internal y desarrollo." *América Latina* (Rio de Janeiro) 6, no. 3 (1963): 15–31.

González Rodríguez, Luis. *Tarahumara: La sierra y el hombre*. Mexico City: SEP, 1982.

Gough, Kathleen. "Comments." *Current Anthropology* 9, no. 5 (1968): 429.

———. "New Proposals for Anthropologists." *Current Anthropology* 9, no. 5 (1968): 403–7.

Gould, Jeffrey. *To Die in This Way: Nicaraguan Indians and the Myth of Mestizaje, 1880–1965*. Durham, N.C.: Duke University Press, 1998.

Graham, Richard, ed. *The Idea of Race in Latin America, 1870–1940*. Austin: University of Texas Press, 1990.

Grünberg, Georg. "Beiträge zur Ethnographie der Kayabí Zentralbrasiliens." *Archiv für Völkerkunde* (Vienna) 24 (1970): 21–185.

———. "Urgent Research in North-West Mato Grosso." *Bulletin of the International Committee on Urgent Anthropological and Ethnological Research* (Vienna) 8 (1966): 143–52.

Grupo de Barbados. "Antecedentes." In *Indianidad y descolonización en América Latina: Documentos de la segunda reunión de Barbados*, 9–16. Mexico City: Nueva Imagen, 1979.

———. "Declaración de Barbados II." In *Indianidad y descolonización en América Latina: Documentos de la segunda reunión de Barbados*, 389–92. Mexico City: Nueva Imagen, 1979.

———. "La política colonialista del ILV." In *Indianidad y descolonización en América Latina: Documentos de la segunda reunión de Barbados*, 397–400. Mexico City: Nueva Imagen, 1979.

Gudschinsky, Sarah. *Manual de alfabetización para pueblos prealfabetas*. Mexico City: SEP Setentas, 1974.

———. "Native Reaction to Tones and Words in Mazatec." *Word* 14 (1958): 338–45.

———. "Toneme Representation in Mazatec Orthograpy." *Word* 15 (1959): 446–52.

Guerrero Guerrero, Raúl. *Otomíes y tepehuas de la Sierra Oriental del Estado de Hidalgo*. Pachuca: Universidad Autónoma del Estado de Hidalgo, 1986.

Guevara Niebla, Gilberto, ed. *La educación socialista, 1934–1945*. Mexico City: SEP, 1985.

Guzmán García, Luis. "Política pastoral de la Iglesia Católica frente a las sectas religiosas." In *Religión y sociedad en el sureste de México,* ed. Leonel Durán Solís, 7:127–201. Mexico City: Cuadernos de la Casa Chata, 1987–89.

Hall, Stuart. "Ethnicity: Identity and Difference." In *Becoming National: A Reader,* ed. Geoff Eley and Ronald Grigor Suny, 339–51. New York: Oxford University Press, 1996.

Hamilton, Michael S. "We're in the Money: How Did Evangelicals Get So Wealthy, and What Has It Done to Us?" *Christianity Today,* 12 June 2000, 36–43.

Hart, John Mason. *Empire and Revolution: The Americans in Mexico since the Civil War.* Berkeley: University of California Press, 2002.

Hart, Laurie. "Story of the Wycliffe Translators: Pacifying the Last Frontiers." *NACLA's Latin America and Empire Report* 7, no. 10 (1973): 15–31.

Hefley, James. *Peril by Choice: The Story of John and Elaine Beekman, Wycliffe Bible Translators in Mexico.* Grand Rapids, Mich.: Zondervan, 1968.

Hefley, James, and Marti Hefley. *Uncle Cam: The Story of William Cameron Townsend, Founder of the Wycliffe Bible Translators and the Summer Institute of Linguistics.* Waco: Word, 1974.

Hernández Castillo, Rosalva Aida. *Histories and Stories from Chiapas: Border Identities in Southern Mexico.* University of Texas Press, 2001.

Hilton, Roseanne. *They Were Considered Faithful.* Orange, Calif.: Promise, 1993.

Hostetter, Douglas. "An Insider's Story: Religious Agencies in Viet-Nam." *NACLA's Latin America and Empire Report* 7, no. 10 (1973): 3–14.

Howe, James. "An Ideological Triangle: The Struggle over San Blas Kuna Culture, 1915–1925." In *Nation-States and Indians in Latin America,* ed. Greg Urban and Joel Sherzer, 173–91. Austin: University of Texas Press, 1991.

Hvalkof, Søren, and Peter Aaby, eds. *Is God an American? An Anthropological Perspective on the Missionary Work of the Summer Institute of Linguistics.* Copenhagen: International Work Group for Indigenous Affairs, 1982.

Jackson, Jean. "Being and Becoming an Indian in Vaupés." In *Nation-States and Indians in Latin America,* ed. Greg Urban and Joel Sherzer, 131–55. Austin: University of Texas Press, 1991.

———. "Traducciones competetivas del evangelio en el Vaupés, Colombia." *América Indígena* 44, no. 1 (1984): 49–94.

James, Daniel. *Mexico and the Americans.* New York: Praeger, 1963.

James, Earl K. *Foreign Policy Reports* 11, no. 9 (1935).

Jaulin, Robert. "Introducción." In *El etnocidio a través de las Américas,* trans. María Dolores de la Peña, ed. Jaulin, 9–14. Mexico City: Siglo Veintiuno, 1976.

———, ed. *El etnocidio a través de las Américas.* Trans. María Dolores de la Peña. Mexico City: Siglo Veintiuno, 1976. Originally published in 1972 in France as *Le livre blanc de l'ethnocide en amérique.*

Johnston, Thelma, ed. *Walking Upright on Foreign Soil: An Anthology.* Waxhaw, N.C.: Summer Institute of Linguistics, 1995.

Joseph, Gilbert. "Close Encounters: Toward a New Cultural History of U.S.–Latin American Relations." In *Close Encounters of Empire: Writing the Cultural History of U.S.–Latin American Relations*, ed. Gilbert Joseph, Catherine LeGrand, and Ricardo Salvatore, 3–46. Durham, N.C.: Duke University Press, 1998.

Joseph, Gilbert, Catherine LeGrand, and Ricardo Salvatore, eds. *Close Encounters of Empire: Writing the Cultural History of U.S.–Latin American Relations*. Durham, N.C.: Duke University Press, 1998.

Joseph, Gilbert, and Daniel Nugent. "Popular Culture and State Formation in Revolutionary Mexico." In *Everyday Forms of State Formation: Revolution and the Negotiation of Rule in Modern Mexico*, ed. Joseph and Nugent, 3–23. Durham, N.C.: Duke University Press, 1994.

——, eds. *Everyday Forms of State Formation: Revolution and the Negotiation of Rule in Modern Mexico*. Durham, N.C.: Duke University Press, 1994.

Juárez Cerdi, Elizabeth. "Yajalón, ciudad confesionalmente pacífica." In *Religión y sociedad en el sureste de México*, ed. Leonel Durán Solís, 3:107–213. Mexico City: Cuadernos de la Casa Chata, 1987–89.

Junqueira, Carmen, and Edgard de A. Carvalho, eds. *Los indios y la antropología en América Latina*. Buenos Aires: Búsqueda, 1984.

Keith, Shirley. "Los indios de América del Norte: Un pueblo en vías de desaparición." In *El etnocidio a través de las Américas*, trans. María Dolores de la Peña, ed. Robert Jaulin, 19–36. Mexico City: Siglo Veintiuno, 1976.

King, Linda. *Roots of Identity: Language and Literacy in Mexico*. Stanford, Calif.: Stanford University Press, 1994.

Knight, Alan. "Racism, Revolution and *Indigenismo*: Mexico, 1910–1940." In *The Idea of Race in Latin America, 1870–1940*, ed. Richard Graham, 71–107. Austin: University of Texas Press, 1990.

——. "The Rise and Fall of Cardenismo, 1930–1946." In *Mexico since Independence*, ed. Leslie Bethell, 241–320. New York: Cambridge University Press, 1991.

——. "Weapons and Arches in the Mexican Revolutionary Landscape." In *Everyday Forms of State Formation: Revolution and the Negotiation of Rule in Modern Mexico*, ed. Gilbert Joseph and Daniel Nugent, 24–68. Durham, N.C.: Duke University Press, 1994.

Krauze, Enrique. *Mexico: A Biography of Power: A History of Modern Mexico*. Trans. Hank Heifetz. New York: HarperCollins, 1997.

Lagarde, Marcela, and Daniel Cazés. "Política del lenguaje y lingüística aplicada: Del segmento fonético al ejército." In Mercedes Olivera et al., *Indigenismo y lingüística: Documentos del foro "La política del lenguaje en México,"* 159–70. Mexico City: Universidad Nacional Autónoma de México, 1980.

Lara, Antonia. "Rural Organizations: Cardenista Freemasonry." Paper presented at Latin American Studies Association International Conference, 16 March 2000.

Lara, Luis Fernando, and Felipe Garrido, eds. *Escritura y alfabetización*. Mexico City: Ediciones del Hermitaño, 1986.

Lewis, Bonnie Sue. *Creating Christian Indians: Native Clergy in the Presbyterian Church*. Norman: University of Oklahoma Press, 2003.

Lombardo Toledano, Vicente. "Como resolvió el régimen sovietico el problema de las nacionalidades oprimidas." In Lombardo Toledano, *El problema del Indio,* 82–108. 1936. Mexico City: SEP Setentas, 1973.

———. *El problema del indio.* 1936. Mexico City: SEP Setentas, 1973.

Lomnitz, Claudio. *Deep Mexico, Silent Mexico: An Anthropology of Nationalism.* Minneapolis: University of Minnesota Press, 2001.

Marino Flores, Anselmo. *Bibliografía lingüística de la República Mexicana.* Mexico City: Instituto Indigenista Interamericano, 1957.

Marroquín Zaleta, Enrique. *El botín sagrado: La dinámica religiosa en Oaxaca.* Oaxaca: Universidad Autónoma Benito Juárez de Oaxaca, 1992.

Marsden, George M. "Fundamentalism and American Evangelicalism." In *The Variety of American Evangelicalism,* ed. Donald Dayton and Robert Johnston, 22–35. Downers Grove, Ill.: InterVarsity Press, 1991.

———. *Understanding Fundamentalism and Evangelicalism.* Grand Rapids, Mich.: Eerdmans, 1991.

Martin, David. *Tongues of Fire: The Explosion of Protestantism in Latin America.* Oxford: Blackwell, 1990.

McFarland, Charles. *Chaos in Mexico: The Conflict of Church and State.* New York: Harper and Brothers, 1935.

McKinlay, Arch. *Visits with Mexico's Indians.* 2nd ed. Mexico City: Wycliffe Bible Translators, 1945.

Mecham, J. Lloyd. *Church and State in Latin America: A History of Politico-Ecclesiastical Relations.* Chapel Hill: University of North Carolina Press, 1934.

Mendieta y Nuñez, Lucio. *El valor económico y social de las razas indígenas de México.* Mexico City: DAPP, 1938.

Meyer, Jean. "El problema indio en México desde indepedencia." In *El etnocidio a través de las Américas,* ed. Robert Jaulin, trans. María Dolores de la Peña, 55–83. Mexico City: Siglo Veintiuno, 1976.

———. *El Sinarquismo: ¿Un fascismo Mexicano?* Trans. Aurelio Garzón del Camino. Mexico City: Editorial Joaquín Mortiz, 1979.

Miano Borruso, Marinella. "Política pastoral de la Iglesia Católica frente a los sectores religiosos." In *Religión y sociedad en el sureste de México,* ed. Leonel Durán Solís, 7:23–126. Mexico City: Cuadernos de la Casa Chata, 1987–89.

Michaels, Albert. "The Modification of the Anti-clerical Nationalism of the Mexican Revolution by General Lazaro Cardenas and Its Relationship to Church-State Détente in Mexico." *The Americas* 26, no. 1 (1969): 47–55.

Millán, Rosario. "Al recibir Águila Azteca Townsend era todo mieles." In Pedro Alisedo et al. *El Instituto Lingüístico de Verano,* 85–86. Mexico City: Proceso, 1981.

Miller, Max. *Mexico around Me.* New York: Reynal and Hitchcock, 1937.

Millett, Richard. "The Protestant Role in Twentieth-Century Latin American Church-State Relations." *Journal of Church and State* 15, no. 3 (1973): 369–73.

Mondragón, Carlos. "Protestantismo, panamericanismo e identidad nacional, 1920–1950." In *Cultura e identidad nacional,* ed. Roberto Blancarte, 305–42. Mexico City: Fondo de Cultura Económica, 1994.

Moore, Thomas. "SIL and a 'New-Found Tribe': The Amarakaeri Experience." In *Is God an American? An Anthropological Perspective on the Missionary Work of the Summer Institute of Linguistics,* ed. Søren Hvalkof and Peter Aaby, 133–43. Copenhagen: International Work Group for Indigenous Affairs, 1982.

NACLA Church Research Project. "The Benevolent Empire." *NACLA Newsletter* 4, no. 4 (1970): 10–18.

———. "Introduction." *NACLA's Latin America and Empire Report* 7, no. 10 (1973): 2.

Nahmad Sitton, Salomón. "La educación bilingüe y bicultural para las regiones interculturales de México." In Mercedes Olivera et al., *Indigenismo y lingüística: Documentos del foro "La política del lenguaje en México,"* 11–34. Mexico City: Universidad Nacional Autónoma de México, 1980.

———. "Gobierno indígena y sociedad nacional." In Nahmad Sitton et al., *Siete ensayos sobre indigenismo,* 5–17. Mexico City: Instituto Nacional Indigenista, 1977.

———. "Oaxaca y el CIESAS: Una experiencia hacia una nueva antropología." *América Indígena* 50, no. 2 (1990): 11–32.

Nahmad Sitton, Salomón, et al. *Siete ensayos sobre indigenismo.* Mexico City: Instituto Nacional Indigenista, 1977.

Negrete, Martaelena. *Relaciones entre la iglesia y el estado en México, 1930–1940.* Mexico City: Colegio de México, 1988.

Newbigin, Leslie. *Foolishness to the Greeks: The Gospel and Western Culture.* Grand Rapids, Mich.: Eerdmans, 1986.

Niblo, Stephen. *Mexico in the 1940s: Modernity, Politics, and Corruption.* Wilmington, Del.: Scholarly Resources, 1999.

———. *War, Diplomacy, and Development: The United States and Mexico, 1938–1954.* Wilmington, Del.: Scholarly Resources, 1995.

Nida, Eugene. *Linguistic Interludes.* Santa Ana, Calif.: Summer Institute of Linguistics, 1947.

Niebuhr, H. Richard. "Fundamentalism." In *Encyclopedia of the Social Sciences,* ed. Edwin R. A. Seligman, 525–27. New York: Social Science Research Council, 1931.

Nolasco Armas, Margarita. "El Instituto Lingüístico de Verano en México." In Mercedes Olivera et al., *Indigenismo y lingüística: Documentos del foro "La política del lenguaje en México,"* 145–52. Mexico City: Universidad Nacional Autónoma de México, 1980.

Ochoa Zazueta, Jesús Angel. "El Instituto Lingüístico de Verano, A.C." Cuadernos de Trabajo, Estudios 11, Departamento de Etnología y Antropología Social, Instituto Nacional de Antropología e Historia, 1975.

Olivera, Mercedes. "Algunos problemas de la investigación antropológica actual." In Arturo Warman et al., *De eso que llaman antropología mexicana,* 94–118. Mexico City: Nuestro Tiempo, 1970.

Olivera, Mercedes, et al. *Indigenismo y lingüística: Documentos del foro "La política del lenguaje en México."* Mexico City: Universidad Nacional Autónoma de México, 1980.

Palomino, Cebero. *El Instituto Lingüístico de Verano: Un fraude.* Lima: Ediciones Rupa Rupa, 1980.

Pérez, Gloria, and Scott Robinson, *La misión detrás de la misión/The Mission behind the Mission*. Mexico City: Claves Latinoamericanas, 1983.

Pérez-Enríquez, María Isabel. *Expulsiones indígenas: Religión y migración en tres municipios de los Altos de Chiapas: Chenalhó, Larrainzar y Chamula*. Mexico City: Claves Latinoamericanas, 1994.

Pérez Francisco, Ernesto. *Ra dathu bin ja (El hambre)*. Mexico City: Summer Institute of Linguistics, 1975.

Pérez Montfort, Ricardo. "Indigenismo, hispanismo y panamericanismo en la cultura popular mexicana de 1920 a 1940." In *Cultura e identidad nacional*, ed. Roberto Blancarte, 343–83. Mexico City: Fondo de Cultura Económica, 1994.

Pike, Eunice. *Ken Pike: Scholar and Christian*. Dallas: Summer Institute of Linguistics, 1981.

———. *Words Wanted*. Chicago: Moody Press, 1958.

Pike, Kenneth. *Axioms and Procedures for Reconstruction in Comparative Linguistics: An Experimental Syllabus*. Santa Ana, Calif.: Summer Institute of Linguistics, 1951.

———. *The Intonation of American English*. Ann Arbor: University of Michigan Press, 1945.

———. *Phonemics: A Technique for Reducing Languages to Writing*. Ann Arbor: University of Michigan Press, 1947.

———. *Phonetics: A Critical Analysis of Phonetic Theory and a Technique for the Practical Description of Sounds*. Ann Arbor: University of Michigan Press, 1943.

———. *Pronunciation*. Vol. 1 of *An Intensive Course in English for Latin American Students*. Ann Arbor: English Language Institute of the University of Michigan, 1942.

———. *Selected Writings to Commemorate the Sixtieth Birthday of Kenneth Lee Pike*. Ed. Ruth Brend. The Hague: Mouton, 1972.

———. *Tone Languages: A Technique for Determining the Number and Type of Pitch Contrasts in a Language, with Studies in Tonemic Substitution and Fusion*. Ann Arbor: University of Michigan Press, 1948.

———. *With Heart and Mind: A Personal Synthesis of Scholarship and Devotion*. Duncanville, Tex.: Adult Learning Systems, 1996.

Pike, Kenneth, and Thomas Headland. "SIL and Genocide: Well-Oiled Connections?" *Anthropology Newsletter*, February 1997, 4–5.

Pittman, Dick. "O King, Live Forever." In *Walking Upright on Foreign Soil: An Anthology*, ed. Thelma Johnston, 2–4. Waxhaw, N.C.: Summer Institute of Linguistics, 1995.

———, ed. *Best of Both Worlds*. N.p.: Summer Institute of Linguistics, 1988.

———. *Fifty Gold Buckles . . . Held It All Together*. Waxhaw, N.C.: Summer Institute of Linguistics, 1988.

———. *Given a Heading: The Symphonics of International Relations*. N.p.: Summer Institute of Linguistics, 1990.

Pittman, Dick, et al., eds. *The Wycliffe Sapphire*. N.p.: Wycliffe Bible Translators, 1991.

Portillo, Jorge H. *El problema de las relaciones entre la iglesia y el estado en México*. Mexico City: Costa-Amic, 1982.

Pozas, Ricardo. *Juan the Chamula*. Trans. Lysander Kemp. Berkeley: University of California Press, 1966.

Prado Gutiérrez, Ana María V., ed. *Monografía del Estado de Hidalgo*. Pachuca, Mexico: Instituto Hidalguense de la Cultura, 1993.

Pride, Kitty. *Bread Is Not Enough*. London: Hodder and Stoughton, 1976.

Purnell, Jennie. *Popular Movements and State Formation in Revolutionary Mexico: The Agraristas and Cristeros of Michoacán*. Durham, N.C.: Duke University Press, 1999.

Raat, Dirk, and William Beezley, eds. *Twentieth-Century Mexico*. Lincoln: University of Nebraska Press, 1986.

Raat, Dirk, and George Janacek. *Mexico's Sierra Tarahumara: A Photohistory of the People of the Edge*. Norman: University of Oklahoma Press, 1996.

Ramírez, Rafael. *La escuela rural mexicana*. Mexico City: SEP Setentas, 1976.

Rappaport, Joanne. "Las misiones protestantes y la resistencia indígena en el sur de colombia." *América Indígena* 44, no. 1 (1984): 111–26.

Read, William. *Latin American Church Growth*. Grand Rapids, Mich.: Eerdmans, 1969.

Reich, Peter Lester. *Mexico's Hidden Revolution: The Catholic Church in Law and Politics since 1929*. Notre Dame: University of Notre Dame Press, 1995.

Robinson, Scott. "Some Aspects of the Spontaneous Colonization of the Selva Communities of Ecuador." In *The Situation of the Indian in South America: Contributions to the Study of Inter-ethnic Conflict in the non-Andean Regions of South America,* ed. Walter Dostal, 108–14. Geneva: World Council of Churches, 1972.

Robledo Hernández, Gabriela. *Disidencia y religión: Los expulsados de San Juan Chamula*. Tuxtla Gutiérrez: Universidad Autónoma de Chiapas, 1997.

Rodríguez, Nemesio J., ed. *Apuntes para la interpretación de una transnacional misionera: El caso del ILV,* tomo 1, programa de etnolingüística. Pátzcuaro: SEP, INI, and CIESAS, 1981.

Romano Delgado, Agustín, and Angel Baltazar Caballero. "Historia evaluativa del Centro Coordinador Tzeltal-Tzotzil." 4 vols. Mexico City: Instituto Nacional Indigenista, 1996.

de la Rosa, Milca and Ana Cecilia Campos Cabrera. "Presbiterianismo en una comunidad otomí de la Huasteca." Licenciatura thesis, Universidad Autónoma de Puebla, 1992.

Roseberry, William. "Hegemony and the Language of Contention." In *Everyday Forms of State Formation: Revolution and the Negotiation of Rule in Modern Mexico,* ed. Joseph and Nugent, 355–66. Durham, N.C.: Duke University Press, 1994.

Rossell de la Lama, Guillermo. *Orientación programática municipal, 1985–1987, Huejuetla, Hidalgo*. Pachuca: Comité de Planeación para el Desarrollo del Estado de Hidalgo, 1987.

Ruiz Guerra, Rubén. "Panamericanismo y protestantismo: Una relación ambigua." In *Cultura e identidad nacional,* ed. Roberto Blancarte, 261–304. Mexico City: Fondo de Cultura Económica, 1994.

Rus, Jan. "The 'Comunidad Revolucionaria Institucional': The Subversion of

Native Government in Highland Chiapas, 1936–1968." In *Everyday Forms of State Formation: Revolution and the Negotiation of Rule in Modern Mexico*, ed. Gilbert Joseph and Daniel Nugent, 265–300. Durham, N.C.: Duke University Press, 1994.

Rus, Jan, and Robert Wasserstrom. "Evangelization and Political Control: The SIL in Mexico." In *Is God an American? An Anthropological Perspective on the Missionary Work of the Summer Institute of Linguistics,* ed. Søren Hvalkof and Peter Aaby, 163–75. Copenhagen: International Work Group for Indigenous Affairs, 1982.

Sáenz, Moisés. *México integro*. Mexico City: SEP Ochentas, 1982 (1939).

Salamone, Frank. "Missionaries and Anthropologists: An Inquiry into Their Ambivalent Relationship." *Missiology: An International Review* 14, no. 1 (1986): 55–70.

Sanneh, Lamin. *Encountering the West: Christianity and the Global Cultural Process*. Maryknoll, N.Y.: Orbis, 1993.

———. *Translating the Message: The Missionary Impact on Culture*. Maryknoll, N.Y.: Orbis, 1989.

Scott, James. *Seeing Like a State: How Certain Schemes to Improve the Human Condition Have Failed*. New Haven: Yale University Press, 1998.

Scott, Lindy. *Salt of the Earth: A Socio-Political History of Mexico City Evangelical Protestants, 1964–1991*. Mexico City: Editorial Kyrios, 1991.

Scott, Ruby. *Jungle Harvest: God's Word Triumphs in Tila Hearts*. N.p.: Conservative Baptist Home Mission Society, 1988.

Shaw, R. Daniel. "Ethnohistory, Strategy and Bible Translation: The Case of Wycliffe and the Cause of World Mission." *Missiology: An International Review* 14, no. 1 (1986): 47–54.

Sierra, Justo. *Obras completas*. Vol. 7, *La educación nacional*. Mexico City: Universidad Nacional Autónoma de México, 1977.

Silva y Aceves, Mariano. "Las cartillas lingüísticas." *Cuadernos lingüísticos* (Mexico City). Nos. 5 y 6, n.d.: 1.

Siverts, Henning. *Oxchuc*. Mexico City: Instituto Indigenista Interamericano, 1969.

Sjollema, Baldwin. Preface. In *The Situation of the Indian in South America: Contributions to the Study of Inter-ethnic Conflict in the Non-Andean Regions of South America,* ed. Walter Dostal, 11–12. Geneva: World Council of Churches, 1972.

Slocum, Marianna, with Grace Watkins. *The Good Seed*. Orange, Calif.: Promise, 1988.

Smith, Richard Chase. "The Summer Institute of Linguistics: Ethnocide Disguised as a Blessing." In *Is God an American? An Anthropological Perspective on the Missionary Work of the Summer Institute of Linguistics*, ed. Søren Hvalkof and Peter Aaby, 121–32. Copenhagen: International Work Group for Indigenous Affairs, 1982.

Spenser, Daniela. *El triángulo imposible: México, Rusia Soviética, y Estados Unidos en los años veinte*. Mexico City: CIESAS and Porrua, 1998.

Stavenhagen, Rodolfo. "Clases, colonialismo y aculturación." *América Latina* 6, no. 4 (1963): 63–103.

Stephen, Lynn. *Zapata Lives! Histories and Cultural Politics in Southern Mexico.* Berkeley: University of California Press, 2002.

Stern, Steve. "The Decentered Center and the Expansionist Periphery: The Paradoxes of Foreign-Local Encounter." In *Close Encounters of Empire: Writing the Cultural History of U.S.–Latin American Relations,* ed. Gilbert Joseph, Catherine LeGrand, and Ricardo Salvatore, 47–68. Durham, N.C.: Duke University Press, 1998.

Steven, Hugh. *Doorway to the World: The Mexico Years: The Memoirs of W. Cameron Townsend, 1934–47.* Wheaton, Ill.: Harold Shaw, 1999.

——. *Manuel, the Continuing Story.* Langley, B. C.: Credo, 1987.

——. *They Dared to Be Different.* 3rd ed. Huntington Beach, Calif.: Wycliffe Bible Translators, 1991.

——, ed. *Pass the Word: Fifty Years of Wycliffe Bible Translators.* Huntington Beach, Calif.: Wycliffe Bible Translators, 1984.

Stoll, David. "¿Con qué derecho adoctrinan ustedes a nuestros indígenas? La polémica en torno al Instituto Lingüístico de Verano." *América Indígena* 44, no. 1 (1984): 9–24.

——. *Fishers of Men or Builders of Empire? The Wycliffe Translators in Latin America.* London: Zed Press, 1982.

——. *Is Latin America Turning Protestant? The Politics of Evangelical Growth.* Berkeley: University of California Press, 1995.

——. "What Should Wycliffe Do?" *Missiology: An International Review* 14, no. 1 (1986): 37–46.

Suárez Argüello, Ana Rosa, ed. *En el nombre del destino manifiesto: Guía de ministros y embajadores de Estados Unidos en México, 1925–1983.* Mexico City: Instituto Mora and Secretaría de Relaciones Exteriores, 1998.

Summer Institute of Linguistics. *Bibliography of Linguistic, Ethnographic, and Literacy Materials by Members of the Summer Institute of Linguistics.* Glendale, Calif.: Summer Institute of Linguistics, 1951.

Svelmoe, William. "The General and the Gringo: W. Cameron Townsend as Lázaro Cárdenas's 'Man in America.'" In *The Foreign Missionary Enterprise at Home: Explorations in North American Cultural History,* ed. Daniel Bays and Grant Wacker, 171-86. Tuscaloosa: University of Alabama Press, 2003.

——. "A New Vision for Missions: William Cameron Townsend in Guatemala and Mexico, 1917–1945." Ph.D. diss., University of Notre Dame, 2001.

Tannenbaum, Frank. *Peace by Revolution: Mexico after 1910.* New York: Columbia University Press, 1966.

Taylor, Clyde, and Wade Coggins, eds. *Protestant Missions in Latin America: A Statistical Survey.* Washington, D.C.: Evangelical Foreign Mission Association, 1961.

Townsend, Cameron. "Cartillas lingüísticas: Lengua nahuatl." *Cuadernos Lingüísticos,* nos. 5–6, n.d., 2.

——. "Cartillas lingüísticas: Lengua nahuatl." *Cuadernos Lingüísticos,* nos. 5–6, n.d., 48–50.

——. "Cuestionario lingüístico." *Cuadernos Lingüísticos* 4, nos. 1–2 (1937): 2.

———. "Go with Them." In Cameron Townsend and Richard Pittman, *Remember All the Way*, 33–41. Huntington Beach, Calif.: Wycliffe Bible Translators, 1975.

———. "Honor to Whom Honor Is Due." In *The Wycliffe Sapphire*, ed. Dick Pittman et al., 86–90. N.p.: Wycliffe Bible Translators, 1991.

———. "How Can We Fit In?" In Cameron Townsend et al., *Being Vectored In: the Harmonics of International Relations*, 66–75. N.p.: Summer Institute of Linguistics, 1989.

———. "I Saw a Lamb." In Cameron Townsend and Richard Pittman, *Remember All the Way*, 42–46. Huntington Beach, Calif.: Wycliffe Bible Translators, 1975.

———. "Keep Those Sailors on Board." In Cameron Townsend et al., *Given a Heading: The Symphonics of International Relations*, 158–64. N.p.: Summer Institute of Linguistics, 1990.

———. *Lázaro Cárdenas, Mexican Democrat*. Ann Arbor: George Wahr, 1952.

———. *Lecciones sencillas para aprender a leer*. Mexico City: Departamento de Trabajo, 1936.

———. "Let Your Light Shine." In Cameron Townsend and Richard Pittman, *Remember All the Way*, 47–57. Huntington Beach, Calif.: Wycliffe Bible Translators, 1975.

———. "Mexico's Program of Rural Education." *School and Society* (Dallas), 30 June 1934, 848–51.

———. *They Found a Common Language: Community through Bilingual Education*. New York: Harper and Row, 1972.

———. *The Truth about Mexico's Oil*. Los Angeles: Inter-American Fellowship and Summer Institute of Linguistics, 1940.

———. "Two Presidents . . . and the Chamulas." In Cameron Townsend et al., *Being Vectored In: The Harmonics of International Relations*, 143–47. N.p.: Summer Institute of Linguistics, 1989.

———. "We're in the People Business." In *The Wycliffe Sapphire*, ed. Dick Pittman et al., 53–58. N.p.: Wycliffe Bible Translators, 1991.

———. "You're Back Again, Uncle Cam." In *Fifty Gold Buckles . . . Held It All Together*, ed. Richard Pittman, 31–38. Waxhaw, N.C.: Summer Institute of Linguistics, 1988.

Townsend, Cameron, and Richard Pittman. *Remember All the Way*. Huntington Beach, Calif.: Wycliffe Bible Translators, 1975.

Townsend, Cameron, et al. *Being Vectored In: The Harmonics of International Relations*. N.p.: Summer Institute of Linguistics, 1989.

Townsend, Elvira. *Latin American Courtesy: A Guide to Manners for Americans South of the Rio Grande*. Mexico City: Summer Institute of Linguistics and Instituto Mexicano de Investigaciones Lingüísticas, 1941.

UNESCO. *Empleo de las lenguas vernáculas en la enseñanza*. Lauzanne: UNESCO, 1954.

Urban, Greg, and Joel Sherzer. "Introduction: Indians, Nation-States, and Culture." In *Nation-States and Indians in Latin America*, ed. Urban and Sherzer, 1–18. Austin: University of Texas Press, 1991.

———, eds. *Nation-States and Indians in Latin America*. Austin: University of Texas Press, 1991.

Valencia, Enrique. "La formación de nuevos antropólogos." In Arturo Warman et al., *De eso que llaman antropología mexicana*, 119–53. Mexico City: Nuestro Tiempo, 1970.

Varese, Stefano. "Inter-ethnic Relations in the Selva of Peru." In *The Situation of the Indian in South America: Contributions to the Study of Inter-ethnic Conflict in the Non-Andean Regions of South America*, ed. Walter Dostal, 115–39. Geneva: World Council of Churches, 1972.

Vaughan, Mary Kay. *Cultural Politics in Revolution: Teachers, Peasants, and Schools in Mexico, 1930–1940*. Tucson: University of Arizona Press, 1997.

Villa Rojas, Alfonso. "La responsibilidad social de los ciéntificos sociales." *América Indígena* 29, no. 3 (1969): 787–804.

Voigtlander, Katherine. "Sketch of the Lord's Work among the Eastern Otomi Language Group of Mexico." Unpublished paper, 1994.

Wallis, Ethel. *The Dayuma Story: Life under Auca Spears*. New York: Harper & Row, 1961.

———. *It Takes Two to Untangle Tongues: The Story of Evelyn Griset Pike*. Huntington Beach, Calif.: Wycliffe Bible Translators, 1985.

———, ed. *The Cakchiquel Album*. Costa Mesa, Calif.: Gift Publications, 1981.

Wallis, Ethel, and Mary Angela Bennett. *Two Thousand Tongues to Go: The Story of the Wycliffe Bible Translators*. New York: Harper and Brothers, 1959.

Warkentin, Clara Neufeld. *Fishers of Men*. Privately published, 1997.

Warman, Arturo. "Comentarios." *América Indígena* 30, no. 4 (1970): 85–93.

———. "Todos santos y todos difuntos: Crítica historica de la antropología mexicana." In Warman et al., *De eso que llaman antropología mexicana*, 9–38. Mexico City: Nuestro Tiempo, 1970.

Weber, Max. *The Protestant Ethic and the Spirit of Capitalism*. New York: Scribner, 1958.

Index

162–64, 168, 172, 174, 177. *See also* Summer Institute of Linguistics

bilingual education. *See* Summer Institute of Linguistics: advocacy of vernacular education and literacy

Bolivia, 158

Bonfil Batalla, Guillermo, 143–46, 151, 153–55, 158, 179, 180

Bower, Bethel, 111

Bravo Ahuja, Gloria, 159

Brazil, 148, 158

Brindís, Leon, 128

British and Foreign Bible Society, 25

Burgess, Don, 139

Cabellero, Armando, 113

Cahuloti, Michoacán, 66

Cakchiquels, xv, xvi, 31

Calles, Plutarco Elías, xix, 21–24, 30–32

Cambodia, 138

Camp Wycliffe, 6, 36, 71, 74, 90, 96, 100, 102

Cárdenas, Cuauhtémoc, 150

Cárdenas, Lázaro: as icon of Mexican Revolution, 8, 32, 89, 150; attitude toward United States, 28, 29, 34–37; strategy of religious substitution, 9, 12, 13, 24, 29–32, 128, 133, 160, 165. *See also* Townsend, Cameron: relationship with Lázaro Cárdenas

Cárdenas family, 156

Carlson, Paul and Ellen, 103

Carpenter, Joel, xiv, xv

Carter, Jimmy, 153

Carrillo, Francisco, 16, 17

Caso, Alfonso, 80, 81, 130, 133, 137

Castellanos, Manuel, 97

Castillo Nájera, Francisco, 27, 28, 35, 36

Castro, Angélica, 82

Catholic Church. *See* Roman Catholic Church

Cazés, Daniel, 136, 142

Ceiba, La, Veracruz, 110

Central American Mission, xv, xvi, 1

Central Intelligence Agency, 91, 133, 137–40, 149, 150, 153, 159, 160

Chafer, Lewis Sperry, xvi, xvii, 6

Chamula. *See* San Juan Chamula

Chamulas. *See* Tzotzils

Chatinos, 151

Chiapas, xix, 22, 75, 81, 156, 157, 164, 168–75, 178, 180

Chilón, Chiapas, 95

China Inland Mission, 74, 91

Chinantecs, 82

Christiansen, L. G., 55

Church of God in the Mexican Republic. *See* Iglesia de Dio en la República Mexicana

Cincinnati Plan, 25

Coatlinchán, México, 68

Colby, Gerard, xvii, xviii, xix, 90, 91, 156

College of Ethnologists and Social Anthropologists, 154–57, 171

Colombia, 148, 149

Columbia Bible College, xv

Comas, Juan, 82

Comité Nacional de Defensa Evangélica. *See* National Evangelical Defense Committee

Communications and Public Works, Ministry of, 84

Congress of Americanists, 58, 130, 142, 144

Constitution of 1857, Mexican, 166

Constitution of 1917, Mexican, xii, 2, 4, 26, 32, 67, 68, 79, 99, 120, 166, 178

convenio between Ministry of Education and Summer Institute of Linguistics. *See* Education, Ministry of: convenio with the Summer Institute of Linguistics

Corralito, Chiapas, 97, 98, 105, 106, 181

Costa Rica, 158

Cowan, George, 134

Jungle Aviation and Radio Service, 10, 153

Keith, Shirley, 142
Kennedy, John F., 90
Kiemele, Mildred, 71
King, Linda, 159
Krauze, Enrique, 63

Labor, Ministry of, 8, 9, 14, 18
Labor Party, 126
Lacandones, 48
Lathrop, Max, 11, 12, 55
Latin American courtesy. *See* Summer Institute of Linguistics: teaching Latin American courtesy
Legters, Brainerd, 47, 48, 73
Legters, Leonard Livingston, xvi, xvii, 1–4, 6, 7, 9, 73, 74
León Portilla, Miguel, 158
Lincoln, Abraham, 12
linguistics, x, xxi, 6, 10, 40, 45, 47, 53–57, 60, 81, 82, 111–13, 126, 128, 131, 135, 151, 152, 155, 161–63, 166, 174. *See also* Bible translation; indigenismo; Mexican Institute of Linguistic Research; Nida, Eugene; Pike, Ken; Silva y Aceves, Mariano; Summer Institute of Linguistics
Linguistic Society of America, 74
Lombardo Toledano, Vicente, 56
López, Justinio, 77
López, Ramón, 102, 105
López Mateos, Adolfo, 130, 131
López Portillo, Alicia, 153
López Portillo, José, 154, 161–63
Lucas, Anastasio, 68
Luther, Martin, 42

Margaín, Hugo, 153
Malmstrom, Elvira. *See* Townsend, Elvira
Marlett, Steve, 159
Marsden, George, xiii
Mártinez, Luis María, 65

Marzialle, Allegro, 149
Matlazincas, 156
Mayas, xv, 55. *See also* Bachajón, Chiapas; Lacandones; San Juan Chamula, Chiapas; Slocum, Marianna; Tzeltals; Tzotzils
Maximilian von Hapsburg. *See* von Hapsburg, Maximilian
Mazahuas, 71, 156
Mazatecs, 82
McKinney, Richmond, 41, 48
Méndez, Martín, 16
Mendoza, Panfilo, 120
Mérida, Yucatán, 158, 161
Methodists, 25
Mexican-American Cultural Relations Association, 27
Mexican Indian Mission, 165
Mexican Institute of Linguistic Research, 7, 8, 14, 54, 55
Mexican state. *See* Cárdenas, Lázaro; Roman Catholic Church: relations with the Mexican state; Summer Institute of Linguistics: relations with the Mexican state; United States-Mexican relations
Mexico-Cárdenas Museum, 153
Mexico City, 129–31
Meyer, Jean, 142
Michoacán, 167
Miller, Max, ix
Miller, Walter, 55
Ministry of the Interior. *See* Interior, Ministry of
Miranda, Horacio, 113
Mission Aviation Fellowship, 149
Mitla, Oaxaca, 131, 163
Mixtecs, 152
Moody Bible Institute, xiv–xvi
Moody Church, xvi, 6
Montgomery, Larry, 160
Morales, Gaudencio, 78
Morelos, ix. *See also* Cuautla, Morelos; Tetelcingo, Morelos
Morrow, Dwight, 22
Múgica, Francisco, 37